T0291345

Unveiling the North Korean Economy
Collapse and Transition

North Korea is one of the most closed and secretive societies in the world. Despite a high level of interest from the outside world, we have very little detailed information about how the country functions economically. In this valuable book for both academic and policy-making circles, Byung-Yeon Kim offers the most comprehensive and systematic analysis of the present-day North Korean economy in the context of economic systems and transition economics. The book addresses what is really happening in the North Korean economy, why it has previously failed and how the country can make the transition to a market economy. It takes advantage of not only carefully reconstructed macroeconomic data but also rich, new data at the micro level, such as quantitative surveys of North Korean refugees settled in South Korea and surveys of Chinese companies that interact heavily with North Korea.

BYUNG-YEON KIM is a professor in the Department of Economics at Seoul National University. He has been recognised with the T. S. Ashton Prize from the Economic History Society of the United Kingdom and the Chungram Award from the Korean Economic Association and as Distinguished Researcher in Humanities and Social Sciences by the National Research Foundation of the Republic of Korea. He is a regular columnist on North Korean issues in a South Korean newspaper, the JoongAng Daily.

Unveiling the North Korean Economy

Collapse and Transition

BYUNG-YEON KIM
Seoul National University

CAMBRIDGE
UNIVERSITY PRESS

University Printing House, Cambridge CB2 8BS, United Kingdom

One Liberty Plaza, 20th Floor, New York, NY 10006, USA

477 Williamstown Road, Port Melbourne, VIC 3207, Australia

4843/24, 2nd Floor, Ansari Road, Daryaganj, Delhi – 110002, India

79 Anson Road, #06–04/06, Singapore 079906

Cambridge University Press is part of the University of Cambridge.

It furthers the University's mission by disseminating knowledge in the pursuit of education, learning, and research at the highest international levels of excellence.

www.cambridge.org
Information on this title: www.cambridge.org/9781107183797
DOI: 10.1017/9781316874882

First published 2017

A catalogue record for this publication is available from the British Library.

ISBN 978-1-107-18379-7 Hardback
ISBN 978-1-316-63516-2 Paperback

Contents

Figures

Tables

Acknowledgements

I owe a debt of gratitude to many people whose knowledge and ideas shaped this book. I am indebted to the scholars whose studies of economic systems and transition economics laid the framework for the analysis of the North Korean economy. In this regard, I would like to give my warm thanks to Joe Brada, Wendy Carlin, Christopher Davis, Mark Harrison, Michael Kaser, Masaaki Kuboniwa, Gérard Roland and Chenggang Xu. This book also draws from the insightful research of Nicholas Eberstadt, Stephan Haggard, Hyung-Gon Jeong, Dongho Jo, Seung-Ho Jung, Suk-Jin Kim, Andrei Lankov, Suk Lee, Seog Ki Lee, Young-Hoon Lee, Sung Min Mun, Marcus Noland, Hyeong-Jung Park, Moon Soo Yang and Hyoung Soo Zang, to whom I am thankful. I am particularly grateful to Gérard Roland and Christopher Davis who first encouraged me to write this book. Furthermore, Christopher Davis and Suk-Jin Kim provided me with detailed comments on several of the chapters, which proved to be very useful in revising the manuscript. I also thank Chaesung Chun who read the Conclusion of this book and gave valuable comments. Special thanks must go to Christopher Davis, Ichiro Iwasaki, Satoshi Mizobata, Shinichiro Tabata and Yasushi Nakamura, who arranged for facilities at their respective universities and provided me with time and accommodation to focus on writing this book.

Collecting data on North Korea required a cooperative effort, and the surveys featured in this book were possible thanks to a number of my colleagues and students. I would like to thank and acknowledge the joint works of my colleagues Sokbae Lee, Jungmin Lee and Syngjoo Choi on surveying North Korean refugees. The help of a group of talented students – Seung-Ho Jung, Jieun Hong, In Jeong Hwang, Yooseon Hwang, Joonhwi Joo, Min Jung Kim, Olivia Kim, Seong Hee Kim, Seo Young Kim, Jongmin Lee and Juntae Park – was also invaluable. A special mention goes to Seung-Ho Jung, who collected unique data by interviewing Chinese businessmen who conducted trade or who invested in North Korea.

The editor of this book, Phil Good, provided valuable support for which I am grateful. The efforts of the production team of this book, which includes the content manager, Emma Collison, are also well appreciated.

I am especially grateful to my parents who have demonstrated integrity and responsibility throughout their lives. As always, I would like to give my utmost thanks to my wife, Heonsook, and two sons, Wooseok and Woojin. Without their love, support and encouragement, this book would not have been written.

I would like to acknowledge that this work was supported by the Ministry of Education of the Republic of Korea and the National Research Foundation of Korea (NRF-2010-342-B00008). Without their generous support over the past five years, writing this kind of the book, which requires a lot of data collection, would not have been possible.

Lastly, the children of North Korea have been constantly on my mind throughout the past five years as I worked on this book. While they may be too young to completely understand the reality of their situation, I hope that they will be able to freely realise their full potential in the future. As such, I dedicate this book to them.

Introduction

North Korea is a small country, with a population of approximately 25 million people. However, North Korea can be considered large in terms of world influence. The number of Google hits on recent news about North Korea is around 30 million, whereas that number for South Korea, with twice the population and 70 times the economic size (GNP), is only 13 million. This phenomenon is understandable if one looks at headline news in the world media from the past three years involving North Korea. In December 2013, Kim Jong-un surprised the world by executing his uncle and a leading political figure in North Korea, Jang Sung-taek. In 2014, the United States accused North Korea of orchestrating the hacking of Sony Pictures Entertainment, despite North Korea's denial. The North Korean government even made threats against cinemas that showed the film 'The Interview', which centres around a fictitious plot to assassinate the North Korean dictator. In early 2016, North Korea conducted its fourth test of a nuclear bomb and tested a long-range ballistic missile, leading to the imposition of one of the strongest United Nations sanctions yet against North Korea. However, in the midst of the sanctions, North Korea appeared to denounce their effect on the regime by holding the 7th Workers' Party Conference in June 2016 and heralding the heroic leadership of Kim's family in protecting North Korea from imperialist invasion.

In spite of its increasing importance, international understanding of the workings of North Korea turns out to be limited. The country's realities are difficult to explore because it allows no independent press or free use of the internet. The presence of several foreign embassies and one Western press office in North Korea is of little help because their access to the real North Korea is known to be quite limited. The absence of solid facts has hampered efforts at developing an unbiased understanding of North Korea and undermined the development of effective policies regarding the nation. It may be that the North Korean authorities have strategically used such secrecy to take advantage of the asymmetrical access to information between North Korea and its foreign counterparts, such as the United States and South Korea.

Data on the North Korean economy are no exception to this severe deficiency of information access. In the early 1960s, North Korea stopped publishing statistical yearbooks, which were routinely published in all other centrally planned economies, and from that date they have failed to regularly provide economic data, including essential statistics on growth rates and per capita income. Even the data they do provide are often incoherent and unconvincing. When international economists work with Soviet data, it is said to be like playing with jigsaw puzzles: data exist, but they are incomplete, hidden and manipulated. Working with North Korean data is more like looking for a needle in a haystack – it is both costly and quite time consuming.

However, without an understanding of the facts of the economy, international policy-makers would have to depend on simple, unreliable practices and personal preferences in determining what policies to follow with regard to the country. It would be naïve to think that such policies would work well in reality. The country's economy affects the livelihood of North Korean people and should be the main consideration for policy-making by Kim Jong-un as he tries to maintain his power. One can certainly argue that understanding the economy is a key to deciphering Kim's intentions. Economic structures generally change slowly unless some dramatic event occurs, which enables the prediction of the future of a country with a fair degree of accuracy.

This book sets out to unveil the real North Korean economy through the use of novel datasets. Currently, approximately 30,000 North Korean refugees live in South Korea. Accounts of their experiences while in North Korea are valuable sources of information on the nation's economy. In addition, China is the most important trade partner of North Korea, and Chinese firms engage in various businesses with North Korea. This book utilises data from surveys of North Korean refugees in South Korea and from Chinese firms that do business with North Korea. In addition, long-term data on growth rates and per capita income are reconstructed and used to evaluate North Korea's economic performance.

This book places the North Korean economy in the context of the socialist economic system and its transition toward a market economy. An economic system is a fundamental institution that determine long-term economic performance. Moreover, the experiences of now-defunct socialist economies imply that the failure of socialist economies and their subsequent transition toward a market economy are not accidental but a predictable historical pattern. Assuming this is an accurate observation, North Korea will also follow such a pattern in the future. This does not necessarily mean, however, that the current North Korean regime will collapse. The current regime could survive if its economy were to transform into a market economy as a result of pressure from the people involved in market activities or from a government decision in favour of a transition, or both. However, regardless of scenario, the collapse of the socialist economy and its transition to a market economy appear to be inevitable.

This book is made up of three chapters. Chapter 1 provides a framework that helps us understand why economic performance depends on an economic system and coherency across the elements of that system. Any economic system should have the following three elements: institutions, a coordination mechanism and the behaviour of economic agents. A socialist economy is grounded on state ownership as the institutional basis and central planning as the coordination mechanism. For the economic system to be coherent, economic agents such as households and firms must follow the rules set by the state. However, the pursuit of self-interests by these agents causes conflict with such rules, and this is a fundamental problem in the socialist economy model. The literature on socialist economies abounds in analyses of the policies of socialist governments, but is relatively limited in terms of investigations of the behaviour of firms and households. In this book I argue that the performance of the socialist economy depends heavily on interactions between the government and households or firms. Reflecting this view, Chapter 1 investigates the inefficiencies, shortages and collapse of the socialist economy, particularly the Soviet Union, focusing on the behaviour of households and firms as they interact with government policies.

Chapter 2 provides a comprehensive analysis of the North Korean economy. This chapter begins with a short history of the North Korean economy, followed by a discussion of its economic system and an evaluation of its performance based on reconstructed data on long-term growth rates and national income per capita. The household sector in North Korea during the current period is examined using data from surveys of North Korean refugees who settled in South Korea. In this discussion, we will give considerable attention to the phenomenon of marketisation in the North Korean economy. The firm sector and its involvement in economic transactions in markets and with China are investigated using the above surveys of the refugees and survey data from Chinese firms doing business with North Korea, respectively. The last section of the chapter focuses on the relationships between corruption and the informal economy, and derives implications bearing on the stability of the North Korean regime.

Chapter 3 discusses transition issues involving the future of North Korea. North Korea is a latecomer in transitioning toward a market economy. Careful examination of other economies' previous transition experiences will be valuable in drafting appropriate policies for North Korea. Having said that, North Korea has unique environmental factors that will influence economic performance during the transition period. The chapter begins with an evaluation of transition strategies, such as big-bang and gradualism, and a comparison of the Chinese experience of economic reforms to those of Eastern European nations and the former Soviet Union. Subsequently, we will discuss transition policies with regard to stabilisation, liberalisation and privatisation as they apply to North Korea. Finally, we will examine scenarios for unification of the two Koreas, together with estimates of benefits and costs for each scenario.

1   An Evaluation of the Socialist Economy

1.1   ECONOMIC SYSTEMS

This chapter first lays a foundation on which an economic system is analysed and evaluated. Subsequently, we will evaluate the performance of socialist economies in the former Soviet Union and Eastern Europe against the objectives of an economic system – namely, efficiency, macroeconomic balance and sustainability. In this analysis we will investigate the behaviour of households and firms, which interact with the socialist government, using theories and empirical evidence. This discussion will provide a framework in which to analyse the North Korean economy.

An economic system is defined as the set of institutions and mechanisms that influence the decisions and the behaviour of economic agents, typically consumers and producers (Gregory and Stuart, 2004). There are three bases of any economic system: property rights (ownership) as an institution, a coordination mechanism and the behaviour of economic actors (that is, households, firms and government). Numerous works suggest the importance of property rights and the coordination mechanism in determining economic performance (e.g. North, 1990, 2005; Greif, 2006; Acemoglu and Robinson, 2012; Acemoglu et al., 2001, 2002). Households and firms are expected to behave in accordance with the rules of ownership and the coordination mechanism.

The history of economic systems is as long as the history of human beings, since human beings require the production and consumption of goods and services for their physical survival. Even a primitive society must have some norms that work as economic institutions: a village that relies on animal hunting will have social norms or traditions that govern which animals to hunt, which tools to use and how to distribute food and materials from killed animals. As the populations increased and the markets expanded, it became difficult to rely on a simple rule or on decisions made by a person, such as a village chief, to manage all of the problems related to the production and consumption of goods and services. Furthermore, the division of labour required that every human being rely on the goods and services produced by others. Accordingly, the institutions and mechanisms that constitute economic systems have gradually become more complex. Several questions arose with these developments, including how to increase production, how to maintain supply equal to demand and how to distribute produced goods and services to consumers.

The modern academic debate on economic systems started with Adam Smith's *The Wealth of Nations*, published in 1776. Instead of creating or envisioning an ideal economic system, Adam Smith described an economic system emerging in reality, which he called 'the system of natural order' or 'the system of perfect liberty', and provided economic justification for it. One of the primary reasons that Adam Smith's book was so influential was that it successfully addressed critical concerns of seventeenth- and eighteenth-century scholars. They were concerned that individuals freed from medieval rules would pursue their unfettered self-interests, leading to societal collapse. Before Adam Smith, scholars had responded to this problem in two ways: (1) by calling for altruism and (2) by suggesting the need for an absolute power. The former argument said that altruism should be emphasised to prevent economic development from destabilising the society. The latter maintained that each person should voluntarily delegate his rights to a strong central authority to avoid a 'war of all against all'.

Adam Smith rejected both claims. In his books, he argued that the individual pursuit of self-interest would lead not to collapse but to the welfare of the society. He distinguished self-interest as the love of oneself without causing harm to others as a result of one's selfishness.

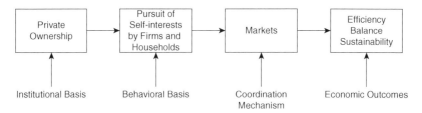

FIGURE I.I The Capitalist Economic System

He illustrated self-interest with this frequently cited sentence: 'It is not from the benevolence of the butcher, the brewer, or the baker, that we can expect our dinner, but from their regard to their own interest' (Smith, 1976, I, ii, 2).[1] Those people pursue their self-interest, but their gain neither reduces others' property nor harms their bodies. According to Adam Smith, this self-interest generates economic growth through an 'invisible hand'. 'By directing that industry in such a manner as its produce may be of greatest value, he intends only his own gain, and he is in this, as in many other cases, led by an invisible hand to promote an end which was no part of his intention' (Smith, 1976, IV, 2, 9).

The economic system described by Adam Smith can be summarised in Figure I.1, which shows that capitalism rests on three bases: private ownership as the institutional basis, the individual's free pursuit of self-interest as the behavioural basis and the market mechanism as the coordination basis. Ownership of productive assets such as land, housing and firms defines an economy's main institutional features. For instance, a constitution, laws and the court system operate to protect property rights. The coordination mechanism concerns how to allocate resources. In a capitalist economic system, a market mechanism – a so-called 'invisible hand' – guides economic actors to rationally behave in accordance with market signals. The behavioural basis refers to the behaviour of economic actors. Households maximise utility and firms profit, whereas government's main role is to provide public goods. In other words, the pursuit of self-interest is widely accepted as capitalism's behavioural basis. These three bases are regarded as a package because without the others, any one would not properly function. Private ownership motivates economic agents to pursue their self-interest. The pursuit of economic agents' self-interest is coordinated by the market mechanism in a way that achieves socially desirable outcomes, such as economic growth and market clearing (an equilibrium of supply and demand).

Socialism contrasts with capitalism in terms of these bases. Karl Marx believed that capitalism was 'the root of all evil'. According to Marx, capitalism leads to class struggle, income inequality, unemployment and business cycles. Given the existence of private ownership of productive assets such as capital and land, class struggle is inevitable, he said, because capitalists exploit a surplus of potential workers' labour. Central planning as the coordination mechanism, he wrote, can be designed to maximise both economic growth and social fairness; if economic agents follow instructions provided through central planning, then central-planning goals will be accomplished. In socialism, therefore, economic agents' behaviour in accordance with instructions set by a central planning mechanism serves as a substitute for the free pursuit of self-interest found in capitalism.

Figure 1.2 shows the structure of the socialist economic system. The three bases are different from those of capitalism. The market mechanism is replaced by central planning. Instead of an individual pursuing his or her self-interest, he or she must follow instructions given by central planning and designed to achieve socially desirable outcomes. State or public ownership enables the state to use resources in accordance with the decisions it makes based on central planning.

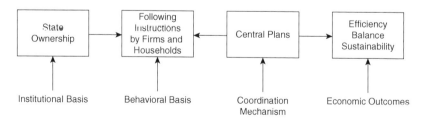

FIGURE I.2 The Socialist Economic System

It is noteworthy that there is another difference between capitalism and socialism: central planning is the initiator of economic decision-making in socialism, as the arrow in Figure 1.2 suggests, whereas in capitalism, individuals initiate decision-making, and markets, as the coordination mechanism, work according to the decisions made by individuals.

Socialism was a grand-scale experiment of an economic alternative to capitalism. Adam Smith described and justified capitalism as a system that had already been put in motion, but Karl Marx designed and initiated implementation of the ideal of socialism. In this sense, the former was based on the natural evolution of society, whereas the latter was based on human design. Unlike capitalism, however, socialism did not last for long. The Soviet economy experimented with socialism from 1918 to 1991, but eventually failed. The failure of this experiment after fewer than 80 years implies that the system had fatal flaws. We next discuss what those flaws were and how they occurred.

Both capitalism and socialism attempt to achieve socially desirable economic outcomes. In other words, the objectives are nearly the same in both economic systems. An ideal economic system should function to maximise efficiency and maintain a macroeconomic balance between supply and demand. Furthermore, it should be sustainable for a sufficiently long period. A more efficient economic system has the ability to produce more output using the same quantity of inputs or the same quantity of output using fewer inputs than an alternative economic system, suggesting higher long-run economic growth rates. The existence of permanent aggregate shortages is undesirable: It causes long queues, an underground economy and reduced incentives to work. The permanent oversupply of goods and services is not desirable, either, because it results in the waste of valuable resources. Finally, an economic system that is doomed to collapse after a short period of time cannot be considered desirable and, if possible, it should not be adopted. Hence, we evaluate the performance of the former socialist countries using the three criteria suggested earlier: (1) the efficiency of the former socialist countries, particularly the former Soviet Union; (2) chronic shortages of consumer goods; and (3) the sustainability of the socialist economic system.

The next section of this chapter begins with a discussion on the performance of the socialist economy, including the growth rates, extent of inefficiencies and shortage of consumer goods. Sections 1.3 and 1.4 focus on the behaviour of economic agents, that is, households and firms. Section 1.5 discusses studies on the causes of the collapse of the socialist economies, particularly that of the Soviet economy. Five theories or hypotheses are presented and evaluated. At the end of the chapter we will discuss the implications of socialist reforms for the stability of the regime.

I.2 THE PERFORMANCE OF THE SOCIALIST ECONOMY

I.2.a Growth Performance

To understand the performance of former socialist economies (FSEs), one must look at growth statistics. However, the reliability of growth statistics on FSEs is limited. Official statistics appear to have several faults: hidden inflation, over-reporting of output and exaggeration of quality improvements. Unofficial estimates are not perfect either, suffering as they do from data deficiencies on prices, quality and volume of outputs. Thus, the cautious approach is to compare all available statistics and understand the lower and upper limits of growth rates. We concentrate on growth statistics for the Soviet economy because more data are available in that area and previous studies have concentrated on the growth of that economy.

An economy's growth can be attributed to two sources: (1) the expansion of inputs such as capital and labour and (2) the better use of given inputs. Growth based on the expansion of inputs is called 'extensive growth', whereas growth based on the better use of inputs refers to 'intensive growth'. Accordingly, growth rates can be divided into one part accounted for by more inputs and another part accounted for by better use of inputs. By subtracting the growth rates of employment and capital from the growth rates of output, one can obtain labour productivity and capital productivity, respectively. Total factor productivity, which is a measure of better use of inputs or efficiency, is computed by subtracting the growth of employment and capital combined from the growth rates.

There are three different estimates of Soviet GDP: official Soviet statistics, the Central Intelligence Agency (CIA) and Bergson's estimates and Khanin's estimates. There are large discrepancies among these estimates. According to the Soviet official statistical office, Soviet economic growth was astonishingly high, amounting to 8.8 per cent per annum during 1928–1985. In contrast, CIA and Bergson estimate annual growth in the same period as 4.3 per cent (Bergson, 1961; CIA, 1991). Khanin, a Russian economist, provides the lowest estimates among the three alternatives: according to him, the Soviet economy grew by 3.33 per cent per annum from 1928 to 1985 (Khanin and Selyunin, 1987; Khanin, 1991; Harrison, 1993). According to the CIA/Bergson estimates, the Soviet economy was approximately two-thirds of the size of the US economy in the late 1980s, assuming that Soviet real national income in 1929 was approximately 20 per cent of the US level. However, Khanin suggests that the Soviet economy was only approximately one-third the size of the economy of the United States in the late 1980s.

These discrepancies result from the different methods used to estimate prices and the volume of output. First, the CIA/Bergson and Khanin methods take into account 'hidden inflation'. These estimates assume that the official Soviet price statistics underestimate actual increases in prices. For example, new products were likely to be introduced at disproportionately high prices that were not fully reflected in the official price index. Second, it was possible for firm managers to overstate quality improvements. Consequently, price increases, at least in part, exceeded what could be justified on the basis of quality improvements. Third, output figures may have been exaggerated. In other words, Soviet firms had an interest in over-reporting their outputs. The CIA questioned the reliability of price and quality improvement data but accepted output statistics given in physical units. Khanin, however, was suspicious of all of those statistics and developed his own methodology for estimation based on both physical and indirect measures of output. Ericson (1990) criticised Khanin's method, asserting that the Khanin estimate represents the extremely low bound because hoarding – which might be difficult to determine in the sample of products on which Khanin based his estimation – increased over time, and Khanin's assumption that labour productivity in the USSR was the same as that in the US twenty years earlier might have underestimated physical outputs.

We use the CIA/Bergson estimates unless stated otherwise, in spite of some criticisms.[2] They are the most reasonable estimates, both because of the methodology used and because they fall midway between the upper and lower bounds.

According to CIA estimates, the Soviet economy grew by 3.5 per cent from 1950 to 1990 (CIA, 1991). Average annual growth rates of the United States and the European countries belonging to the Organisation for Economic Co-operation and Development (OECD) recorded for the same period were 3.2 and 3.7 per cent, respectively. That is, the Soviet growth rate during this period was slightly higher than that of the US, but lower than that of the European OECD countries. However, given the larger capital stock per capita in the US and European OECD, the Soviet growth rates would be expected to be higher than those of the other countries. All of this leads us to conclude that Soviet economic growth was not impressive during this period.

Another interesting and important feature is that Soviet growth was slightly faster than that of Western industrialised countries from 1950 to 1970. More specifically, annual growth rates for the Soviet economy were estimated at 5.2 and 4.8 per cent in the 1950s and the 1960s, respectively, while European OECD countries grew by 5.1 and 4.4 per cent during those same periods. This trend, however, reversed after the 1970s, and the deterioration in economic growth intensified over time until the Soviet economy disintegrated. The Soviet average annual growth rate declined from 2.4 per cent in the 1970s to 1.7 per cent in the first half of the 1980s, and fell further to 1.3 per cent in the second half of the 1980s.

The trend of deterioration in growth following a rapid increase is found in other Eastern European economies (Kornai, 1992). For example, Czechoslovakia grew by 4.7 per cent (2.8 per cent)[3] per annum during 1971–1980, according to official net material product statistics. However, the growth rate declined to 1.7 per cent (1.2 per cent) from 1981 to 1985. The same pattern is found in Poland: the Polish annual growth rate from 1971 to 1980 was 5.3 per cent (3.6 per cent), but it was only 0.1 per cent (0.6 per cent) from 1981 to 1985. The Hungarian growth rate decreased from 4.7 per cent (2.6 per cent) in 1971–1980 to 1.8 per cent (0.7 per cent) in 1981–1985.

What was the source of this downward trend in growth rates for former socialist countries? Very low efficiency lies at the heart of the problem. Comparison of the productivity of the Soviet Union and the United Kingdom shows that factor productivity of the former was lower than that of the latter. The average British factor productivity, which had been modest among the Western European economies, was 1.6 per cent from 1950 to 1990 (Crafts and Toniolo, 1996), whereas the average Soviet factor productivity during the same period was 0.2 per cent, just 12.5 per cent of the British level (Schroeder, 1997). In other words, the Soviet economic system was less efficient than capitalist countries; it had to utilise more inputs to achieve the rates of economic growth achieved by an advanced market economy. This was true not only in the period after the 1970s, when the Soviet economy began to deteriorate, but also in the period of the 1950s, which can be considered the 'Soviet golden age' in terms of growth performance. Moreover, the Soviet factor productivity became negative from the 1970s to the economy's demise, suggesting that the level of inefficiencies intensified over time.

1.2.b   Inefficiencies

To what extent were FSEs less efficient than comparable capitalist countries? Bergson (1987) assessed the efficiency level of seven capitalist countries and four socialist countries (the Soviet Union, Poland, Hungary, Yugoslavia). Bergson estimated a modified Cobb-Douglas function, which includes an economic-system dummy, that is, socialism and capitalism, using data for 1975. He found that the four socialist economies were 25 to 34 per cent less efficient in 1975 than were advanced market economies in the same year. The magnitude in the gap depends on whether one controls for the skill level. This suggests that a country's GDP decreases by at least one-fourth when it adopts socialism instead of capitalism, although capital, land, the number of workers and skill are the same as they were before adoption. In his later article, taking possible overestimation of outputs and capital into account, Bergson (1992) revised his estimates and suggested that the productivity shortfall of FSEs relative to market economies would reach approximately 40 per cent.

The cause of this inefficiency in socialist economies is the matter of an old debate between Oskar Lange and the Austrian school of economics. The Austrian school of economics, represented by von Mises and Hayek, argued that a socialist economy is intrinsically inefficient. It argued that information about the value of resources requires private ownership and markets, without which the efficient allocation of resources would not be feasible. Private ownership motivates economic agents to evaluate the value of goods and services. Markets collect such evaluations from many agents, and as a result the economic scarcity of resources is reflected in prices found in markets. Because socialism lacks private ownership and the price mechanism, the argument goes, it cannot allocate resources efficiently.

Oskar Lange refuted this argument and claimed that socialism was able to mimic the price mechanism through 'trial and error'. His idea is explained in a model developed by Heal (1969). Lange argued that central planning can be optimal in that planners can allocate inputs in the most efficient manner. Assume that central planners maximise social welfare subject to an input constraint. One simple example involves maximising the sum of two outputs produced by two firms. The two firms use the same input, so the quantity of input used by either firm is flexible, subject to the fixed quantity of total input. Next, the central planner requests information on marginal output when each firm obtains one more unit of output. Given this information, the central planner allocates more input to the firm whose productivity is higher than the other, and this 'trial and error' continues until marginal output is the same across the two firms. In this way, socialism has the ability to maximise total output.

However, several problems exist in this model when it is applied to real-world situations. One main problem concerns incentives and information. If the firms defend their own interests and the central planners are partially ignorant of the situation within the firms, no efficient allocation of resources takes place. If a firm's manager is interested in running a bigger firm and believes that the central planner cannot detect his lie, he may exaggerate the marginal output of an additional input. Although the central planner has the ability to monitor firms, monitoring would require some cost. Such monitoring costs increase when the economy becomes more complex and the number of firms in the economy increases. All of this makes it extremely difficult for central planners to require that all firms honestly report their marginal output. Similarly, central planners have interests of their own that might lead them to favour certain firms. Nevertheless, the Heal model assumes that neither central planners nor firms are interested in maximising benefit to their own interests.

1.2.c   Balance: Shortage of Consumer Goods

Most of the economists agreed that socialist economies were more inefficient than advanced market economies. However, before the collapse of FSEs in the late 1980s and the early 1990s, there was no consensus among scholars on the macroeconomic balance between supply and demand in those economies. Some economists, including Nove and Kornai, have argued that socialist economies suffered from disequilibrium between consumer demand and the supply of consumer goods. In contrast, Portes and his colleague have asserted that there is no evidence of macroeconomic shortage of consumer goods in socialist economies.

The existence of chronic shortages in FSEs is an important issue. It suggests that FSEs failed to balance demand and supply. It also indicates that the socialist economic system is not durable. As we will discuss later, the shortage of consumer goods may have a spillover effect on the supply side of labour. More importantly, it has implications for the credibility of the economic system. If households often failed to be able to purchase the consumer goods that they desired, they were likely to lose faith in the socialist economic system, and that may have influenced the socialist countries' political systems. This led numerous economists to examine the issue of whether, and to what extent (if any), there was a macroeconomic shortage in socialist economies.

With respect to the existence of shortages in the consumer market, some economists have relied on anecdotal evidence such as long queues and increasing bank savings over income. This anecdotal evidence would be difficult to consider as *prima facie* evidence of the existence of shortages, not only because it lacks rigorous verification but also because a surfeit of some goods and a shortage of other goods might exist at the same time.

Accordingly, economists have endeavoured to understand whether macroeconomic shortages existed in FSEs, and if so, the extent of those shortages. Several economists have attempted to develop econometric models that might be able to test the existence of shortages. The best-known examples are the works of Portes and his colleagues (1981, 1987, 1988). Their model estimates the supply-and-demand function of consumer goods and the minimum condition.[4] On the basis of this approach, they found that consumer markets in FSEs were actually in a state of excess supply rather than excess demand during 1955–1980. The approach of Portes et al., however, suffers from a critical problem. It implicitly assumes that central planners prefer the lack of shortages in consumer markets over other goals, such as rapid industrialisation and stable retail prices. This assumption is difficult to justify on the basis of real-world conditions.

The other way to measure shortage in centrally planned economies (CPEs) is a reduced-form approach based on shortage indicators. This approach has been used by Charemza (1989, 1990), IMF et al.

(1991), Chawluk and Cross (1994) and Kim (1997a, 1999). There are several reduced-form approaches, depending on the functions and indicators used. Economists have adopted shortage indicators to estimate money demand or consumption functions with proxies of rationing (shortage indicators). The significance of the coefficient of these proxies with a correct sign is regarded as suggesting the existence of a shortage in a consumer market. IMF et al. (1991) estimate a consumption function with a shortage indicator of the price ratio between prices in the official market and those in the secondary market, and they find little evidence of shortages in the Soviet consumer market from 1965 to 1985. Instead of a shortage indicator based on the price ratio, Chawluk and Cross (1994, 1997) use a shortage indicator based on the ratio of income over retail inventories in the official market to estimate a money demand function. Based on this approach, Chawluk and Cross (1994) find evidence of shortages in Poland: the size of the monetary overhang in Poland amounted to approximately 33 per cent of the household money stock before price liberalisation in 1990.

One serious drawback of using the ratio of free market prices to official prices as a shortage indicator is that it wrongly assumes that the share of spillover into the secondary market in forced savings is constant across years. For example, an increase in forced savings in the official markets may lead to a rise in consumption in the second (informal) economy, and thus an increase in free market prices. Hence, there is a positive correlation between forced savings and the shortage indicator. However, greater consumption in the second economy, given the same amount of forced savings, means not an increase, but a decrease in total shortages (which is not consistent with a higher shortage indicator). Thus, a consumption function approach that uses this indicator is unlikely to give accurate shortage estimates. The shortage indicator using the ratio of income to retail inventories also has an important problem: it fails to consider the role of the second economy in absorbing a portion of the monetary overhang.

Secondary consumer markets, where prices are determined by supply and demand, might be able to reduce or even eliminate shortages in the official market. In this regard, Alexeev (1988) argued that, in concept, there should have been no shortages if secondary markets existed in CPEs. In other words, consumers who failed to purchase their desired goods on the official market must have purchased them on the secondary market. According to Kornai (1992), however, another possible option for consumers is to abandon the intent to purchase when they face shortages in the official economy.[5] That is, it is possible for consumers to accumulate unspent money and then attempt to make the purchase later at an official retail shop, when supplies match their notional demand. This suggests that purchasing a consumer good in the secondary market is affected by consumers' characteristics – that is, whether they are time-sensitive or price-sensitive.[6] This, in turn, means that the transfer to the secondary market of all demand that is unfulfilled by the official market secondary market is not a general phenomenon. Instead, it may represent a special case when consumers expect either that goods will become unavailable in the official sector or that price liberalisation is imminent. The presence of the secondary market does not necessarily mean that it will absorb all of the official market's unfulfilled demand.

The discussion above implies that a proper shortage indicator should reflect not only the shortage intensity in the official market and secondary market, but also the size of the spillover effect on consumers' effective demand from the official market to the secondary market. Kim (1997a) proposes a shortage indicator that consists of two parts: the magnitude of unfulfilled demand that remains in the official market without entering the secondary market and the magnitude of unfulfilled demand in the official market. Based on this discussion, Kim (1997a, 1999) estimates a savings equation with the above shortage indicator, using the co-integration test and the dynamic error-correction mechanism. According to Kim's estimate (1999), the monetary overhangs in the Soviet Union in 1989 and in Russia in 1991 were 23 and 38 per cent of the total money stock held by households, respectively.

As regards the main causes of shortage of consumer goods in the Soviet market, Kim (2002) suggests retail price subsidies and the 'siphoning effect'; that is, the purchasing of consumer goods using enterprises' money without official authorisation. Retail price subsidies, which were introduced in 1965 to keep basic prices stable, rapidly increased from 1965 to 1989, rising from 4 per cent of state budget expenditures in 1965 to 20 per cent of those expenditures (or 12 per cent of GDP) in the late 1980s. Such increases in retail price subsidies had two negative effects on the Soviet economy. First, any increases in demand for consumer goods had to be met with increases in the supply of consumer goods. Second, investments, which were a main item in state budget expenditures, had to be squeezed. Anything else would have increased the budget deficit.

The siphoning effect in the Soviet Union increased rapidly starting in 1965. Traditionally, the state bank had regulated every transaction between enterprises to prevent passive money in the enterprise sector from transforming into active money with real purchasing power. However, the 1965 Economic Reform, which aimed to provide more autonomy in firm management and incentives for innovation, weakened state control over enterprise transactions. Without retail price subsidies, firms' purchases of consumer goods would have increased prices by reducing the remaining supply of goods. However, retail price subsidies caused the unofficial siphoning effect to intensify disequilibrium in the consumer market.

The role of central planning in balancing supply and demand was further hampered by the involvement of households in informal economic activities, which will be explained in more detail in the next section. Any shortage of consumer goods tended to encourage households to engage in various informal activities, such as cultivating private plots, engaging in informal trade and smuggling. These activities were difficult to account for in central planning, so the central planning effort was less effective at balancing supply and demand for consumer goods in the presence of the informal economy than it would have been otherwise.

1.2.d   Conflicts between Institutions and Behaviour of Economic Agents

The most important factors leading to inefficiencies and shortages in FSEs are inherent conflicts between institutional settings and the behaviour of economic agents. In order for FSEs' central planning to work, economic agents must follow the instructions given by central planning. There is no guarantee, however, that firms and households will behave in accordance with such instructions. Both firms and households are tempted to pursue their own self-interests when those interests conflict with instructions from central planning. This means that central planners have to motivate economic agents by means of moral and material incentives and then have to monitor their behaviour. However, increases in the complexity of the economy over time raise monitoring costs. As a result, the socialist economy based on state ownership and central planning encounters a serious mismatch between institutional economic interests and the behaviour of economic agents.

This indicates that, even in the socialist system, economic performance is determined not just by the government (i.e. central planners) but also by firms and households. The latter interact with the central planners, but respond to current economic conditions in a way that best addresses own benefit. Through this process, actual outcomes may turn out to be less optimal for society overall. Thus, it is essential to discuss the interactions among the three actors when analysing a socialist economy. In the following discussion, we analyse the behaviour of households and firms in economic environments established by the central planners.

1.3   HOUSEHOLDS IN SOCIALIST ECONOMIES

1.3.a   Informal Economic Activities

The economic sectors with high priority in FSEs were normally heavy and defence industries, while the consumer sector attracted limited attention from central planners in the allocation of resources. The supply of consumer goods often failed to satisfy demand, and their quality and variety were limited, compared to Western countries. These circumstances led households to engage in various informal activities to obtain food and goods that were not available in the official retail network. The cultivation of private garden or farming plots is a prime example of such activities. Kolkhoz markets were allowed to trade food. Despite prohibitive laws, the informal trading of manufactured goods was frequently used to obtain goods during shortages. Private builders (shabashniki) were also employed by households to build houses and dachas (summer houses). Illegal distillation (samagon), private tutoring, private medical services and private consumer services also played a part in the informal economy, and Western music, cosmetics and clothing that were prohibited by Soviet law were smuggled into the Soviet Union. Illegal production and transactions were often accompanied by bribes and favours (blat). Raw materials, spare parts and other inputs for production were reported as stolen from firms (Grossman, 1977), and then traded in informal markets.

Grossman (1977) pioneered research on the Soviet informal economy (i.e. the second economy). He defined the second economy as one for 'all production and exchange activities that fulfil at least one of the two following tests: (a) being directly for private gain; (b) being in some significant respect in knowing contravention of existing law' (p. 25). However, more systematic estimates of the magnitude of the Soviet informal economy were provided only after the data on Soviet households became available. Using data from Soviet immigrants to Israel, Ofer and Vinokur (1992) estimate that the share of private income in Soviet households was 11.5 per cent of total income and that 18.1 per cent of all consumption expenditures were paid to private individuals. Grossman (1987) provides higher estimates: private income of urban households made up between 28 and 33 per cent of total household income. However, results from a non-random sample of immigrants should be interpreted with caution. Using unpublished Soviet family budget surveys representative of the Soviet population, Kim (2003) found that the informal economy was large. The average share of informal income (or expenditure) as a percentage of total income (or expenditure) from 1969 to 1990 was 16.3 per cent (or 22.9 per cent). He classified informal economic activities into three areas: informal production, illegal production and rent seeking. According to this study, some increases in these activities were observed at the end of the 1980s, but such increases were modest.

The significant informal economy in FSEs might distort information used for central planning. It would be difficult to draw a plan to balance between supply and demand for consumer goods, considering consumer goods produced in the informal economy, given the nature of informal economic activities. Demand for consumer goods in the official economy might have been affected by the informal economy in part because demand for consumer goods may have shifted from the official economy to the informal one, or vice versa. Household demand for consumer goods could change because of income from informal economic activities, which would not have been reflected accurately in central planning. As the informal economy provided business opportunities for private gains, some inputs from the official economy could be stolen and then used for such a business. This could be a partial explanation for why central planning became less effective in controlling the consumer market. This would imply that central planning that is 'optimal' according to official documents cannot be optimal in the presence of an informal economy.

1.3.b Shortage and the Labour Supply

Barro and Grossman (1971, 1974) emphasised the interconnections between the labour market and the goods market when they discussed various macroeconomic regimes. They classified macroeconomic regimes as Walrasian, Keynesian unemployment, classical unemployment or repressed inflation, with the Walrasian regime referring to macroeconomic conditions in which the two markets are at equilibrium. The Keynesian unemployment regime applies to the conditions in which excess supply exists in both the goods and the labour markets. In contrast, unemployment in the labour market together with excess demand in the goods market denotes the classical unemployment regime. Finally, demand exceeding supply in both markets is a feature of the repressed inflation regime. Barro and Grossman argued that shortage in the consumer market leads to a decrease in labour supply in the regime of repressed inflation. This is called a 'supply multiplier'.

FSEs belong to the repressed inflation regime because excessive demand in both markets is their main feature. Given the interconnection of these two markets, the disequilibrium school asserts that shortages in the goods market will reduce output through decreases in labour supply. In other words, when households' consumption plans are frustrated, they will generally substitute leisure and therefore supply less labour at any given real wage, which will decrease output. This theoretical prediction implies that FSEs suffering from shortages in the consumer market are unstable.

Empirical evidence on the supply multiplier is mixed. For example, Howard (1976), testing the effects of shortages on savings and labour supply in the Soviet Union, found that households were forced to save rather than reduce their labour supply, given the system's consumer-goods shortages. He attributed this to Soviet practices that made it difficult for Soviet workers to reduce their working hours freely because of heavy regulations and harsh penalties. By contrast, Gaddy (1991) maintained that workers were able to steal time from their workplace, whereas firm managers were reluctant to apply penalties because of a shortage of labour.

Davis (1988) suggested that one of the reasons for the lack of responsiveness in the labour supply was the prevalence of informal economic activities in the Soviet Union. That is, money had real purchasing power in the informal economy, where consumers were able to buy goods that were unavailable to them through the official economy. Households that faced shortages in the official market – but not necessarily in the secondary market – could increase their labour supply either in the official economy or in the second economy, depending upon wage rates, their preferences, etc. Similarly, the informal economy and shortages reflect flaws in central planning. Households were able to behave in a way that exploited these flaws for their own benefit. As a result, allocation of resources became sub-optimal, indicating that the behavioural basis for FSEs failed to work in accordance with the central planners' ideology.

1.4 FIRMS IN SOCIALIST ECONOMIES

1.4.a Firms under Asymmetric Information

Central planners need to know the production capacity of firms before they can decide on output targets. The behavioural basis of socialism assumes that firms honestly report their production capacity and then follow the instructions given by central planners. However, firms are interested in receiving more inputs together with low output targets, and thus want to conceal their true production capacity from central planners.

What happens if the firm manager defends his or her own interest and the central planners suffer from asymmetric information on firm's input/output capacity? As an example of incentive problems in FSEs, Weitzman (1980) developed a model that shows the potential interdependence of plan targets and performance levels in succeeding periods. This model assumes that firms' true capacity is not directly known to the central planners, and that the central planners therefore derive information about the firms' true capacity from their past performance, given a particular performance target. In other words, the central planners intend to impose increased output targets based on the difference between a firm's planned output and its actual output from the previous period, because they assume that the firm has some amount of extra capacity to produce more output.

In response to this 'ratchet' principle, firm managers choose not to exert a high level of effort to maximise production, since a high level of output during one period will lead to a decrease in utilities for subsequent periods. Effectively, the ratchet mechanism has a negative effect on enterprises' contemporaneous output. This model assumes that the extent to which a gap between a planned output target and actual output is an exogenous variable decided by the planners. If the central planners understood the negative correlation between this ratchet and a firm's performance, how would they react? According to the model, a decrease in the extent of the ratchet mechanism may actually increase output. However, when we combine this decrease with the economy's being more complex, it may lead to declining growth – or even collapse (Harrison, 2002; Gregory, 2004). This phenomenon is analysed in the section addressing the collapse of the socialist economy.

1.4.b   Firms in the Shortage Model

The relationship between central planners and firms in FSEs were regarded as special in the sense that the former act as guardians for the latter. This point was taken by Janos Kornai (1971, 1986a, 1986b), who attributed the inefficiency of socialist firms to the soft budget constraint (SBC). The SBC denotes paternalistic relations between the state bureaucracy and enterprises. According to Kornai, the perfect SBC includes price-setting activity by enterprises, a soft tax system, free state grants, a soft credit system and risk sharing with outsiders, especially with the state. Firms in CPEs are exclusively concerned with investment (called 'investment hunger') and quantity of production ('quantity drive') rather than sales and the quality of products. Enterprises in CPEs are inevitably inefficient because they operate in a seller's market, experience chronic shortages of inputs and suffer from technological bottlenecks.

Kornai explains how the SBC causes problems such as chronic shortages in inputs and outputs. The SBC encourages firms to invest more and to become bigger because they do not need to worry about bankruptcy. This causes shortages in inputs to become a permanent feature in CPEs, which in turn results in low levels of innovation, forced substitution and hoarding of inputs. On the output side of the firm, quantity becomes the most important concern for firms' operation, so managers pay little attention to the quality of output. Sellers' markets and output shortages result from firms' behaviour under the SBC.

The shortage school, on the basis of the above analysis, claims that inefficiency in FSEs results from institutional arrangements. The central planning system specifies that firms are under its control, and therefore any problems in the firms are the responsibility of the central planners. This problem is aggravated by the fact that all firms are owned by the state and, as a result, a firm's bankruptcy is regarded as the state's failure.

The institutional aspect of the SBC was emphasised by Dewatripont and Maskin (1995). According to them, the SBC is the result of a dynamic commitment problem in which a funding source finds that an *ex ante* financial plan is not optimal any longer *ex post* and thus fails to make a credible commitment not to refinance the firm. For a funding source, an investment or loan in the previous period is a sunk cost when it must renegotiate *ex post* about whether the investor will decide to bail the firm out instead of liquidating it. Understanding this dynamic commitment problem, a firm's manager submits bad loan or investment projects to a funding source. According to Kornai et al. (2003), simple changes to governments' or banks' loan policies are likely to fail to harden budget constraints. Instead, it requires the creation of a different institutional setting such as privatising banks and allowing competition among regional governments and firms. However, such changes were deemed as being inconsistent with socialist ideology and institutions.

I.4.c Government Responses

In response to firm behaviours that cause inefficiencies, the Soviet government introduced several measures, ranging from the self-accounting system to institutional reforms. Central planners concluded that a fundamental problem in the system lay in the fact that the rigid central planning mechanism failed to motivate firms to run efficiently. The self-accounting system (khozraschet) was emphasised in the Soviet Union beginning in 1957 with a view toward making firms self-supporting and not reliant on government subsidies. Firms were required to be financially responsible, although most of the firms' profit still had to be remitted to the government budget.

The 1965 Economic Reform in the Soviet Union can be regarded as the most far-reaching reform in the country before perestroika. Reform measures involved the planning system and regulations on wages, prices and bonuses. The essence of this reform was to enlarge the autonomy of firms by reducing the number of plan targets and allowing firms a certain degree of latitude in setting wages and prices, and providing material incentives in the form of bonuses. However, the reform was not radical enough to change the coordination mechanism and to transform property rights. In addition, the price system was not set rationally, because price reform was limited to wholesale prices without consideration for supply and demand (Adam, 1989).

Decentralisation was also used to respond to increased ineffi-ciencies in the economy. The 1965 Economic Reform can be viewed as decentralisation intended to partially shift decision-making and responsibility from the upper hierarchy to firms. Regional decentrali-sation was another attempt. Part of the role of central planners was taken up by regional planners, who made plans for their region. This regional planning was adopted by Khrushchev in the late 1950s, but ended without much success when he lost power in the early 1960s.

Some of the reform measures during perestroika were more radical than the 1965 Economic Reform. One example is the Law of the State Enterprise, which allowed firms to enter into contracts with other firms without approval from upper administrators. The Law on Private Economic Activity is another example. It allowed individuals to engage in private business activities with the condition that they obtain a licence. Furthermore, state employees were permitted to establish cooperatives for the produc-tion of consumer goods, with profits to be distributed to the mem-bers of the cooperative. In this sense, perestroika altered some of the key institutions of FSEs: coordination by central planners and state ownership. Nevertheless, these reforms can be regarded as falling within the socialist ideology because the main components of the system were still based on central planning and state ownership. This does not necessarily deny the possibility that the reforms could be the beginning of a transition toward a market economy, but the reform measures were not coherently implemented and resistance was quite strong. Consequently, perestroika ended abruptly, without allowing sufficient time to observe its effects.

Brus and Laski (1989) put forward the following evaluation of economic reforms which attempt to combine some elements of market economy with the socialist economic system:

> ... we still strove for a compromise solution, blending macroeconomic central planning with autonomy of market-regulated state enterprises. Subsequent, continuous and careful observation of the tortuous reform process ... brought us to the conclusion that such compromise was conceptually unviable. (Preface)

Kornai (1992) concurs with this diagnosis, arguing 'Nor can there be a comprehensive and consistently radical transformation in the other spheres while the key feature of the old classical structure, the Communist party's power, remains' (p. 566). The negative assessment of partial reforms such as perestroika, from the perspective of coordination failure, will be presented in next section.

I.5 SUSTAINABILITY AND COLLAPSE OF THE SOCIALIST ECONOMY

I.5.a Causes of Collapse

In the previous section, we discussed various theories that attempt to account for the inefficiency of socialist economies. Different theories identify different causes for that inefficiency. The work on incentives and information suggests that an information gap between central planners and firms, together with the incentive problems faced by firm managers, are the sources of inefficiency. The shortage model also claims that the relationship between the centre and the enterprise sector is important, but with a different emphasis. The shortage model ascribes the cause of inefficiency to SBC, meaning that it would not have been possible to eliminate inefficiency in socialist economies even if the knowledge and incentive problems had not existed. In contrast to these two models, the disequilibrium model maintains that the reduced labour supply of households confronted with shortages in the consumer market was the main source of inefficiency. In other words, this model argues that the cause of the trouble lies in the household sector rather than in the enterprise sector.

1965 Economic Reform

Although the three theories that we discussed in the previous section can account for socialist economies' inefficiencies, they are less relevant to the overall collapse of the socialist economies. Clearly, the collapse of an economy is a dynamic process. A theory for the collapse of an economy does have to explain why the economy's performance deteriorated over time, but neither the theory based on information/incentives nor that based on shortages appears to be useful for a theory of collapse. These theories are applicable to the period of a typical socialist economy system such as the Stalinist command economy, during which information asymmetry between central planners and enterprises was the most severe and the SBC affected enterprises to the greatest extent. However, Eastern European countries, including the Soviet Union, experienced further deterioration in efficiency when they implemented economic reforms that provided enterprises with more autonomy. For example, the Soviet Union introduced the 1965 Economic Reform that abolished many targets, including the mandatory output target, and switched the centre-dominated system to a more autonomous system in which firms were allowed some freedom to set prices and wages. Nevertheless, economic performance either failed to improve or deteriorated. Furthermore, the economies even collapsed when socialist control became more relaxed. The disequilibrium theory based on the supply multiplier can account for the dynamics of economic growth; shortages led to decreasing output through a reduction in labour supply, which further intensified shortages, causing even lower output levels. It is not clear, however, whether the supply multiplier operated in socialist economies. In the presence of a substantial informal economy, households may have had an incentive to earn more income despite shortages in the official economy. Moreover, in socialist economies, the extent to which households were allowed to reduce their labour supply might have been limited.

To account for the collapse of the Soviet economy, we need a theory that captures its dynamic process. The theory should also be able to explain how economic collapse is related to political disintegration. Five theories or hypotheses can be considered as possible explanations for the collapse of socialist economies:

i Coordination failure: the partial replacement of central planning with a less-controlled market brought to light shortcomings in the coordination mechanism.

ii Informalisation: the Soviet economy disintegrated because of ever-increasing informal economic activities.

iii Quantity of corruption: a relaxation of rules in an authoritarian regime spurred the process of disintegration because of a rampant increase in corruption.

iv Quality of corruption: the application of a lower degree of tautness to the plan led to greater use of resources for personal consumption rather than inputs for production.

v Forced surrender: the tendency of rising costs of monitoring and punishment caused the authorities to abandon the socialist system.

Coordination Failure

Murphy et al. (1992) have argued that partial reform – which is defined as the coexistence of state firms and private firms, the coexistence of free and controlled prices, and the free choice of customers – can lead to economic collapse due to diversion of substantial inputs from higher-to lower-value uses. Murphy et al. provide such a case by using the example in which one input industry – that of timber – supplies inputs to industries, that is, housing and boxcars. Before reform, the central planners allocated timber to these industries efficiently; in other words, timber was rationed between the two sectors so that the marginal valuation of timber was the same in the two sectors.

Partial reform privatised the housing industry, which consequently enjoyed greater financial resources. However, the boxcar industry was still state-owned and thus financially constrained. The allocation of timber was now partially liberalised in the sense that timber could be sold at the offered price, but the controlled price remained the same as before. In addition, decision-makers in the timber industry were able to choose to whom to sell timber. Under this partial reform, the housing industry had the ability to offer a timber price higher than the official price and could thus buy timber until the valuation of timber represented by its demand curve was equal to the official price. Consequently, more timber was allocated to the housing industry, while the boxcar industry received the timber that remained after sales to the housing industry. Welfare, measured in terms of consumer surplus, decreased as a result of this partial reform because it diverted resources from higher- to lower-value uses (i.e. from the boxcar industry to the housing industry). If not enough boxcars are produced, other industries that require boxcars as inputs will suffer. As a result, the total output in the economy may decrease.

Murphy et al. (1992) suggested that a partial reform causes a vacuum in the coordination mechanism: neither plans nor markets operate as a dominant coordination mechanism. It destroyed central planning's role as the coordination mechanism, but at the same time failed to bring in true markets as a substitute. Murphy et al. ascribe this coordination failure to Gorbachev's partial reform, *perestroika*, which contributed to the collapse of the Soviet economy.

One question arises, however: why was China's partial reform successful? Murphy et al. argued that China's partial reform was different from *perestroika* in that the Chinese government required the traditional socialist sector to continue to follow the plan, whereas the new private sector was allowed to be coordinated by markets. One critical condition for the applicability of China's partial reform to other countries, then, is that the state must be able to require input firms to sell the same (pre-reform) amount of input at pre-reform prices (Roland, 2008). If this condition had not been met, the Chinese partial reform would have caused significant corruption while creating confusion in the coordination mechanism.

Informalisation

According to the informalisation hypothesis, the Soviet system collapsed because the socialist economy was informalised in a way that allowed private economic activity, misappropriation, corruption and organised crime to become prevalent (Treml and Alexeev, 1994; Grossman, 1998). For example, Treml and Alexeev (1994) claimed that the negative effects of the informal economy – such as loss of productivity and the malfunctioning of the central planning system – became larger than its possible positive effects, such as 'greasing the wheels'. This hypothesis is clearly presented in Grossman (1998): 'the USSR's shadow economy and the rest of its underground in the end contributed to the system's collapse' (p. 24).

The effects of the informal economy, also called the 'second economy', may be both positive and negative. Positive effects include an increase in the production of goods and services. In addition, free secondary markets might reduce the disincentive effects of shortages on the labour supply. However, the informal economy can have a depletive effect by switching inputs necessary for the official sector to the secondary sector. Information used by central planners can also be distorted, which causes a weakening of state control over the economy.

The informalisation hypothesis may account for the collapse of the Soviet economy if the informal economy was large enough and had been increasing substantially. Estimates from Ofer and Vinokur (1992), Grossman (1987) and Kim (2003) on the share of informal expenditures in household total expenditures range from 18 to

33 per cent. These figures appear to be sizable, though it is reasonable to question whether they are large enough to cause the collapse of a socialist economy. However, Kim (2003) found that the informal economy as a percentage of GNP did not increase over time. There were some increases in informal economic activities in the late 1980s, but such rises were modest.

Quantity of Corruption

Shleifer and Vishny (1993) suggest that a regime collapses because of relaxation of authoritarian rules. More specifically, a dictator is able to maintain the regime by collecting bribes for him- or herself, but preventing others from doing so, whereas a partial liberalisation of the authoritarian regime will allow multiple agents to maximise bribes independently, leading to a deterioration of production activities and eventual economic collapse.

Shleifer and Vishny (1993) define corruption as 'the sale by government officials of government property for personal gain' (p. 599), and they classify corruption into two types: corruption without theft and corruption with theft. The former refers to the case in which an official pays the government the official price for the good, whereas in the latter case the official does not pay anything to the government. Between these two types, corruption with theft is the more difficult to eradicate because the interests of buyers and sellers are aligned. In contrast, corruption without theft is a less persistent problem because the buyers become worse off than they would have been without corruption, so the interests of buyers and sellers are in conflict.

Competition among officials and buyers can increase corruption. An official who intends to take bribes will offer bribes to his or her superior. If the job is indeed allocated to the official who gives the largest bribe, an honest or less corrupt official is not able to take the job. Competition among buyers also spreads corruption. In the case of corruption with theft, a company can outperform its competitors by paying bribes and thus avoid taxes, which are more costly. As a result, a company that pays taxes honestly will be forced out of the market.

The size of corruption depends on the type of political regime. A fully operational democracy can effectively prevent corruption from spreading because of the development of institutions. Complaints from voters, political competition among parties, the independent press and political minorities will contribute to the disappearance of corrupt officials. It is also said that dictatorships can effectively control corruption because the dictator him- or herself receives bribes but uses his or her power to severely penalise corrupt inferiors.

Shleifer and Vishny indicated that a relaxation of authoritarian rules in the Soviet Union contributed to its collapse. When Gorbachev relaxed the rules, allowing greater freedom among ministries and officials, those ministries and officials were able to engage in corrupt behaviour without expecting severe penalties from above. Previously, the KGB had been an effective policing mechanism to monitor bureaucrats' actions, but it became less effective as the society became more liberalised.

This analysis implies that in terms of efficiency, dictatorial control of the number of the ruling elites and monitoring of their actions by means of policing mechanisms is better than a liberalised but non-democratic government. Similarly, reforms that introduce some elements of market economies into a traditional socialist state may destabilise the system by allowing more officials to engage in corrupt activities.

Quality of Corruption

Although Shleifer and Vishny's argument may account for the collapse of the former Soviet economy, no empirical findings to support their theory have emerged. Moreover, it is questionable whether reforms in the Soviet Union (*perestroika*, for example) led to a dramatic increase in corrupt behaviour, as suggested by Kim (2003), given that rent-seeking activities, measured in terms of transfers between households as a proportion of GDP, increased only modestly during the latter half of the 1980s.

Harrison and Kim (2006) provided another explanation of corruption as a cause of the collapse of the Soviet regime. According to them, Soviet economic performance was affected by the *quality* of corruption rather than its *quantity*, that is, the way in which corrupt incomes were used by enterprise managers. The researchers illustrated how changes in a government control mechanism may influence the quality of corruption, and how that can translate into changes in economic performance. According to their model, enterprises are able to generate some corrupt resources, but these resources may in turn be applied either to the purposes of personal enrichment or to those of production-related activities in the enterprise. They suggest that reductions in plan tension during the 1970s changed the quality of corruption from a production orientation to a personal enrichment orientation, which contributed to the collapse of the Soviet economy.

More specifically, some enterprises obtained discretionary cash through activities that were illegal and officially prohibited. The managers behaved corruptly not just for their own private interests, though, but also as a way to increase production and help their enterprises fulfil their plans. It was possible for the managers to use the cash at their disposal to get their employees to work longer and to purchase inputs from unofficial *tolkachi* (supply agents) or in the retail market. In this way, the corrupt money softened resource constraints, enabling firms to produce more for a given amount of official money and a given amount of effort.

A reduction in plan tension during the 1970s meant that it was no longer necessary for enterprises to use discretionary liquidity for production. Combined with planners being less strict about allowing price increases, this enabled firms to increase prices in order to fulfil their output targets. This resulted in the use of siphoned funds, not for improvements in production but for personal enrichment, causing more severe shortages. Inflation also increased due to hidden inflation. In other words, the firms produced less real output and set inflation rates higher, leading to an economic crisis. Harrison and Kim provided evidence that siphoning was used more for personal gain than for purchase of inputs for production in retail markets. As plan tension relaxed in 1980, 1985 and 1989, siphoning for personal consumption purposes (such as for tobacco and food) increased faster than siphoning for general-purpose goods, such as light automobiles, which could be used as inputs for production.

Forced Surrender

One problem with previous explanations is that unlike the hypotheses' prediction, the Soviet economy did not experience severe recession before its collapse. This implies that the Soviet collapse was caused partially by an intentional action. Harrison (2002) focuses on the rise of monitoring costs and punishment costs in the economy and argues that it was those costs that led Soviet authorities to abandon the socialist system.

In Harrison's model, the players in the command system are defined as self-interested producers and a dictator, maximising their own payoffs. If certain conditions are met in the forward-looking game, high coercion by the dictator and high effort by the producer will be at equilibrium. In other words, when the cost of monitoring is smaller than the value of rents stolen by the producer, paying a reward can be the dictator's best long-run strategy.

This discussion implies that the costs of monitoring disintegrate the socialist system. In a socialist system, monitoring costs are quite likely to increase over time as the number of firms increases, as firms' characteristics become more complex and as the volume of information that must be monitored soars. When monitoring costs exceed the value of stolen rents, the dictator has no incentive to retain the system, and so gives up. By this reasoning, a Soviet-type system cannot be sustainable; eventual collapse is more or less an inevitability as the cost of monitoring rises. However, the collapse of the Soviet system was forced despite the failed efforts of the last Soviet leader, Gorbachev, to preserve the system until the last moment. The next question to consider is why was the collapse of the Soviet system so sudden.

Harrison ascribes the sudden collapse to the dictator's weakened reputation as a cruel leader. In such a situation, producers, who believe that the dictator is less likely to mete out punishment, steal rents. Although the dictator monitors the producers so long as the monitoring costs are smaller than the value of stolen rents, he or she will forgive and condone a producers' strike if he or she perceives the potential cost of punishment to be high enough. If the producer understands that there will be no punishment, he or she becomes likely to steal rents, and the dictator will abandon the system.

This discussion suggests that two factors cause the disintegration of the socialist system. Because of monitoring costs, the Soviet system was destined to end naturally over time. Another factor is the loss of political control; the system may break down if the dictator loses his or her credibility as a brutal leader and, consequently, the producers expect no punishment. The sudden collapse of the Soviet economy can be accounted for by the latter: confronted with a strike movement and no possibility of restoring efficient penalties, the dictator was forced to abandon monitoring and to surrender.

1.5.b Reforms and the Collapse of a Socialist System

All of the theories we have discussed suggest that relaxation of state control over the economy has negative effects on the stability of the regime in a socialist state. All of the theories other than informalisation directly relate the relaxation of control over the economy to regime collapse. Informalisation does so indirectly, because firms and households are more likely to be involved in illegal economic activities when the punishment for such activities decreases due to the relaxation of authoritarian rules.

A question may arise about why the socialist authorities would have wanted to reform the economy at all. As we examined in the introduction, the primary reason was that the system was found to be too inefficient and over time inefficiencies had increased. A seeming alternative was to reform the economy by introducing elements of a market economy, providing enterprises with greater autonomy and offering society more freedom. However, such reforms endangered the stability of the system rather than strengthening it, and pushed the economy to the point of collapse.

These theories contribute to an accounting for the collapse of the socialist economy. The central planning system required that producers be monitored, but monitoring costs rose and coordinated planning turned out to be more difficult because the economy became too complicated to accommodate a consistent, coherent plan. The mismatch between plan and reality was sufficient excuse for firm managers to adopt corrupt practices and to rely more on other informal mechanisms. Shortages of consumer goods in official markets contributed to the informalisation of the economy. These economic conditions, in turn, justified economic reforms intended to allow more autonomy for firms in setting wages, prices, etc. The reforms then further destabilised the economy, however, as firms made the most of opportunities to enrich themselves rather than boost production. The change to a view of the political leader as more democratic and rule-based then triggered the ultimate process of collapse, reinforced by the economic factors discussed above.

The five theories we have discussed can be classified into three groups, depending on which actors are involved. Three theories – including coordination failure, quality of corruption, and forced surrender – base their arguments on the relationships between firms and the government. The quantity-of-corruption model examines changes in officials' behaviour in response to different political regimes. Although our discussion did not pay explicit attention to the role of the government, informalisation can be regarded as households' and firms' response to changes in government policies. In terms of active players, the former group of theories suggests that the government or dictator is more important than firms. In contrast, informalisation suggests the possibility of change from below, as increases in informal economic activities transform both the incentives and the behaviour of officials and firms.

The framework for analysing a socialist economy will be applied to North Korea in Chapter 2. Following a discussion of North Korea's economic system, we will look at the three actors in that economy. The dictator decides the economic system and the policies that

determine economic performance. Households and firms make decisions about their behaviour given economic system and performance,
and government policies. In turn, households' and firms' behaviours
influence the decisions of the dictator or the government.
By transforming the economic system and the incentives of the actors,
this dynamic process has implications for regime stability.

NOTES

1. The numbers after the year of the publication refers to book, chapter,
   and paragraph, respectively, according to the original divisions. This also
   applies to the subsequent citation from Smith.
2. Boretsky (1987) argues that the CIA underestimated Soviet economic
   growth for the following reasons; the Soviet authorities might have
   intentionally withheld information about products whose output had been
   rapidly growing, and output index in physical units would not adequately
   account for improvements in the quality of the goods produced. However,
   there was a wide belief that the CIA overestimated Soviet economic
   performance (GAO, 1991).
3. Alternative GDP statistics according to CIA estimates are given in
   parentheses.
4. The minimum condition is needed because the observed market
   transactions are the smaller of supply and demand. The supply and demand
   of consumer goods are not directly observable, but by using the minimum
   condition with the functions, one can estimate whether supply or demand
   is larger or smaller than the other. This approach was adopted and tested by
   Portes and his colleagues to identify shortages in FSEs.
5. According to Kornai (1992), the other options for consumers to take include
   forced substitution, search and postponement of purchase.
6. Kim (1997a) classifies consumers into two types in terms of the extent of
   disutility of queuing: consumers with low disutility of queuing and
   consumers with high disutility of queuing. The former are more likely than
   the latter to buy a consumer good in the secondary market, and the latter's
   evaluation of the price difference between the official market and
   the second one is larger than their discount factor.

2   The North Korean Economy

2.1   THE NORTH KOREAN SOCIALIST ECONOMIC SYSTEM

2.1.a   Brief Economic History

Establishment of a Socialist Economic System in the Democratic People's Republic of Korea up to 1953

Korea was unified in 676 AD when Silla, one of three kingdoms located in the Korean peninsula and Manchuria, defeated Goguryeo and Baekje and drove Tang, a Chinese dynasty that attempted to conquer the three kingdoms, away from the Korean peninsula. The Korean people preserved their history, language and culture under the same political authorities during the subsequent dynasties, Goryeo and Chosun. The last emperor of the Chosun dynasty, however, was forced to sign an annexation treaty with Japan in 1910, which saw the beginning of the Japanese occupation.

The Japanese occupation ended in 1945 following Japan's defeat in World War II, which led to the liberation of Korea. However, Korea was divided as a result of the negotiation between the United States and the Soviet Union, despite strong opposition from South Koreans. The Soviet army, which remained in the northern part of Korea, installed a socialist state and established the Democratic People's Republic of Korea (DPRK). The southern region of Korea adopted a market economy and democratic political institutions under the tutelage of the United States, although a fully functioning democracy was not established until the 1980s. The division left about two-thirds of Korea's total population (15.6 million out of 23.5 million people) in South Korea and the remaining one-third (7.9 million) in North Korea. The division brought about not only political problems but also a massive economic shock. About 92 per cent of the electrical power used in South Korea had been supplied by power plants in the North, but North Korea stopped supplying electricity after the division. In addition, South Korea lacked mineral resources, most of which were located in North Korea. On the other hand, the bulk of agricultural land and light industries were located in the South, so North Korea suffered from a lack of food and consumer goods. For instance, in 1945 the shares of steel and chemical production were 95 per cent and 85 per cent in the North versus 5 per cent and 15 per cent in the South, respectively. In contrast, in the same year, the shares of food and consumer goods production were 65 per cent and 80 per cent in the South and only 35 per cent and 20 per cent in the North (Lee, 1984). The division of Korea into the South and the North disintegrated their previously interdependent economic structure.

The Soviet Union appointed Kim Il-sung, who had led a group of Korean guerrillas against Japan and served as an officer in the Soviet army before the liberation of Korea, as the leader of North Korea. His attempt to build a socialist state was aided both economically and politically by the Soviet Union and other socialist states (Kimura, 2001). The DPRK was established in the North on 9 September 1948. Earlier in the same year, in May, the South held its first general election, after which the founding of the Republic of Korea was declared there on 15 August 1948.

The two Koreas did not maintain a peaceful coexistence. In 1950, North Korea invaded South Korea with the support of the Soviet Union. The Korean War was one of the deadliest manifestations of the Cold War between the American and Soviet blocs, the latter of which included China. The war ended in 1953 with an armistice agreement signed among the United Nations (UN), North Korea and China. The South Korean government opposed this agreement.

Prior to the Korean War and under the supervision of the Soviet Union in the late 1940s, land in North Korea had been confiscated from its owners and transferred to farmers. The nationalisation of large enterprises in the North occurred soon after the division of the two Koreas. The Central Bank (Chosun Joongang Eunhaeng) was established in the North in 1946 and was managed according to the principles of a socialist economic system. The process of transforming North Korea into a socialist state occurred rapidly, mainly because of Soviet influence. However, the Korean War prevented the further transformation of the North Korean economy into a full-fledged Soviet-type socialist economy before 1953.

Mass Mobilisation and Daean Management System, 1953–1983

After the war, North Korean authorities accelerated the process of transforming North Korea into a socialist economy. They took away farmers' land and nationalised it. Collectivisation in agriculture began in 1953 and came near completion in 1958. Small-scale enterprises that were privately owned before the Korean War were also nationalised after the war. The change in ownership proved to be easier, however, than establishment of a fully working, centrally planned economy, because North Korea lacked the necessary requirements for developing such an economy. North Korea had neither reliable data on the nationalised firms nor the capacity to organise economic institutions and agents according to a socialist framework. Moreover, the North Korean authorities' efforts to set up a system of central planning was hindered by a worsening of the relationship between North Korea and the Soviet Union after Stalin's death.

The death of Stalin in 1953 and the appointment of Khrushchev as the First Secretary of the Communist Party of the Soviet Union discouraged North Korea from pursuing a Soviet-type socialist economy because North Korea viewed Khrushchev's attempt to reform the Stalinist economy as being revisionist. Furthermore, conflicts between the Soviet Union and China after the death of Stalin compelled North Korea to balance its policy between both countries. As a result, the subsidies and technical help from the Soviet Union to North Korea were reduced substantially, which interfered with North Korea's goal of establishing a 'scientific', centrally planned economy according to detailed planning mechanisms similar to those used in the Soviet system. Consequently, North Korea relied on inaccurate approximations of figures when developing its plans and combined its central plans with a mass mobilisation policy that was geared toward economic development.[1] One such plan was 'Chullima Movement' ('Movement of horse running 400 kilometres'), which was implemented from 1958 to 1961.[2] This movement was intended to maximise the effort of industrial workers by means of a form of 'speed battles', something like the Great Leap Forward in China, which occurred during the same period. The North Korean authorities were having difficulty securing investment resources because of a sharp decrease in the amount of aid received from other socialist states, so they used this movement to increase their supply of resources for production. The mass mobilisations were also used to overcome certain inadequacies of the central plans. For instance, households were mobilised to produce fertiliser during a fertiliser shortage; in another case, authorities forced firms and organisations to mobilise resources to construct power plants.

After certain problems with running a centrally planned economy became apparent to North Korean authorities, they adapted the economic system to emphasise the common effort of workers to increase the productivity and self-reliance of firms. This was called the Daean management system, named for an electronics firm that Kim Il-sung visited in December 1961.[3] Daean management followed three principles: the first was to place political priorities above economic ones, the second was to focus on moral and spiritual incentives rather than material rewards and the third emphasised the role of the Workers' Party Committee over that of management in the supervision of firms. The supreme decision-maker in any business became the firm's Workers' Party Committee, of which the firm's manager was a member. Workers' Party dominance in the operation of firms was strengthened by the establishment of these committees.

The Daean management system also initiated other practical changes. For example, several firms that supplied raw materials and intermediate goods were established in an attempt to solve the chronic shortage of inputs. Kim Il-sung viewed the lack of inputs as a result of the incompetency and bureaucracy of existing firms, and decided instead to transfer the responsibility for supplying inputs to specially designated firms.

Attempts to Change Economic Management, 1984–1990

Unlike China, which follows a multi-divisional form (M-form) organisation, North Korea adopted the unitary form (U-form) economic organisation model of the Soviet Union.[4] In order to exploit the economies of scale, firms in a given region were organised to supply goods and services not only to other firms that were in the same region, but also to firms in other regions. Specialisation was the key principle in grouping the firms. The decentralisation of the regional planning mechanism was introduced in 1981, but only lasted until 1983. In 1985, North Korea implemented a new policy to integrate firms universally, something like the kombinat policy that was introduced in East Germany. Combined enterprises, which were called 'Yeonhap Giupso', were designed to integrate firms vertically or regionally.[5,6]

All of these attempts, including the Daean management system, regional decentralisation and Yeonhap Giupso, can be viewed as reactions to the severe difficulties North Korea faced in supplying raw materials and intermediate goods to firms, a problem prevalent not only in North Korea but also in other socialist countries, including the Soviet Union. Nevertheless, the extent of this problem in the Soviet Union was arguably less severe than in North Korea because Soviet plans were more coherent and realistic than North Korean plans. Given its incapacity to plan a coherent economy, as time passed and the economy became more complex, North Korea faced increasingly serious problems in supplying inputs according to plan.

Notable changes were eventually observed in external aspects of the North Korean economy, particularly in the mid-1980s. These changes were related to North Korean authorities' previous, failed attempts to deal with external relations in the 1970s. Following the path of Eastern European countries, in the early 1970s North Korea adopted an import substitution policy in which capital goods such as large plants and machinery were imported using money that was borrowed from Western countries. The purpose of this policy, which was similar to that of Eastern European countries, intended to allow North Korea to rapidly catch up with Western economies by importing their technology. However, plunging prices for nonferrous metals, a main export item for North Korea, resulted from the first oil shock and prevented North Korea from paying back its debt in the late 1970s. In response to this problem, Kim Il-sung emphasised the importance of exports during his New Year's Day speech in 1979, saying that 'we should make it a top priority to produce exportable goods in all sectors of the national economy'.[7]

To achieve this end, North Korea created the Joint Operation Act in 1984 to increase foreign direct investment. Under this Act, North Korea attracted 148 instances of foreign investment with a combined value of approximately US$200 million (Nanto and Chanlett-Avery, 2008). However, the majority of these investments (131 cases, or 88.5 per cent) were made by pro-North Korean residents of Japan. North Korea had failed in its attempt to obtain a large sum of foreign direct investment from a wide group of foreign investors.

Despite suffering from a long-term economic decline since the 1960s, the North Korean economic system did not undergo substantial change until the mid-1990s. North Korea remained a mass-mobilised, centrally planned economy, even though the country's central planning lacked detail and consistency. Faced with economic decline and a shortage of consumer goods, the authorities emphasised an economic accounting system similar to that used in the Soviet Union (khozraschet) as well as self-reliance of firms in terms of providing consumer goods to their workers. Large firms were integrated to facilitate the timely and sufficient provision of inputs to firms that were producing intermediate or final goods. However, these attempts did not yield the hoped-for positive outcomes.

Arduous March, Forced Economic Changes and Struggle
to Survive since 1990

The collapse of the Soviet bloc in the late 1980s and the early 1990s resulted in a crisis in North Korea. The industrial structure of the North Korean economy relied heavily on heavy manufacturing, which required the import of energy from other countries. Until its collapse in the early 1990s, the Soviet Union had been a main supplier of oil for North Korea. After the Soviet Union's collapse, North Korea was unable to meet its oil demand, partly because Russia now demanded hard currency in exchange for its oil exports instead of agreeing to a traditional, barter-type settlement. The direct effect was a standstill in North Korean industries. Given that power plants were unable to function without an adequate oil supply, the country's electricity output fell and firms in the extractive industry were unable to produce sufficient natural resource products, which were the main inputs for other industries as well as important export items. An undisclosed source suggests that the capacity utilisation ratio of North Korean firms in the mid-1990s fell by approximately 50 per cent in the late 1980s (Park, 2002).

North Korea also experienced an extreme food crisis from 1995 to 1998. Robinson et al. (1999) interviewed 440 North Korean adult migrants in China in 1998 and found that the crude death rates in North Korea increased from 28.9 per 1,000 persons in 1995 to 45.6 per 1,000 in 1996, and to 56.0 per 1,000 in 1997. At the same time, the average size of households that included a person who had recently migrated to China declined from 4.0 at the beginning of 1995 to 3.4 at the end of 1997. Based on these survey results, Robinson et al. estimated that roughly 12 per cent of the population in North Hamkyung Province, which was the most heavily affected during the famine, had died between 1995 and 1997. This estimate is in line with the testimony of Hwang Jang-yop, who had served as the Chairman of the Standing Committee of the Supreme People's Assembly in North Korea and defected to South Korea in 1997.

Hwang claimed that approximately 500,000 people starved to death in North Korea in 1995, a number that increased to 1 million in 1996 and to 2 million in 1997. Recent empirical studies, however, indicate that such reported death tolls were exaggerated. Goodkind and West (2001) used nutrition surveys from the World Food Programme in 1997 and 1998 as well as calibrations based on the changes in population during China's Great Leap Forward and created an adjusted model that included implied infant mortality rates for North Korea, estimating the total number of deaths from 1995 to 2000 at approximately 600,000. By comparing data from the 1993 Population Census to official North Korean data that were submitted to international organisations, Lee (2004) inferred that around 630,000 to 660,000 people died between 1994 and 2000 when the narrow category of excess deaths was applied. Park (2012) used data from the 1993 and 2008 Population Censuses and found that the total loss from 1993 to 2008 amounted to 880,000, of which 490,000 people died from starvation, 290,000 resulted from a decreased fertility rate, and 100,000 were attributable to migration. Overall, empirical studies using nutrition surveys or the population census suggested that the number of deaths exceeded 500,000 to 600,000, approximately 2 to 2.5 per cent of the total North Korean population at the time.

North Korean authorities attributed this famine to the natural disasters of the mid-1990s, but the fundamental causes of the famine were actually structural rather than natural. Aside from the poor incentives for working on collective farms, North Korean agriculture was input-intensive and relied heavily on the use of electrically powered irrigation, chemical fertilisers and insecticides. The so-called 'Juche method of agriculture' encouraged the expansion of cultivated land, meaning that many trees were cut down from the mountains to create additional farming plots.[8] This left the agricultural areas of North Korea heavily exposed to natural disasters such as floods.

North Korean authorities decided to reduce the food ration provided through the Public Distribution System (PDS) by 10 per cent in 1987, before the collapse of the Soviet bloc and the floods of 1995. The food ration was reduced by a further 10 per cent in

1992, with an exception for military personnel (Lee, 2004). Essentially, the famine itself was triggered by a variety of unexpected events such as the disintegration of the Soviet bloc and natural disasters, but the country's agricultural production was already unable to cope with the increase in population even before these events occurred. This sense of the situation was confirmed by Noland et al. (2001), who applied computable general equilibrium model techniques and found that the restoration of land and capital that were lost in the flood had only a minor effect on the production of food.

In response to the serious economic crisis, North Korean authorities were compelled to implement several important changes in their management of the economy. These changes focused on four areas.

First, North Korean authorities implicitly allowed trading in markets. Market trading, except in small-scale collective farm markets, had been heavily repressed by the authorities. Unlike Soviet authorities, who even under Stalin had become more generous toward informal trading in kolkhoz markets, North Korean authorities had continued a strict prohibition on trading in markets before the 1990s (Kim, 2003; Lim, 2009).[9] However, the famine forced people to trade food, consumer goods and other essential materials for simple survival. Households were compelled to cope with the famine by collecting food from fields and mountains, selling assets and trading in the market.

After realising that they had failed to supply sufficient food through the PDS, the North Korean authorities substantially reduced their restrictions on the market. Furthermore, public anger against the regime intensified and was expressed more visibly during the Arduous March in the mid- and the late 1990s. It may be that the authorities also considered the possibility that a backlash could result from strict repression of market activity. As will be shown in Section 3 of this chapter, market trading in North Korea expanded significantly during this period. This 'bottom-up marketisation' (Haggard and Noland, 2007) or 'forced marketisation' of the North Korean socialist state has become an essential feature of the contemporary North Korean economy and has important implications for the future of the country.

Second, the North Korean authorities partially opened the economy up to the outside world after appealing for aid from the international community during the food crisis. They also announced establishment of Special Economic Zones (SEZs). Of these, the Rajin–Seonbong region located near the Chinese border was the first to be announced. Kumgang Mountain, which was created as part of an agreement between North Korea and the South Korean company Hyundai Asan, was announced as an SEZ in 1998. Kaesong Industrial Complex (KIC), also formed in 2000 as a result of an agreement between North Korea and Hyundai Asan, is another example. The KIC, located within 10 km of the northern line of the Demilitarized Zone (DMZ), began operations in 2004.[10] North Korean workers were also dispatched to various foreign countries where they operated various businesses such as restaurants and export agencies and worked in foreign-owned firms to generate hard currency.[11] North Korean organisations and institutions were similarly allowed to trade with companies from other countries. This policy was introduced to allow these organisations and institutions to seek their own means of securing resources for operation and for paying their workers. North Korean authorities never intended to fully liberalise the country's foreign trade, however, but rather to issue licences only to certain companies or organisations that it would allow to engage in foreign trade.

Third, the central government decentralised the planning process to the level of firms and districts. The fiscal collapse that resulted from the economic crisis prevented North Korean authorities from devising centralised plans to cover all firms and regions. Instead, they instructed individual firms to find inputs for themselves, with no expectation that the national government would supply such resources. Regional governments were also asked to independently seek inputs, food and consumer goods. As a result, planning was conducted from the bottom up instead of from the top down (Park, 2002). This decentralisation was related to both the marketisation and external liberalisation of the North Korean economy.

Fourth, the North Korean government implemented a major reform in 2002 known as the 'July 1st Economic Management

Improvement Measures' (or, more simply, the 'July 1st Measures'). This reform was based on the principle of a less-centralised decision-making structure which gave enterprises some autonomy in aspects of their planning of production targets, setting of prices, selling of goods in markets and purchase of inputs and spare parts. These measures are summarised in Table 2.1. The measures were comprehensive and ranged from changes in prices and wages to modifications in plans and firm management. Nevertheless, they did not include more fundamental reforms such as de-collectivisation and the creation of non-state firms, as were observed in China during the late 1970s and the 1980s. In addition, no measures were taken to legalise market exchanges.

The issue of whether the July 1st Measures were a step toward the transition of North Korea to a market economy has been extensively debated in South Korea.[12] A current evaluation suggests that such measures were implemented to normalise the socialist economy rather than to make a transition of the economy toward a market economy. Comparing the July 1st Measures with the reforms in the former Soviet Union and Eastern Europe, Kim (2005b) found that the measures adopted by the North Korean authorities were not sufficiently radical to be considered a step toward transition to a market economy and that such reforms were actually within the boundaries of reformed social-ism. In other words, the two core elements in a market economy – private ownership and market coordination – were not introduced in these reforms. Instead, these reforms concentrated on providing incen-tives, allowing more autonomy for firms and reducing planning.

In this sense, the North Korean reforms did not differ from reforms made by former socialist countries in the Soviet Union and Eastern Europe. For instance, the 1965 Economic Reform in the Soviet Union allowed firms to keep a part of their profits so that firms could use the profits to increase the welfare of workers by providing bonuses. However, this policy failed to contribute to growth because of the lack of market mechanisms and private ownership.

Table 2.2 suggests that all of the policy measures in the July 1st Measures had been implemented in the Soviet Union and Eastern

Table 2.1 *The July 1st Economic Management Improvement Measures: Comparison of Practices and Policies before and after their Implementation*

	Before implementation	After implementation
Prices	Prices in farmer's markets exceeded the official prices by tens or several hundreds of times.	Official prices rose vis-à-vis the market prices.
Wages	The average monthly wage ranged between 100 won and 150 won.	The average wage level of workers increased to 2,000 won.
Price setting method	Production cost was only considered when setting prices, and the prices were set by the central and regional administrative bodies.	International market prices, domestic supply and demand, and production cost were all considered in setting the prices. Some autonomy was given to the enterprises in setting the prices of their produced goods.
Plan formulation	The National Planning Committee had exclusive authority to formulate economic plans in accordance with the principles of consistency and detail.	The National Planning Committee was in charge of formulating plans for nationally and strategically important industries, provincial industrial outputs and investments in construction. The authority for other industries and plans was given to related institutions, enterprises and local administrative bodies.

Table 2.1 (*cont.*)

	Before implementation	After implementation
Management of plants and enterprises	Plants and enterprises were heavily controlled by the state using fiscal control (control by won) and the state adhered to a loose self-accounting system.	The heavy state control over factories and enterprises was loosened. The self-accounting principle was strengthened. Factories and enterprises independently obtained inputs and spare parts.
Markets for raw materials and spare parts	Only those transactions between firms that were in accordance with plans were allowed.	Markets for raw materials and spare parts were created. Some parts of raw materials and spare parts were allowed to be sold in markets, but the authorities still specified the types of goods that could be sold in markets, and transactions had to be made through banks.
Method of distribution	The spirit of equal distribution was emphasised.	Distribution was based on earned income. Bonuses were given based on profitability. The mobilisation of labour on national projects became paid labour.
Social security system	Food, other basic consumer goods and housing were provided by the government, nearly for free.	People had to pay for food, daily essentials, education and housing.

Source: Modified and translated by the author from Bank of Korea (2002)

Table 2.2 *Comparison of Reforms in North Korea with those in Former Socialist Countries*

North Korean reforms	Former socialist reforms	(Expected) results from these reforms
Partial introduction of incentives for producers	The 1965 Economic Reform in the Soviet Union	Negligible effects on output, due to the lack of market mechanisms and changes in ownership/competition
Allowing enterprises to set prices to a limited extent	The 1965 Economic Reform in the Soviet Union/New Economic Mechanism (NEM) in Hungary	May generate 'growth without growth' due to the lack of market mechanisms and changes in ownership/competition
Partial introduction of markets for raw materials and spare parts	Perestroika in the late 1980s	May induce a vacuum of coordination
Limited liberalisation of prices	NEM in Hungary	Increase in income inequality
Partial claim of profits	The 1965 Economic Reform in the Soviet Union/NEM in Hungary/Yugoslavian self-management	Temporary boom in investment, but increase in income inequality/disparities in growth between industries
Reduction in planning	The 1965 Economic Reform in the Soviet Union/NEM in Hungary/Yugoslavian self-management	Reduction in or abolition of planning, but no increase in output

Source: Extracted and translated from Kim (2005b)

Europe without success. In other words, the North Korean authorities failed to recognise the fact that such measures would not contribute to the recovery of the economy. At the same time, the characteristics of these reforms indicated that the North Korean authorities were unwilling to make radical reforms and were extremely cautious about the potential effects of such reforms on the stability of the regime. This stance conflicted with the first two changes that emerged from the crisis in North Korea in the 1990s: namely, forced market-isation and external liberalisation. The North Korean authorities' unwillingness to take on radical reform continued to hinder the insti-tutionalisation of marketisation and external liberalisation. However, marketisation and liberalisation intended to improve economic wel-fare and efficiency are considered likely to be in conflict with the authorities' political goal of maintaining power (Kim, 2014a).

Kim Jong-un, who is the third son of Kim Jong-il, took power following the death of his father in December 2011, but no fundamen-tal change in the economy has yet been observed. Instead, there have been some attempts to revive the economy. First, repression against market activities was reduced, which represents a reversal of policy concerning market activities during 2005–2009. Second, it appears that incentives were strengthened, in the form of a reduction in the number of farm households that are in charge of a common plot of land. Although the scale of this reform is not yet clear, three to five households were assigned to a common land and instructed to share returns among themselves, after having divided it between the state and the farmers according to some rule.[13] Third, nineteen small-scale economic development zones in various provinces were announced in 2013–2014. These include industrial, agricultural and tourism zones. Fourth, some large-scale construction projects have been implemen-ted. One example is a ski resort in Masikryeong, which was con-structed mainly to attract foreign tourists.

Annual economic growth rates appeared to be positive from 2011 to 2014. This growth might be ascribed at least in part to increased trade and market activities. An agricultural reform which introduced incentives based on the reduced number of individuals in one production team may have contributed to some extent to an increase in agricultural production. In contrast, other policies implemented by Kim Jong-un turned out to be ineffective, as the inflow of both foreign investments and foreign tourists is still quite limited. Furthermore, it is unlikely that the positive growth seen over the past years will continue if there is no institutionalisation of market activities or introduction of private property rights.

2.1.b The North Korean Economic System

Juche Ideology and Pseudo-Central Planning System Combined with Mass Mobilisation

North Korea claims that its economic system is based on the Juche ideology. Introduced in 1955, the term 'Juche' refers to the principle of 'we-centred' or 'self-reliance'.[14] Hwang Jang-yop, who conceptualised the Juche ideology in North Korea and later defected to South Korea, argued that the ideology was formulated in order to counter the principles of 'flunkeyism' and 'dogmatism', but was actually designed to prevent Soviet intervention in North Korean affairs (Free North Korea Radio, 2008). After the death of Stalin in 1953, Kim Il-sung saw a need to reduce Soviet influence over North Korea, especially after considering Khrushchev's criticisms against Stalin, which implied that even socialist ideology could no longer be used to justify the absolute dictatorship of Kim Il-sung and that his dictatorship could be challenged by both the Soviet Union and China (Yang, 2001). Moreover, conflicts between the Soviet Union and China during the Khrushchev era accelerated the establishment of a unique and independent socialist ideology in North Korea. The Juche ideology served two main purposes. First, the ideology indirectly justified the absolute dictatorship of Kim Il-sung by claiming that Soviet socialism was neither ideal nor relevant to North Korea. Second, the ideology allowed North Korea to maintain an equal distance between the Soviet Union and China as well as to ensure the survival of the regime, which would have been critically undermined if support from either country had been reduced. Therefore, the scope of the Juche ideology could be surmised as being very political, and not particularly designed to guide government policies for benefit of the economy.

The Juche ideology has no clear definition in the economic domain – none has been presented by the North Korean regime. The major elements of the North Korean economic system are similar to those in the Soviet Union: state ownership, the central planning system, collectivised farms and the monobank system were implemented in North Korea by the Soviet Union. Moreover, the essential instruments for the implementation of the Juche ideology, such as control of won (won is the North Korean currency), passive money in the enterprise sector, the self-accounting system (khozraschet) and consistent and detailed planning all were borrowed from the Soviet Union.[15] The term 'Juche' is only applicable to minor matters, such as some areas of technology or methods of production. Juche iron and the Juche method of agriculture are examples.[16] Only a few studies have indicated that the North Korean socialist economy is strictly managed according to the Juche ideology. Instead, the economy is similar to that of the Soviet Union in terms of its design.

Despite its being based on the Soviet type of socialist economy, the North Korean economic system encounters a fundamental problem when operating as a Soviet-type economy. Soviet-type central planning requires detailed data from firms and industries. Such data need to be processed by qualified technocrats who then formulate efficient plans for material balancing. In other words, high-quality data and well-trained technocrats are prerequisites for operation of a Soviet-style 'scientific' socialism. North Korea was incapable of creating, collecting and processing data because it lacked properly trained technocrats.[17] This was partly a result of the country's low level of economic development and partly a result of the Soviet Union's withdrawal of technical support for coherent central planning after the conflict between the two countries in the late 1950s.[18]

Instead of focusing on the collection of accurate data, North Korea relied on the mass mobilisation of the public, which was necessary to conceal the deficiencies in planning. Mass mobilisation helped the North Korean authorities overcome the country's economic and political crises and at the same time increase their control over the masses (Yang, 2001). For example, the Chullima Movement in the late 1950s began during a period of economic and political crises caused by sharp decreases in outside economic aid and conflicts between North Korea and the Soviet Union.[19]

The North Korean authorities also emphasised moral incentives rather than material incentives (an approach based in Confucian culture) to initiate mass mobilisation and develop socialism. This Confucian connection partially explains why China and North Korea share a tendency to use mass mobilisation, which was employed only temporarily and on a smaller scale in the Soviet Union and Eastern Europe. However, several important differences still exist between China and North Korea in terms of the characteristics of their mass mobilisation. First, unlike in China, mass mobilisation has been a constant feature in the North Korean economic system. North Korea has witnessed large-scale mass mobilisation in specific periods, such as the Chullima Movement, as well as smaller-scale mass mobilisation in other periods. North Korean university students and soldiers have frequently been mobilised in economic programmes such as rice planting, harvests and construction projects. This sort of activity has also been observed in other groups in society. Second, North Korean mass mobilisation was fully controlled by the authorities, whereas in China the mass mobilisation was extreme and exceeded the scope of control of the authorities. Both the Great Leap Forward and the Cultural Revolution, which affected the lifestyles of people from every level of society, demonstrated this intensity in mass mobilisation movements in China. Consequently, transformations in the Chinese economic system resulting from mass mobilisation were quicker and more dramatic, whereas similar transformations in the North Korean economic system were not observed until the 1990s.

Coherent central planning is incompatible with mass mobilisation: central planning is built on measurable and predictable data, whereas the outcome of mass mobilisation is difficult to predict. The existence of mass mobilisation in a socialist state indicates that the country is unable or unwilling to devise and implement coherent central planning. Recognising this, China opted for economic decentralisation while maintaining political centralisation (Xu, 2011). North Korea, however, invests its leader with absolute power, and that seems to necessitate a high level of centralisation in both the economic and political spheres. This degree of central planning is inherently handicapped with inconsistencies and inaccuracies and is difficult to operate without mass mobilisation. In effect, the North Korean economic system is a pseudo-centrally planned economy combined with a pattern of mass mobilisation of the public. The former aspect mimics the Soviet-style planned economy, while the latter is similar to the Chinese economy before its reform in the late 1970s.

Juseok Fond and Spot Guidance

Juseok Fond and Spot Guidance are unique elements in the North Korean economic system.[20] Juseok Fond is a fund or quota that is used at the discretion of Juseok, the president of DPRK, and includes both material inputs and currency. Firms are required to produce a certain amount of inputs for the Juseok Fond as their highest priority, which guarantees that all requirements are fulfilled. The requirements of the Juseok Fond are sometimes included in the national planning system but can also be ordered on an *ad hoc* basis (Yang, 2001).[21]

Juseok Fond was introduced in the early 1970s when Kim Il-sung became President of DPRK after the North Korean constitution was changed to appoint the 'president' as the supreme leader. Yang (2001) argued that Juseok Fond was used to ensure a sufficient supply of inputs for high-priority sectors. This explanation appears valid, considering that numerous complaints were raised even by high-priority sectors about the insufficient supply of inputs.[22] North Korean authorities also made adjustments to the economic system, such as the Daean management system, in attempts to improve the timely supply of sufficient inputs, recognising problems there as a major concern. Given these problems, the authorities could have acknowledged that the goal of establishing consistent and detailed planning was unrealistic. Instead, they attempted to seek an alternative mechanism to provide inputs to high-priority sectors.

The existence of a feature like Juseok Fond, administered and doled out by the nation's top leadership, is unique among socialist countries. The Juseok Fond has been used as a way to circumvent the bureaucracy associated with central planning (Kim, 2006), decreasing the power of the bureaucracy in North Korea by depriving that bureaucracy of complete control over resources. Another function of the Juseok Fond was to strengthen the power of the political leadership. Through exercise of their control over allocation of Juseok Fond resources, Kim Il-sung and the other top leaders demonstrate a unique ability to influence and govern the country.

The intention is to create political idolisation, and in this way Juseok Fond is closely related to Spot Guidance, a practice through which the top leaders of North Korea bestow special attention and instructions or directions when they visit an organisation, firm or institution. The top leader issues on-site instructions and directions on several matters, such as the production method in firms, restaurant menus and army uniforms. When he visits a place, he tends to provide special resources or special presents. His visits are broadcast by the North Korean mass media with great emphasis on the wise, kind and accurate guidance of the President as well as on the gratefulness of people who work at the site. In this manner, Spot Guidance has been used for political propaganda.[23] In the case of a firm, mass media often reports substantial increases in production after the leader has given Spot Guidance instructions.[24] However, these production increases may just as well have resulted from increases in the amount of inputs bestowed by the top leader from his Juseok Fond.

Table 2.3 shows the number of instances of Spot Guidance that were performed by Kim Jong-il in different sectors from 1994 to 2009. A total of 1,447 instances were conducted during this period, about 90

Table 2.3 *Number and Pattern of Spot Guidance Instances Performed by Kim Jong-il, 1994–2009*

	Economy												
	Agriculture	Fishery	Foodstuff	Light manufacturing (excluding foodstuff)	Electricity, power plant	Heavy manufacturing	Others	Sum	Politics	Education/ Culture	Military	Others	Total
1994												3	3
1995						1	1	2	10	9	7	6	34
1996				1	4			5	2	15	23	8	53
1997	1							1	5	22	22	5	55
1998	4		1	3	11	15	1	35	3	16	34	8	96
1999	17	7	3	9	9	7	1	53	6	8	27	6	100
2000	15	5	3	7	13	7		50	6	8	14	9	87
2001	14	6	11	5	11	8		55	1	17	27	7	107
2002	14	3	9	5	7	11		49	6	24	19	8	106
2003	9	2	5	4	9	1		30	4	9	40	4	87
2004	10	4	3	1	6	4		28	3	13	39	3	86
2005	6	2	5	5	4	10	1	33	1	25	48	1	108
2006	4		5	3	7	4		23	2	20	58	2	105
2007	4	1	4	7	7	13		36	7	17	28	7	95
2008	12	2	10	5	2	9	2	42	8	19	43	8	120

Table 2.3 (cont.)

	Economy								Politics	Education/ Culture	Military	Others	Total
	Agriculture	Fishery	Foodstuff	Light manufacturing (excluding foodstuff)	Electricity, power plant	Heavy manufacturing	Others	Sum					
2009	14	6	13	18	9	41	1	102	17	50	19	17	205
Total	124	38	72	73	99	131	7	544	81	272	448	102	1,447
Share (%)	8.6	2.6	5.0	5.0	6.8	9.1	0.5	37.6	5.6	18.8	31.0	7.0	100.0

Sources: Korea Institute for National Unification (2011); Central News Agency of Democratic People's Republic of Korea (various years); Rodongshinmun (North Korean official newspaper of the Workers' Party, various years).

Note: We counted the total number of visits in those cases in which Kim Jong-il visited multiple sites in the economic sector during one Spot Guidance instance. Hence, the actual number of Spot Guidance instances in the economy may have been overestimated.

every year. The annual number of Spot Guidance visits increased from 30 to 60 visits between 1995 and 1997 up to 80 to 120 visits between 1998 and 2008, and further increased to more than 200 visits in 2009. In terms of the share of total visits, the most frequent sites for Spot Guidance were in the economic sector (37.6 per cent), the military (31.0 per cent) and the educational/cultural sector (18.8 per cent).

The total number of visits in the military and economic sector between 1995 and 2008 were 429 and 442, respectively. These numbers reflect the attempts of Kim Jong-il to respond to two main problems: military strength and economic survival. With regard to the former, Kim Jong-il announced the 'Military First' (Songun) policy in the mid-1990s, and his frequent visits to military sites suggest that Spot Guidance was used to implement his policy. The number of visits in the economic sector also increased rapidly in the late 1990s, when the country was facing an economic crisis. This trend may reflect both the necessity of implementing economic policies to overcome the crisis and the necessity of preserving the political power of Kim Jong-il by maintaining his image as a hardworking leader who cares for the hardships of his people. Within the economic, agricultural and energy industries, power plants received the greatest number of visits from Kim Jong-il. This may reflect the major concerns of the authorities (i.e. to provide a sufficient supply of food to the people and to supply energy to those firms that lacked the necessary amount for operation), but there are no significant correlations between actual economic performance and the share of Spot Guidance visits to the economic sector, when time trend is controlled.[25] This indicates that Spot Guidance has not had much effect on economic performance and shows that, while both political power and the means of implementing main policies are concentrated in the hands of North Korea's leader, the exercise of neither of these has actually contributed to economic growth.

A fundamental problem in the planned economic system was the top leader's arbitrary intervention in the planning mechanism. The Juseok Fond and Spot Guidance actually disrupt the allocation of resources and production in accordance with the plans, meaning that the two interventions are incompatible with the centrally planned economy. Given that the Juseok Fond and Spot Guidance are assigned such high priority, firms tend to focus on their production for the Juseok Fond at the expense of the planned output, if the two targets are in conflict. Firms also seek to obtain resources from the Juseok Fond rather than from the plans. At the same time, firms compete to be selected as a site for Spot Guidance. All of this means that the North Korean economic system can be characterised as a 'plan-less' planned economy. The existence of the Juseok Fond and Spot Guidance also indicates that the North Korean economy is heavily subordinate to political priorities and that proper consideration is not given to economic efficiency.

Partial Marketisation and External Liberalisation
The traditional North Korean economic system was maintained without fundamental transformation until the 1990s. The economic crisis in the middle and late 1990s resulted in forced marketisation and external liberalisation that were not institutionalised by the authorities. These changes had important effects on the North Korean economic system. The traditional central planning system has virtually collapsed, with only some fragments surviving and controlling a few components of the economy. Substantial aspects of the economy have been replaced by informal markets and businesses with foreign companies. Recently, state ownership of productive assets in some areas has been transformed into unofficial, *de facto* private ownership of property. Such transformations have been most noticeable in the real estate sector. Sales of new flats and the trading of existing flats and houses among individuals indicate an implicit recognition of the existence of private property. Private financiers (called donju) are believed to be financing the construction of flats. Moreover, the planned economy itself has become intertwined with the marketised economy and interactions with foreign businesses (Kim and Yang, 2012). For example, some firms pay taxes to the government and

wages to their workers by selling their outputs in domestic or foreign markets. Some firms also allow their workers to be absent from their official workplace so they will be able to engage in market activities. In return, these firms receive some pseudo-taxes for allowing such absences.[26] As we will discuss later, North Korean households now earn more than 60 per cent of their income from informal market activities. They also spend more than 70 per cent of their income in markets, rather than receiving rations or spending their money in official retail networks.

The North Korean authorities have demonstrated a 'zigzag' policy for markets since 2002. The establishment of general markets, which were opened after the July 1st Measures, could be interpreted as an attempt to institutionalise the informal markets. By recognising the informal markets, authorities then became able to control and levy taxes on market activities. However, given the possible negative effects of such market activities on the stability of the regime, new anti-market policies were introduced in 2005 and then intensified since 2007. In 2008, Kim Jong-il criticised the markets and called them 'the residing place of anti-socialism'.[27] However, these anti-market policies, such as restrictions on the age of female traders participating in market activities and controlling the markets' opening time, were largely ineffective, due at least in part to government officials' turning a blind eye to violations in exchange for bribes from market participants.

This situation served as the backdrop for implementation of the currency reform of November 2009. North Korean authorities implemented policies intended to hit market activities directly, circumventing the need to rely on the cooperation of corrupt bureaucrats to repress markets. By changing the old North Korean won to the new won at the rate of 100 won to 1 new won, yet setting a maximum limit on the amount of old won that one could exchange, the currency reform seems to have been designed to shrink market activities in a way that would cause the suppliers to lose money from their business and cause their customers to experience a decrease in purchasing power.[28] The currency reform also enabled authorities to print extra money, since the existing stock of money had decreased substantially.

In addition to implementing currency reform, North Korean authorities also closed the markets and forbade market trading within the country. However, public anger and negative shocks to the economy compelled the authorities to reopen the markets, to acknowledge the currency reform as a failure, and to execute a high-ranking Workers' Party official as a scapegoat. Since then, market activities in the country have largely been tolerated. However, the sustainability of any coexistence between the market system and the socialist system remains uncertain.

Market activities are closely related to foreign trade and investment. The partial decentralisation of the North Korean economy also occurred in the external sector. In the 1990s, firms with trade licences were allowed to engage in export and import activities. In this way, the external sector became the main source of revenue and the ability to obtain inputs for a number of firms. Those firms that produce exportable goods such as natural resources and fish, as well as the institutions that are in charge of those firms, clearly became the winners during this period.[29] In some cases, firms leased their assets to individuals who were able to use those assets in a profitable manner (Kim and Yang, 2012). One beneficiary group included companies that owned trucks. Because transportation has become more important as markets have continued to develop, and given the limited supply of means of transportation in North Korea and market traders' need for faster and more reliable transportation for their goods, circumstances prompted producers to lease trucks from companies that had them. Firms found that they could also profitably lease cafeterias, shops and bathhouses to individuals.

Most of the consumer goods sold in North Korean markets are imported or smuggled from China (Kim and Yang, 2012). Foreign trade or business dealing with foreign customers is arguably the largest source of revenue for North Koreans and represents a critical source of purchasing power in domestic markets. In this way, external business relations and domestic markets reinforce each other. In addition, activities that are related to markets and foreign businesses also increase income inequality among North Koreans and, as a result, decrease social cohesion. Given that engagement in foreign business is lucrative and provides the most important source of income, it follows that institutions, firms and individuals in North Korea will compete against each other for the right to participate in foreign business transactions. The execution of Jang Sung-taek, the uncle-in-law of Kim Jong-un, may have been related to the intensified competition among North Korean elites to make material gains by engaging in foreign trade.[30]

The above discussion on the North Korean economic system is summarised and compared with conditions in the Soviet Union and China in Table 2.4. As discussed before, economic systems are based in institutions and the coordination and behaviour of economic agents. The most important institution, in terms of classifying economic systems, is property rights. Besides this, the extent to which institutionalised, centralised planning and control affects the decision-making and coordination of economic activities is an important factor. The behaviour of economic agents, which include firms and households, is affected by the type of incentives available in the economic system. The Soviet economy presented a typical centrally planned economy. It was based on state ownership, central planning, political and economic centralisation and a U- (unitary) form organisation based on functional activities. It also motivated economic agents to use both moral and material incentives for their own benefit. In contrast, China was less centralised economically but more heavily centralised politically. Furthermore, the main form of organisation in China followed an M- (multi-divisional) form, in which the country had multiple, self-autonomous economic regions. To motivate the economic agents, China relied more on mass mobilisation such as the Great Leap Forward and the Cultural Revolution, which can be regarded as an extreme form of moral and political propaganda, than did the Soviet Union. North Korea initially followed the Soviet system

Table 2.4 *Characteristics of the Economic Systems in Three Socialist Countries: The Soviet Union, China and North Korea*

Basis of economic systems	Components of economic systems	Soviet Union	China	North Korea
Institutional basis	Property rights	State-owned, but allowed cooperative ownership in the late 1980s	State owned, but allowed non-state ownership after 1978	State-owned with some primitive form of unofficial *de facto* private ownership, which appeared mostly in the 2000s
	Political centralisation	Centralised	Centralised	Highly centralised
	Economic centralisation/Form of organisation	Centralised/U-form	Decentralised/M-form	Highly centralised, but was decentralised in the 1990s/ Mainly U-form
Coordination basis	Coordination and decision-making mechanism/Key decision-makers	Relatively coherent and comprehensive central planning/ Politburo and bureaucrats	Relatively not coherent central planning with some regional decentralisation/ Politburo	Not coherent central planning, with Juseok Fond and Spot Guidance. Central planning virtually collapsed in the 1990s/Top leader

Table 2.4 (cont.)

Basis of economic systems	Components of economic systems	Soviet Union	China	North Korea
Behavioural basis	Incentives	Mostly material, with some moral incentives, particularly during the Stalin period	Both material and moral, with moral incentives being particularly strong during the Great Leap Forward and the Cultural Revolution	Moral (greater than in the other two countries); material incentives are of secondary importance

in terms of property rights and central planning. However, economic coordination according to central planning has frequently been disrupted by the use of Juseok Fond and Spot Guidance, elements that were found neither in the Soviet Union nor in China. North Korea is highly centralised politically, but economic centralisation has substantially weakened since the 1990s. The traditional form of organisation is U-form, but interlinkages between institutions and firms have loosened significantly because of the lack of resources to sustain such linkages.

2.2 PERFORMANCE OF THE NORTH KOREAN SOCIALIST ECONOMIC SYSTEM

2.2.a Long-Term Growth Performance of the North Korean Economy

North Korea regularly published a statistical yearbook until the early 1960s.[31] Since then, economic data for North Korea have become rare, although some official data were occasionally released. Lee (2007a) attributed this lack of economic data to the deterioration of North Korean economic performance. During the Arduous March in the 1990s, North Korea provided some economic data to international organisations in exchange for economic aid. However, these data were not consistently published.

Determination of long-term growth rates for North Korea is important when we try to evaluate the country's economic performance, but we are hindered by two critical problems when we attempt any such estimation. First, we lack consistent economic data on North Korea, as discussed above. Second, the growth rate of any socialist country is exaggerated because of the absence of an adequate price deflator. Statistical authorities apply official prices to the volume of output when computing for GDP, but these official prices tend to underestimate any actual increases in price (refer to Chapter 1). This phenomenon, which has been termed 'hidden inflation', causes overestimation of growth rates.

Several studies investigated the GDP/NMP (Net Material Product) of North Korea in years before the economic data became rare (Niwa and Goto, 1989; Lee, 2000). For example, Niwa and Goto (1989) estimated the GDP of North Korea from 1956 to 1959 following the CIA/Bergson method, which was based on the end use of GDP. Other economists estimated the GDP growth rates for North Korea until 1989 – that is, until the Bank of Korea (the central bank of South Korea) started publishing official estimates of the GDP and growth rates of North Korea (Hwang, 1993; Jo, 1993; Yoon, 1986). However, most studies rely on various assumptions that are difficult to justify, such as an absence of inflation during the estimation period, equal levels of inflation between North Korea and Eastern European socialist countries and a correlation between the official won/US$ exchange rate and the US wholesale price index. The existing literature claims that North Korean growth rates remained high until 1975, with some studies estimating that the North Korean GNP/NMP increased by more than 10 per cent per annum from 1953 to 1975.

According to most of the existing estimates, North Korea achieved reasonably rapid growth until the mid-1980s in spite of its declining trends. However, these estimates are inconsistent with the following two observations. First, the well-known severe economic crisis in the 1990s is a clear sign of North Korea's poor economic performance before the 1990s. It is difficult to believe that North Korea could suddenly have plunged into a huge economic crisis in the 1990s after having realised such favourable growth into the late 1980s. Second, Kim Il-sung mentioned in 1965 that the production per capita of North Korea had not increased for several years (Kim, 1982, vol. 20, p. 9). The gradual withdrawal of official statistics from the public domain since 1961 also indicates that the economic performance of North Korea has likely not been encouraging since the early 1960s.

These limitations prompted Kim et al. (2007) to assess the annual growth rates of North Korea from 1954 to 1989 using the approach of Maddison (1998), who used output volume instead of the amount of output in estimating China's growth rates. Kim et al. used the output volume of agricultural production of North Korea as officially published by either North Korea or South Korea. For greater detail, they combined North Korea's official data from 1954 to 1960 with South Korea's official data, as provided by either the Ministry of Unification or the Ministry of Agriculture, Food and Rural Affairs, from 1961 onwards. Official North Korean data on total industrial output growth rate, which had been published until the end of the 1980s, were utilised as well. However, these reported growth rates tend toward overestimation as a result of hidden inflation. The authors corrected this problem by assuming that the North Korean economy was similar to the Soviet-type economy in terms of its structure for generating hidden inflation.[32] They also assumed that the growth rate of the service sector was equal to the average of the growth rates of agricultural and industrial output, weighted by the GDP shares of the respective industries.

Kim et al. (2007) used these data to calculate the GDP growth rates of North Korea by weighting the GDP contributions of each industry – that is, agriculture, manufacturing and service. As regards the respective share of the three industries, they used data submitted by North Korean authorities to the United Nations Development Programme (UNDP) in 1992.[33] Assuming these shares to be equal to those for 1989, they estimated the average annual growth rates of North Korean GNP and per capita GNP from 1954 to 1989 to be 4.4 and 1.9 per cent, respectively. They also found that North Korea had experienced an economic slowdown, beginning as early as the early 1960s.

The Bank of Korea has estimated the North Korean GDP since 1990 using data on the volume of North Korean goods, multiplied by South Korean prices for the same goods. Data on the volume of goods and services produced in North Korea are collected using various methods, including satellite and intelligence information. Finally, North Korean GDP is estimated using the System of National Accounts of the Republic of Korea, in which the value-added ratio for South Korean industries is applied to the corresponding North Korean industries.[34] Given the severe lack of data on prices, alternative methods for estimating the GDP of North Korea are hard to find.

The Bank of Korea method described above suffers from several drawbacks, though its estimated growth rates are less problematic than its GDP estimates. First, the assumption that prices for North Korean products are similar to those for South Korean products may not be valid, considering that North Korean products are of inferior quality. Second, no geometric average between South Korean products and North Korean prices as well as between North Korean products and South Korean prices is used in the estimations. Instead, products from North Korea (a poorer country) are multiplied by prices from South Korea (a richer country), which induces an overestimation of the North Korean GDP. Third, changes in the ratio of value-added in South Korean industries may affect the North Korean GDP and growth rates. Moreover, the weight of specific industries that contribute to the North Korean GDP depends on the extent of the value that is added in the corresponding South Korean industries.

We updated and extended the estimated growth rates of Kim et al. (2007) from 1954 to 1989 to cover the years 1990 to 2013.[35] For this purpose, we estimated growth rates first and then used these to generate GDP per capita figures for all years except a reference year, for which GDP per capita is assumed.[36] Our estimates of growth rates have some advantages over those of the Bank of Korea because ours are not affected by the application of South Korean prices and value-added ratio.

Table 2.5 shows GDP shares for the three industries (agriculture; manufacturing and mining; and services, construction and others) and growth rates from 1954 to 2013. The GDP per capita in purchasing power parity (PPP) and in nominal exchange rates, both of which are expressed in 2012 US dollars, is also presented.

Table 2.5 shows that the North Korean economy experienced rapid growth from 1954 to 1960, possibly as a result of the country's recovery from the Korean War and an influx of aid from the Soviet

Table 2.5 *Annual Growth Rates, Industrial Structure and GDP Per Capita of North Korea, 1954–2013*

Year	GDP share		Services, construction, and others	GDP growth rate	GDP per capita	
	Agriculture	Manufacturing and mining			Purchasing power parity (2012 international US$)[a]	Nominal (2012 US$)
1954	0.439	0.169	0.392	9.22	1357	628
1955	0.433	0.175	0.392	9.37	1433	655
1956	0.433	0.175	0.392	7.77	1504	680
1957	0.430	0.178	0.392	13.38	1638	728
1958	0.433	0.175	0.392	16.49	1848	803
1959	0.394	0.210	0.396	-0.34	1783	780
1960	0.405	0.198	0.397	10.02	1889	818
1961	0.408	0.196	0.397	7.28	1978	850
1962	0.391	0.211	0.397	0.14	1932	833
1963	0.386	0.217	0.398	1.33	1907	825
1964	0.381	0.221	0.398	3.97	1919	829
1965	0.378	0.224	0.398	4.03	1958	843
1966	0.384	0.218	0.398	1.50	1935	835

Table 2.5 (cont.)

Year	GDP share			GDP growth rate	GDP per capita	
	Agriculture	Manufacturing and mining	Services, construction, and others		Purchasing power parity (2012 international US$)[a]	Nominal (2012 US$)
1967	0.378	0.224	0.398	4.35	1966	846
1968	0.374	0.228	0.398	4.12	1994	856
1969	0.377	0.225	0.398	0.60	1953	841
1970	0.361	0.240	0.398	5.88	2013	863
1971	0.356	0.246	0.399	3.15	2014	863
1972	0.348	0.253	0.399	4.84	2050	876
1973	0.338	0.263	0.399	4.17	2075	885
1974	0.330	0.271	0.399	4.56	2110	897
1975	0.315	0.285	0.400	6.32	2183	923
1976	0.315	0.286	0.400	2.07	2190	926
1977	0.308	0.291	0.401	3.53	2229	940
1978	0.292	0.306	0.402	2.79	2139	908
1979	0.292	0.307	0.402	7.57	2381	994
1980	0.242	0.351	0.408	-4.74	2230	940
1981	0.248	0.345	0.407	11.53	2447	1018

Table 2.5 (cont.)

| Year | GDP share | | | GDP growth rate | GDP per capita | |
	Agriculture	Manufacturing and mining	Services, construction, and others		Purchasing power parity (2012 international US$)[a]	Nominal (2012 US$)
1982	0.249	0.354	0.398	6.86	2573	1063
1983	0.238	0.364	0.398	-0.37	2523	1045
1984	0.244	0.357	0.399	4.80	2602	1073
1985	0.224	0.376	0.400	-2.26	2502	1038
1986	0.215	0.385	0.400	0.36	2483	1031
1987	0.214	0.386	0.400	2.82	2524	1045
1988	0.217	0.383	0.400	3.78	2589	1069
1989	0.220	0.380	0.400	3.83	2658	1093
1990[b]	0.208	0.392	0.400	-7.01	2443	1017
1991	0.237	0.359	0.403	-3.63	2323	974
1992[c]	0.255	0.341	0.404	-10.27	2054	877
1993	0.246	0.349	0.404	-5.76	1906	824
1994	0.261	0.334	0.405	0.21	1890	818
1995	0.241	0.353	0.406	-9.36	1698	750
1996	0.265	0.327	0.408	-2.74	1618	721

Table 2.5 (cont.)

| | GDP share | | | | GDP per capita | |
Year	Agriculture	Manufacturing and mining	Services, construction, and others	GDP growth rate	Purchasing power parity (2012 international US$)[a]	Nominal (2012 US$)
1997	0.282	0.309	0.409	-11.21	1422	651
1998	0.303	0.287	0.410	3.61	1464	666
1999	0.301	0.289	0.410	9.40	1591	711
2000	0.273	0.315	0.412	-6.18	1480	672
2001	0.281	0.307	0.412	6.73	1565	702
2002	0.291	0.296	0.412	1.03	1569	703
2003	0.291	0.296	0.412	2.84	1602	715
2004	0.292	0.296	0.412	1.18	1610	718
2005	0.293	0.294	0.412	4.82	1677	742
2006	0.290	0.297	0.413	-0.13	1664	738
2007	0.272	0.314	0.413	-4.78	1575	706
2008	0.279	0.307	0.414	4.85	1646	731
2009	0.276	0.311	0.414	-3.39	1581	708
2010	0.276	0.311	0.414	-0.25	1569	704

Table 2.5 (cont.)

| Year | GDP share | | | GDP growth rate | GDP per capita | |
	Agriculture	Manufacturing and mining	Services, construction, and others		Purchasing power parity (2012 international US$)[a]	Nominal (2012 US$)
2011	0.289	0.297	0.414	3.01	1609	718
2012	0.295	0.291	0.414	3.58	1658	735
2013	0.294	0.290	0.416	1.45	1667	739

Notes:

[a] An international dollar is used to equalise purchasing power between the United States and the cited country. In other words, with one international dollar, a person in the cited country would buy a comparable amount of goods and services a US dollar would buy in the United States.

[b] From 1954 to 1989, the manufacturing and mining industry includes not only the manufacturing and mining industries, but also the forestry, fishery and energy industries. This group only includes the manufacturing and mining industries from 1990 onward.

[c] According to the data submitted to the UNDP (1998) by North Korea, the GDP shares of the agriculture, mining and manufacturing industries and the others in 1992 were equal to 22, 38 and 40 per cent, respectively. We use such information for the share of the three industries in GDP in 1989.

bloc. However, the GDP growth rate of the country decreased substantially in the 1960s. The conflict between the Soviet Union and China hindered North Korea's development of its economy according to a well-organised central planning system. The Juche ideology was used to guide the direction of the economy, but ambiguities and a lack of coordination caused significant deterioration in the country's economic performance. The average GDP growth rate for North Korea from 1961 to 1969 amounted to 3.04 per cent, and its GDP per capita showed a slight decrease during the same period.

North Korean economic performance improved in the 1970s, with its annual average GDP growth rate remaining at 4.48 per cent on average from 1970 to 1979. Such an improvement may have been caused by two factors: import substitution policy and foreign direct investment. This notion is in line with Eberstadt's (2009) view that the share of total imports that are capital goods, which are correlated with economic growth, peaked in the mid-1970s. As Eastern European authorities did in the 1970s, the North Korean authorities adopted an 'import substitution' strategy, importing machinery and technology from Western countries to facilitate economic growth. In addition, they attempted to attract foreign direct investment, notably from ethnic Koreans living in Japan. Although these efforts increased the growth rate to some extent, they turned out to be unsustainable. Contrary to the expectations of North Korean authorities, foreign direct investment failed to bring a large amount of investments into the country. What investments there were came mostly from ethnic Koreans living in Japan, and the amount of available resources was limited. What is more, the import substitution strategy increased North Korea's external debt because the country needed to pay for that imported machinery and technology. In response, the North Korean authorities announced a moratorium on import substitution in the late 1970s, which halted the growth engine.

Although the North Korean GDP per capita increased from US$2,230 (in PPP) in 1980 to US$2,658 in 1989, the country's economic growth for the most part fluctuated during this period.

The unstable, largely stagnant North Korean economy of the 1980s was further affected by the collapse of the Soviet bloc in the early 1990s, which substantially decreased imports of oil and gas from the Soviet Union as well as international trade among the Soviet bloc countries. As a result, the output of energy-intensive industry in North Korea decreased by two digits in 1991 and 1992. Moreover, the country's agricultural production also dropped substantially because the collective farms of North Korea depended so much on energy inputs. To make matters worse, natural disasters such as droughts and floods affected the country's agricultural production in the mid- and late 1990s. For example, agricultural production decreased by 16.3 per cent in 1995, partially because of severe flooding.

During the critical economic crisis, North Korean authorities appealed for international aid and actively engaged in international trade. The economic recovery observed starting in 1998 resulted from both aid and trade (Lee, 2006; Kim, 2011). Nevertheless, the North Korean economy remained generally stagnant between 1998 and 2013, with an average annual growth rate of 1.74 per cent. Although the GDP per capita (in PPP) in 2012 constant international dollars increased from US$1,464 in 1998 to US$1,667 in 2013, the level of GDP per capita in 2013 was similar to that seen in the late 1950s. This indicates serious long-term economic stagnation in North Korea. The North Korean GDP per capita in 2012 amounted to US$735 in current nominal US dollars, which ranked North Korea as 168th out of 189 countries in the world in terms of GDP per capita. According to the World Bank database, those countries whose GDP per capita (current US dollars) in 2013 was similar to that of North Korea included Haiti (US$775), Nepal (US$699) and Afghanistan (US$687).

Most studies suggested that the North Korean GDP per capita was higher than that of South Korea until the mid-1970s (Ministry of Unification, 1990; Hwang, 1993; Cummings, 1997), but these studies disregarded the overestimation of growth rates in the official statistics furnished by North Korea. Assuming that the two Koreas shared the same GDP per capita in 1954, Kim et al. (2007) show that the South

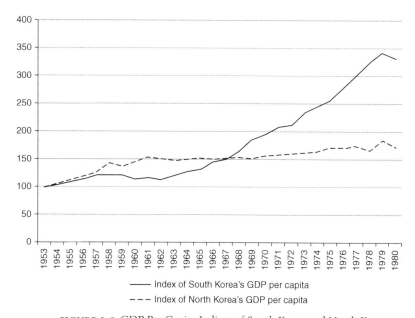

FIGURE 2.1 GDP Per Capita Indices of South Korea and North Korea, 1953–1980
Sources: Table 2.5; National Statistical Office of Republic of Korea
Note: The index was constructed based on the assumption that the GDP per capita of the two Koreas was the same in 1954 (1953 = 100).

Korean GDP per capita must have surpassed that of North Korea in the 1960s. Figure 2.1 shows the GDP per capita indices of the two Koreas from 1953 to 1980. According to the estimates of Kim et al. (2007), the average annual growth rate of North Korea (9.3 per cent) was greater than that of South Korea (4.7 per cent) in the 1950s. However, a reversal was observed in the growth performance of the two Koreas in the late 1960s. Specifically, the South Korean economy grew by 6.7 per cent from 1960 to 1969, whereas the North Korean economy grew by 4.1 per cent during the same period. The South Korean GDP per capita was lower than that of North Korea from 1954 to 1967, but managed to catch up in 1968. The South Korean economy attained rapid growth in the 1970s, expanding the gap between the GDPs of the two Koreas.

We compare our estimated North Korean GDP per capita from 1990 to 2013 with three other major estimates during the same period. The Bank of Korea (various years) provides North Korean GDP per capita estimates in both South Korean won and US dollars from 1990 to 2010, but only in South Korean won from 2011 onward.[37] The United Nations also provides estimates of the North Korean GDP per capita.[38] North Korean authorities report the GDP per capita of their country from time to time in interviews of high-ranking officials or in materials that are submitted to international organisations, although the figures they give are not always consistent.

Overall, our estimates of North Korean GDP per capita are closer to those given by the UN than those of the Bank of Korea. One main reason for substantial differences between our estimates and those of the Bank of Korea is the inconsistent methods of estimating GDP per capita used by the Bank of Korea: they derive the ratio of North Korean GDP to that of South Korean GDP by applying the PPP method, but convert the North Korean GDP in PPP into GDP in market exchange rates by applying the market exchange rates of South Korean won against US dollars. Although our estimates in current US dollars are substantially different from those of the UN in 1994, 1995 and 2009, the differences in most years do not exceed more than US$150.

In terms of growth rates, our estimates suggest that the North Korean economy decreased by 0.9 per cent per annum from 1990 to 2013, whereas the Bank of Korea estimated a 0.6 per cent annual decrease in the economic performance over the same period. However, the trends of both estimates are similar.[39] Figure 2.2 shows the trend of the North Korean GDP from 1989 to 2013 following a 'U' shape, with the latter stage still occurring. The North Korean GDP deteriorated rapidly until the late 1990s, but began to recover, although not fully, from the late 1990s onward. Our estimates suggest that the actual economic crisis in North Korea is more severe than is shown by Bank of Korea estimates. Specifically, we estimate that the North Korean GDP decreased by roughly 40 per cent from 1989 to 1997, whereas the Bank of Korea estimates a decrease of

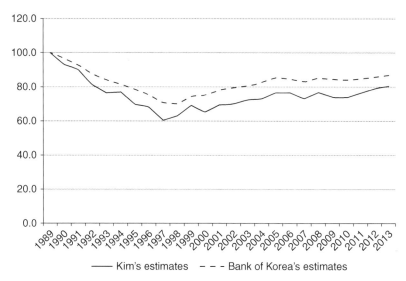

FIGURE 2.2 Trends of the North Korean GDP: Estimates from this Study and the Bank of Korea (1989 = 100)
Source: Table 2.6

approximately 30 per cent from 1989 to 1998. However, both estimations suggest that the North Korean economy has been stagnant since 2005 despite the positive growth shown in the most recent three years. These estimations also indicate that the North Korean economy is far from recovering to pre-crisis (1989) economic performance. The North Korean GDP in 2013 as a percentage of 1989 GDP is 80.5 and 86.8 per cent, respectively, according to the estimates of our study and of the Bank of Korea.

2.2.b   Extent of Economic Inefficiency

The previous section claims that one important goal of the North Korean authorities' economic management efforts is to strengthen the power of North Korea's political leaders. The political leaders' arbitrary intervention using Juseok Fond and Spot Guidance is a prime example of such management. The resultant extent of inefficiency of the North Korean economy, compared to that of a socialist

Table 2.6 *Estimates of Annual Growth Rates and GDP Per Capita of North Korea, 1990–2013*

| | Annual growth rates (%) | | GDP per capita (US$)[a] | | | | | |
| | | | Kim | | | Bank of Korea | UN | Official North |
	Kim	Bank of Korea[b]	PPP (2012 int'l US dollars)	Market exchange rate (2012 US$)	Current US$[c]	(current US$)[d]	(current US$)	Korean sources (current US$)
1990	−7.01	−4.3	2443	1017	654	1146	735	N.A.
1991	−3.63	−4.4	2323	974	641	1115	663	N.A.
1992	−10.27	−7.1	2054	877	592	1013	593	990
1993	−5.76	−4.5	1906	824	568	969	503	991
1994	0.21	−2.1	1890	818	576	992	384	722
1995	−9.36	−4.4	1698	750	538	1034	222	587
1996	−2.74	−3.4	1618	721	527	989	479	482
1997	−11.21	−6.5	1422	651	481	811	462	464
1998	3.61	−0.9	1464	666	499	573	456	458

Table 2.6 (cont.)

| | Annual growth rates (%) | | GDP per capita (US$)[a] | | | | | |
| | | | Kim | | | Bank of Korea (current US$)[d] | UN (current US$) | Official North Korean sources (current US$) |
	Kim	Bank of Korea[b]	PPP (2012 int'l US dollars)	Market exchange rate (2012 US$)	Current US$[c]			
1999	9.40	6.1	1591	711	544	714	452	454
2000	-6.18	0.4	1480	672	526	757	462	464
2001	6.73	3.8	1565	702	559	706	476	478
2002	1.03	1.2	1569	703	571	762	468	490
2003	2.84	1.8	1602	715	593	818	471	524
2004	1.18	2.1	1610	718	615	914	473	546
2005	4.82	3.8	1677	742	656	1056	548	N.A.
2006	-0.13	-1.0	1664	738	671	1108	575	N.A.
2007	-4.78	-1.2	1575	706	655	1152	597	N.A.
2008	4.85	3.1	1646	731	689	1065	551	N.A.
2009	-3.39	-0.9	1581	708	670	932	494	N.A.
2010	-0.25	-0.5	1569	704	679	1074	570	N.A.
2011	3.01	0.8	1609	718	706	n.a	638	N.A.

Table 2.6 (cont.)

| | Annual growth rates (%) | | GDP per capita (US$)[a] | | | | | |
| | Kim | Bank of Korea[b] | Kim | | | Bank of Korea (current US$)[d] | UN (current US$) | Official North Korean sources (current US$) |
			PPP (2012 int'l US dollars)	Market exchange rate (2012 US$)	Current US$[c]			
2012	3.58	1.3	1658	735	735	N.A.	643	N.A.
2013	1.45	1.1	1667	739	749	N.A.	666	N.A.

Sources: Table 2.5, Statistics Korea (http://kosis.kr/nsikor), Statistics Korea, Main Statistics of North Korea (various years), UN Data (http://data.un.org) http://unstats.un.org/unsd/snaama/), Lee (2007a), Kim (2014a)

Notes:

[a] GDP is interchangeably used with GNI (Gross National Income) but the differences between these two are insignificant for most countries. However, GDP per capita might be lower than GNI per capita during recent years in North Korea due to favourable terms of trade and increased revenue by North Korean workers from abroad.

[b] The estimates by UN source from 1990 onward provide growth rates that are equal to those of the Bank of Korea.

[c] The estimates of North Korean GDP per capita in current US dollars were derived by applying a US implicit price deflator to Kim's estimates in market exchange rates in 2012 US dollars.

[d] The Bank of Korea does not provide estimates of North Korean GDP per capita in US dollars from 2011 onward.

economy such as the Soviet Union, might be greater, but this needs to be evaluated.

Kim et al. (2007) compared the efficiency levels of the USSR and North Korea, while Bergson (1987) compared the efficiency of different economic systems, such as those of capitalist and socialist countries. Using a Cobb–Douglas function applied to panel data, Kim et al. compared the performance of the Soviet economy from 1928 to 1971, excluding the period from 1940 to 1948, and that of North Korea from 1954 to 1989. Different periods are used for the two countries in order to account for the different stages of economic development in the countries. One can argue that the South Korean GNP per capita in 1954, estimated by Maddison (1995) at $1,153 in 1990 US dollars, is similar to that of North Korea for the same year, that is, one year after the end of the Korean War. Similarly, Maddison (1995) estimated the Soviet GNP per capita in 1928 to be $1,370 in 1990 US dollars.

They find that the productivity of the North Korean economy was considerably lower than that of the Soviet economy, by a factor of 33 per cent. It suggests that that the shortcomings in North Korean productivity reflected the extreme inefficiency of the North Korean economy when compared to a socialist economy at similar stages of development. Combined with the revised estimates of Bergson (1992), who suggests that the productivity of former socialist economies is approximately 40 per cent lower than that of advanced market economies, our estimates indicate that the gap between the North Korean socialist economy and a market economy should be roughly 60 per cent. In other words, the North Korean economy has been extremely inefficient, even when it appeared to operate in a normal way, before the 1990s.

Appendix: Estimates of North Korean GDP and Growth Rates

Kim et al. (2007) compute GDP growth rates of North Korea by weighting the GDP contributions of agriculture, manufacturing and service from 1954 to 1989. To update these growth rates for the subsequent period, we use estimated growth rates of industrial production from the Bank of Korea, since North Korea has not provided these data since 1989. Unlike the Bank of Korea, however, we do not use the value-added in the sector – instead, we use changes in the volume of production. In addition, the weights that we give to the agriculture, industry and service sectors are different from those assigned by the Bank of Korea. Those are affected by value-added of South Korean industries, whereas our weights use the share of industries in total GDP in 1992 as reported by North Korea. Unlike the estimates from 1954 to 1989, we assume no hidden inflation here because these estimations were provided by South Korean institutions. We continue to use agricultural production estimates from official South Korean sources for 1990 onwards. Shares for the industries are calculated based on the different growth rates of each industry.

As regards North Korean GDP per capita, the Bank of Korea (various years) publishes the GDP per capita of both South and North Korea in South Korean won according to an assumption of price parity between these two countries. For example, the GDP per capita for South Korea and North Korea in 2012 were estimated at 25.59 million won and 1.37 million won, respectively (Korea National Statistical Office, 2013).

The North Korean GDP per capita figures are known to be overestimated or underestimated, however, for several reasons. Basing North Korean GDP figures on South Korean prices, for one thing, may cause overestimation because the weights that are attached to each product are based on different (South Korean) prices and output structures. For example, the CIA estimated the Soviet GDP in 1989 to be 66 per cent of the US GDP when calculated in US dollars, the currency of the more-developed country, but 39 per cent of the US GDP when calculated in rubles, the currency of the less-developed country. The gap between these estimates is smaller for 1976 than for 1989, but is still large. The Soviet GDP in 1976 was estimated at 42.8 and 27.6 per cent of the US GDP when evaluated in US dollars and rubles, respectively (GAO, 1991). The CIA used a geometric average of the two numbers to get its final number on Soviet GDP. The unweighted average of the two geometric averages in 1976 and 1989 is 0.786. Looking again at the two Koreas, the Bank of Korea's estimates could inflate the North Korean GDP figure by 21.4 per cent just by applying South Korean prices to North Korean volume of output.

Looking at things a different way, the Bank of Korea may underestimate North Korean GDP by failing to include value-added that is produced in the informal economy. As we will discuss in Section 3 of this chapter, the share of income from informal sources is estimated at about 70 per cent of total household income from the mid-1990s to the present. It is extremely difficult to estimate the value-added produced in the North Korean informal economy, however, on account of the lack of relevant data. Indirect evidence based on Soviet data can be used as a basis for approximation. According to Kim (2003), the informal economy, which was estimated at 23 per cent of household expenditure, would increase the actual Soviet GDP by 6.8 per cent. By applying the ratio of the latter to the former to North Korean data, we would see an increase of 23.7 per cent in the North Korean GDP.

It is difficult to accurately estimate the extent of all the biases operating in both directions. Because the magnitude of the biases arising from overestimation and underestimation appear to be similar in extent, as we discussed above, it may be reasonable to assume that the extent of overestimation is cancelled out exactly by that of underestimation, and that is the assumption we will make.

The GDP per capita of South Korea in PPP, in current international dollars, was estimated in 2012 to be US$32,150 (World).[40] By applying the ratio of South Korean GDP per capita, in won, to North Korea derived from Bank of Korea's estimate in the same year, we estimated the GDP per capita of North Korea in 2012 in PPP at US$1,658. GDP per capita for the other years is computed using our estimates of GDP growth rates and North Korean population growth rates.

We can compute the GDP per capita in 2012 US dollars, expressed in nominal (market) exchange rates, as follows. These are indirect estimates based on the relationships for developing countries between Gross National Income (GNI) per capita in PPP and GNI per capita in current US dollars. That is, we regress GNI per capita in current US dollars on GNI per capita in PPP in 2012, using the data from 35 low-income countries. The World Bank defines 'low-income countries' as those whose GNI per capita is less than US$1,035 when computed using the Atlas method. We run a binary regression, as previously explained, and then obtain the coefficient of GNI per capita in PPP and the constant, both of which are statistically significant.[41] We subsequently apply these values to the North Korean GDP per capita in PPP to compute the GDP per capita of the country in 2012 US dollars, expressed in nominal exchange rates.

In order to check the validity of our estimates, we compare them with the estimate given by Maddison (1995), which finds that South Korean GDP per capita in PPP in 1954 was US$1,153, measured in 1990 international dollars. It is reasonable to assume that the sheer destruction of the Korean War brought the GDP per capita of the two Koreas in 1954 to similar levels, at extreme poverty. Based on this assumption, Kim et al. (2007) estimated that GDP per capita in 1989 was $2,258 in 1990 international dollars. Our method of estimation for North Korea's GDP per capita is different from that of Kim et al. (2007) in that the two methods use the Bank of Korea's GDP per capita estimate in 2012 and that of Maddison in 1954, respectively. We can derive an estimate of North Korean GDP per capita in 1990 international dollars by applying the ratio of the growth of GDP per capita in nominal US dollars, from 1989 to 2012, to that in PPP for the same period. The estimate of North Korean GDP per capita in 1989 in 1990 international dollars was US$ 2,265, which is very close to the US$2,258 estimated by Kim et al. (2007) for the same year. Similarly, the conversion of GDP per capita in 1954 in 2012 international dollars (shown as $1,357 in Table 2.5) into 1990 international dollars gives us US$1,156. This is also very close to Maddison's estimate of US$1,153 in 1990 international dollars.

2.3 HOUSEHOLDS: SURVIVING IN INFORMAL MARKETS

2.3.a *Introduction*

North Korea adopted a socialist economic system in which households worked in official workplaces and received basic consumer goods rationed by the government. These official workplaces included state organisations, state-owned enterprises and collective farms. In an ideal socialist economy, households should work in the official sector, and no informal sector must exist independent of central planning. Nevertheless, informal sectors have coexisted with official sectors in all socialist economies, although the size of these sectors differs for each country (Grossman, 1977; Kim, 2003).

The PDS for grain in North Korea was introduced in 1946 after independence of Korea from Japan. This system expanded further in the 1970s to include other basic consumer goods. The consumer goods that were distributed to households through PDS included not only agricultural products (e.g. grain, vegetables, soybean sauce, soybean paste, fruits and fish) but also manufactured goods (e.g. soap, footwear and clothes). Households were allowed to purchase these goods at highly subsidised prices upon the presentation of a ration card. However, the amount of distributed products and goods differed according to the type of work, age, rank and residence of individuals. For example, a blue-collar worker could receive 900 grams of grain per day, whereas a white-collar worker could only receive 700 grams of grain per day. Moreover, high-ranking officials could purchase consumer goods that were unavailable in conventional state shops because of shortages, and were able to buy them in exclusive state shops at highly subsidised prices (Kim, 1997b). High-ranking officials and residents in Pyongyang could obtain a larger ration of rice than residents in other regions of North Korea.

The household sector of North Korea has experienced a dramatic transformation since the 1990s. The economic crisis of the 1990s contributed to this change. The transformation started with modifications in the PDS. North Korean authorities reduced the amount of daily distributed grain in the 1990s, decreasing the average amount of rationed grain per day for a civilian adult from 700 grams in 1972 to 492 grams in 1992 (Lee, 2004).[42] Furthermore, the ration of food and consumer goods was reported to have ceased in several parts of North Korea during the mid- and late 1990s. The virtual collapse of the PDS induced numerous households to rely on market activities that were previously repressed by the authorities. Upon realising the necessity of allowing households to rely on markets for their survival, the authorities applied a more lenient approach to markets and tolerated such activities. Consequently, market activities dramatically increased during the Arduous March in the mid- and late 1990s.

Despite the consensus on increasing the market activities of North Korean households, the magnitude of such activities in contemporary North Korea remains uncertain. Two contrasting views on North Koreans' market activities exist. According to the estimates of most existing studies, a substantial share of total household income is derived from informal market activities, ranging from 70 to 90 per cent (Lee, 2007b; Kim and Song, 2008; Kim, 2009b; Haggard and Noland, 2010; Kim and Yang, 2012; Jeong, et al., 2012).[43] These studies also report that 90 per cent of total household expenditures are made in these markets. The majority of these studies, however, use survey data from North Korean refugees who are settled in South Korea, and the question of whether these refugees can be taken to represent the whole population of North Korea has not been fully explored. Additional problems include the small sample size and the use of refugees who arrived in South Korea in different years as the sample.

Another source of information on the North Korean household economy is reported by the United Nations, which provides specific data on how North Koreans obtain food. According to one report, 62 per cent of food is obtained from official sources (e.g. PDS or state shops), and food purchased from markets accounts for only 1 per cent of total expenditures (Food and Agriculture Organization of the UN/World Food Programme (FAO/WFP), 2012). These figures are derived from interviews with 95 North Korean households conducted by an FAO/WFP team dispatched to North Korea. These data have both advantages and disadvantages. The data are collected from North Korean households living in North Korea. This means that the data have less of a tendency to incur a sample selection problem than the data gathered from the refugee sample. However, the households may not have reported honestly on their grain purchase from markets, since grain market transactions were prohibited. Reports actually mention that the interviewees were uncomfortable answering questions about market activity or described exchanges of cereals (FAO/WFP, 2012; 2013). For these reasons, these data, which may underestimate the extent of marketisation in North Korea, should be considered with due care.

We primarily use the two recent quantitative surveys of North Korean refugees conducted in 2009 and 2011 to analyse the market activities of North Korean households and their effects on the economy. North Korean refugees were asked about their economic life in North Korea, including their income, expenditure, official job and market activities. We improved on the existing studies in four ways. First, we purposefully selected the refugee sample to reduce errors in retrospective memory by using North Koreans who did not spend much time in South Korea. Likewise, we confined our sample to those who did not spend considerable time abroad (e.g. in China) before they arrived in South Korea. We recruited newly arrived North Koreans who had spent only a short time yet between living in North Korea and arriving in South Korea. This period, for most of the survey participants, was less than a year. Second, we controlled for yearly fluctuations in market activities in North Korea by using the sample of the refugees who escaped from North Korea in the same or similar years. If marketisation is volatile, averaging the extent of marketisation across several years will fail to reveal the changes in market activities in North Korea. Third, we used gang surveys instead of mail and telephone surveys to reduce response errors. We arranged for 25 to 30 respondents to participate in the surveys at one time at a designated facility. A moderator conducted the surveys with the aid of at least five assistants. Fourth, we used a structured questionnaire in which questions on market activities were carefully organised. For example, we asked about not only the sum of household income but also the components of such income in order to check on the consistency of responses.

The sample selection issue was considered as follows. First, we compared refugees with favourable backgrounds to those who had less favourable backgrounds. The former group included Workers' Party members and the educated in North Korea. Second, we checked on their reasons for escaping from North Korea and compared the market activities of refugees who fled North Korea for economic survival with those of refugees who left for political freedom and to join family members who had arrived in South Korea earlier, among others. Third, we analysed regional disparities in market activities. We recognised that if certain regions in North Korea experienced more widespread market activities than others and if the majority of the refugee sample was from those regions, the estimates from the surveys of the refugees would be biased. We used regional weighting to correct this sort of bias.

2.3.b   North Korean Refugees in South Korea

The number of North Korean refugees in South Korea dramatically increased in the late 1990s. A total of 947 North Koreans had arrived in South Korea by 1998. The number of refugees arriving in South Korea increased substantially after that, by more than 300 per year from 1999 to 2001 to more than 1,000 per year from 2002 to 2005 and more than 2,000 per year from 2006 to 2011. After increasing by 2,914 in 2009, the number of North Korean refugees who settled in South Korea decreased slightly, and this number fell further to 1,500 from 2012 to 2013. The recent decrease in the number of North Korean refugees is attributable mainly to the North Korean authorities' strict policy against refugees exercised. In total, 23,100 North Korean refugees settled in South Korea by 2011. By the end of 2013, this number increased to 26,122. Female refugees (70 per cent) outnumbered male refugees (30 per cent).[44] Table 2.7 indicates the trend and gender composition of North Korean refugees who have arrived in South Korea.

Table 2.7 *Number and Gender Composition of North Korean Refugees (Persons, Per Cent)*

	Until 1998	1999–2001	2002–2003	2004–2005	2006	2007	2008	2009	2010	2011	2012	2013	Total
Men	831	565	984	1050	515	573	608	662	591	795	404	369	7,947
Women	116	478	1443	2,232	1,513	1,981	2,195	2,252	1,811	1,911	1,098	1,145	18,175
Total	947	1,043	2,427	3,282	2,028	2,554	2,803	2,914	2,402	2,706	1,502	1,514	26,122
Share of men (%)	88	54	41	32	25	22	22	23	25	30	27	24	30
Share of women (%)	12	46	59	68	75	78	78	77	75	70	73	76	70

Source: Ministry of Unification of Republic of Korea. www.unikorea.go.kr/content.do?cmsid=1440 (as of June 2016)

We used the data from the two surveys of North Korean refugees aged above 15 conducted in 2009 and 2011. The total number of survey participants was 361, which comprised 227 and 134 individuals in 2009 and 2011, respectively. For the first survey, the survey team visited Hanawon (i.e. House of Unity), where North Korean refugees are educated for three months in preparation for settlement in South Korea.[45] The second survey was conducted at Seoul National University. We sent out invitation letters and contacted potential participants by telephone to recruit newly arrived refugees from North Korea. The target group of the surveys was made up of the individuals who had left North Korea less than a year before their arrival in South Korea. Approximately 95 per cent of the 361 participants in our surveys escaped North Korea from 2007 to 2011. We excluded those who left before 2007 to control the effects of their having left North Korea in different years on the economic life of the North Korean refugees. As a result, we used 342 North Korean refugees in this analysis, and we surveyed 2.6 per cent of those who had arrived in South Korea in the aforementioned five years.

The two surveys employed several questions in common so that we could merge the datasets. The following table provides descriptive statistics on the refugee sample used in the analysis. In addition, the data from the population census conducted in 2008 are reported to compare with the data from the surveys.[46]

Table 2.8 suggests that men are oversampled in our survey compared with the population of the refugees displayed in Table 2.7. The majority of the sample arrived in South Korea within a year after their escape from North Korea. Approximately 85% of the refugees lived in provinces such as Hamkyungdo and Yanggangdo. The geographical proximity to China and the Tumen River, which can be easily crossed, can be regarded as the main reasons for the dominance of refugees from these provinces. The level of education of the refugee sample is at least equivalent to that of the whole population. The average share of Workers' Party membership is 16.9 per cent in our sample, which is close to that in the whole population. Overall, the characteristics of our

Table 2.8 *Summary Statistics of Survey Data Compared with the Population Census*

	2009 survey	2011 survey	Population census (2008)
Gender (male=1; female=0)	0.39	0.38	0.49
Age (median) among those aged 15 or above	35	32	39
Location of residence in North Korea			
Pyongyang and Pyongando	6.2%	12.0%	43.0%
Hamkyungdo	56.9%	60.1%	23.1%
Hwanghaedo	4.3%	0.8%	18.9%
Gangwondo	2.4%	0.8%	6.3%
Jagangdo	0.0%	0.8%	5.6%
Yanggangdo	27.3%	24.8%	3.1%
Others	2.9%	0.7%	0.0%
Education			
Less than high school	3.8%	9.0%	7.1%
High school completed	72.3%	58.7%	71.9%
College, university or above	23.9%	32.3%	21.0%
Workers' Party membership (yes=1; no=0)	18.9%	13.6%	16.2%*
Year of arriving in South Korea (average)	2008	2010	
Departure year (number of persons)			
2007	43	1	
2008	163	1	
2009	3	8	
2010		112	
2011		11	
Reasons for leaving North Korea			
Famine and economic hardship		30.8%	
Personal threat		6.8%	
Recommendation from the neighbourhood in North Korea		2.3%	
Recommendation from the people who had already been in South Korea		4.5%	

Table 2.8 (*cont.*)

	2009 survey	2011 survey	Population census (2008)
With family members escaping North Korea		6.0%	
To seek family members who were already in South Korea		9.0%	
To earn more money		3.7%	
To seek political and social liberty		9.8%	
Antipathy toward the North Korean regime		20.3%	
To give a good future to my children		6.8%	
Perceived living standard in North Korea			
Very poor (bottom 20%)	9.0%	9.8%	
Poor (20%–40%)	14.0%	15.0%	
Middle (40%–60%)	53.0%	45.9%	
Rich (top 20%–40%)	20.0%	26.3%	
Very rich (top 20%)	4.0%	3.0%	
Number of survey participants	209	133	

Note: The share of Workers' Party Membership in the total population is not exactly known. Chung (2007) suggested that the number should range between 2.0 million and 3.2 million in the 1980s. We assumed that the current number amounts to 3 million and we divided this figure by the population aged 15 or above.

sample do not differ substantially from those of the population except for the regional and gender distribution.

One reason why several characteristics of the refugee sample are similar to those of the whole population is that the North Korean refugees who recently settled in South Korea are not confined to those who considered economic survival difficult in North Korea. Only 30.8 per cent of the total sample replied that they had left North Korea because of famine and economic hardship. The other reasons the refugees gave for escaping North Korea include antipathy toward the North Korean regime (20.3 per cent), a desire to seek political and social liberty (9.8 per cent), and a desire to seek family members who were already in South Korea (9.0 per cent). The reasons for leaving North Korea are now sufficiently diversified. The decrease in the number of refugees who escaped North Korea because of economic hardship over time was confirmed by other surveys conducted by a group of researchers in 2014 and 2015. According to those surveys, the share of such refugees in the total number of refugees was 60 per cent before 2000 but decreased to 43 per cent after 2000.[47] This share further decreased to only 29.9 per cent during the post-2007 period. This figure is similar to that indicated in Table 2.8.

The standard of living perceived by the respondents indicates that, on average, refugees do not tend to belong to a poor group. Approximately half of the respondents in the two surveys replied that their living standard in North Korea was neither rich nor poor. In addition, 24.0 and 29.1 per cent of the refugees from the 2009 and 2011 surveys, respectively, assessed that they belonged to the top 40 per cent. From this we get the sense that most of the North Korean refugees who settled in South Korea are not from economically marginalised groups in North Korea. This indicates that data from the refugees can provide accurate information on the North Korean economy when surveys are properly designed and executed.

2.3.c Participation of North Koreans in Official and Informal Economy

Survey questions were designed to provide information on the economic life of the North Korean refugees a year before their departure. For example, a North Korean woman who escaped from North Korea in May 2007 was asked about her economic activities during May 2006. In this manner, we controlled for the possible disruptions in his or her life that were caused by his or her intention to escape or actual escape from the country.

Table 2.9 presents the participation rates of North Koreans in the official and informal economy according to various categories.[48]

Table 2.9 *Participation Rates in the Official and Informal Economy*

	Participation rate in the official economy	Participation rate in the informal economy
Total sample	50.6	71.2
2009 survey (%)	49.0	68.8
2011 survey (%)	53.0	75.0
Difference (P-value)	0.55	0.22
Workers' Party membership		
Members (%)	84.2	71.9
Non-members (%)	43.8	70.6
Difference (P-value)	0.00***	0.84
Regions		
Hamkyungdo (%)	52.8	70.2
Non-Hamkyungdo (%)	47.6	72.5
Difference (P-value)	0.34	0.64
Education		
Up to high school (%)	49.4	69.2
College, university or above (%)	53.8	76.3
Difference (P-value)	0.47	0.20
Reasons for escape		
Left due to economic hardship (%)	43.9	78.0
Left due to other reasons (%)	56.5	73.6
Difference (P-value)	0.18	0.59

Note: *** refers to the significant difference at the 1 per cent significance level.

A summary of the main findings follows. First, North Koreans tend to participate more in the informal economy than in the official economy. The participation rate in the official economy is 50.6 per cent, whereas that in the informal economy is 71.2 per cent. These figures are similar to those reported by Kim and Song (2008), who used the refugee sample that left North Korea from 1997 to 2004 and noted the participation rates in the official and the informal economy to be 53.5 and 78.0 per cent, respectively. On this basis we can infer that the North Korean economy is highly informalised in terms of participation rate. Second, informal economic activities are conducted indifferently by all categories of the groups. The tendency to participate in the informal economy between party members and non-members and between the more and less educated has no significant difference. Furthermore, only a small variation between Hamkyung province (Hamkyungdo) and non-Hamkyung provinces is evident. Therefore, the sample selection bias that emerged from the dominance of refugees from Hamkyungdo may not be a serious issue in terms of the participation rate in the informal economy. This result concurs with Haggard and Noland's (2010) finding that market activities are ubiquitous and uniform across heterogeneous groups of the population. Third, the only significant difference noted between party members and non-members is regarding participation in the official economy: the former tended to participate in the official economy to a greater extent than the latter. The participation rate of party members in the official economy is approximately twice that of non-members. This finding is in harmony with the ideas that party members should work formally (in the official economy), except for housewives and the retired, and that their formal work is strictly monitored by the authorities. Nevertheless, party members also rely heavily on informal economic activities. On the one hand, their official salary may be insufficient for survival. On the other, they may have additional, lucrative opportunities through the informal economy and may be able to avoid penalties through the use of their power and influence.

Table 2.10 lists the characteristics of North Korean households' official economic activities. The official monthly salary that workers actually receive is KPW 2,171, which is equivalent to less than US$1, according to the informal market (jangmadang) exchange rates in 2007. The actual working hours per week in official workplaces are

Table 2.10 *Official Economic Activities of North Korean Households*

Categories	Figures
Average official monthly salary (won)	2,171
Rationing	
Share receiving rationed food or goods among those who worked officially (%)	40.5
Share receiving rationed grain among those who worked officially (%)	20.5
Share receiving rationed food except grain among those who worked officially (%)	9.7
Share receiving rationed non-food consumer goods among those who worked officially (%)	13.5
Working hours (per week)	
Official	49.5
Actual	45.8
Share of those who worked less than official working hours (%)	58.4
Reasons for working less than the official working hours (%)	
Insufficient work to do	47.5
Worked elsewhere as 8·3 workers	34.7
Others (illness, leave of absence, etc.)	17.8
Salary per hour (won)	47.4

five hours less than the official working hours per week. A total of 58.4 per cent of workers responded that they worked less than the official working hours, mainly because of insufficient work to do or because they worked elsewhere as 8·3 workers, a term that refers to those who pay enterprise managers to be absent from their official work.

Survival is extremely difficult for households with such salary unless the PDS provides sufficient rationed food and goods to those who work officially. However, only 40.5 per cent of those who work officially receive rationed food or basic consumer goods. Furthermore, only 20.5 per cent of the refugees with official jobs replied that they received grain through PDS. These figures indicate that the PDS failed to cover the majority of North Korean households. In addition, the amount of food distributed to households may be insufficient to meet their daily calorie requirements (FAO/WFP, 2012; 2013). According to Jung (2009), the lack of any means to survive during the Arduous March caused by the collapse of the PDS prompted North Koreans to participate in informal economic activities (Jung, 2009).

The breakdown of the official economy induced households to rely on the informal economy for survival. Table 2.11 presents the informal economic activities of North Korean households. The average monthly income from the informal economy is approximately 80 times that from official jobs. This finding indicates that the informal economy serves as the main domain for economic survival of North Korean households, rather than the official one.[49] The average working hour total per week is 45.4 hours, which is similar to the number of hours in the official work. North Koreans can earn KPW 3,805 per hour by working informally, whereas they receive KPW 47.4 if they work at an official job. Therefore, households prefer working in the informal economy unless they are restricted and monitored or provided with material compensation by PDS or other means.

The average duration of informal working is 6.7 years, which appears to be sufficiently long in the context of the North Korean socialist state. Approximately 30 per cent of those who worked in the informal economy started their work at least 10 years ago. Evidently, the informal economy is deeply rooted in North Koreans' daily lives, despite its being neither protected nor encouraged by the government.

The most popular types of informal work are trading, smuggling and providing personal services, which involve approximately half of the informal workers. Reselling, smuggling, selling food and knitting account for 93.3 per cent of these types of informal work. Cultivating kitchen gardens and private plots is the second-most popular type of informal economic activity; this type attracts one-third of the informal workers. Approximately 30 per cent of informal economic

Table 2.11 *Informal Economic Activities of North Korean Households*

Categories	Figures
Average monthly income from informal economic activities (won)	172,758
Working hours (per week)	45.4
Income per hour (won)	3,805
Years of working (average)	6.7
Types of informal work[a]	
Share of cultivating kitchen gardens or private plots (%)	33.5
Share of cattle feeding (%)	20.7
Share of trading, smuggling, repair service and other services (%)	46.7
Share of informal production (%)	29.3
Types of trading and service provision[b]	
Reselling (%)	56.3
Smuggling (%)	13.6
Food sales (%)	11.7
Knitting (%)	11.7
Others (%)	6.7
Items of informal production (% of informal producers)	
Food (%)	42.7
Alcohol (%)	23.6
Clothes and footwear (%)	19.2
Soap, toothpaste, pencil (%)	4.2
Tobacco (%)	4.2
Others (%)	6.1
Reasons for working informally	
Insufficient income to live (%)	61.6
Making money for business (%)	16.6
Helping relatives or friends (%)	3.9
Intending to purchase necessary things (%)	4.4
Saving for the future (%)	11.4
Others (%)	2.1

Notes:
[a] Multiple answers are permitted.
[b] These figures only used data from the 2009 survey because the 2011 survey questionnaire did not include this question.

Table 2.12 *Informal Economic Activities: Comparison of Our Surveys with Population Census*

	Shares of those who cultivate kitchen gardens or private plots	Shares of those who raise cattle or poultry
Our surveys (%)	23.9	14.7
Population census (%)	56.2	46.5

Note: We included those who spend at least one hour or more per week on household economic activities, as reported in the population census.

activities are associated with the production of goods. Popular items that include food, alcohol and footwear and clothes account for 85.5 per cent of the informal production. This finding suggests that informal production concentrates on areas that require simple work, and thus cannot add a high value.

The most important reason for working informally is the lack, otherwise, of sufficient income for survival, which was indicated by 61.6 per cent of the respondents. Survival is a predominant motive in informal economic activities. Nevertheless, one-third of the respondents participated in the informal economy in order to earn money for business, save for the future and purchase necessary items. If business-related motives expand in the future, the informal economy may become an important incubator for entrepreneurs in North Korea.

The population census conducted in 2008 includes data on household economic activities. However, the census may refer to legally accepted informal activities, such as working in kitchen gardens or private plots and cattle feeding. Trading in markets and informal production are at best tolerated but generally prohibited, and thus such activities are not likely to be revealed in a census. Household economic activities listed in the census include fruit and vegetable gardening, fishing and raising livestock and/or poultry, gathering firewood, fetching water and other economic activities. The first two activities among these are similar to the categories of cultivating kitchen gardens or private plots and feeding cattle or poultry. Therefore, we can compare the shares of such activities according to our survey data with those from the population census.

According to the population census, 56.2 and 46.5 per cent of the population aged 16 or above participates in cultivating kitchen gardens and private plots and raising cattle or poultry, respectively. These figures confirm our findings, based on the surveys conducted on North Korean refugees, that informal activities are widespread in North Korea. The shares reported in the population census are even higher than those from our surveys. One main reason for the difference in figures is that the surveys inquired about secondary jobs, whereas the population census used information on the working hours for the informal economy. The respondents could have answered that they worked for some hours in the informal economy, but reported that they did not have a secondary job.

The North Korean government levies taxes, such as market fees (jangse), in some market activities. Market fees are paid by traders who have a trading table (maedae) on which goods are displayed to be sold as well as by sellers who enter the covered markets built by the government. Sellers who do not pay the market fee are called 'Grasshopper Traders (meddugi jangsa)', because of their need to quickly pack up to evade policemen or security agents.

Approximately 41.1 per cent of the participants paid the market fee and 58.9 per cent did not. The participants who refused to pay the market fee argued that 'market trading itself is prohibited' (47.7 per cent), 'securing permission to trade is difficult' (17.7 per cent) and 'they need to save money' (16.3 per cent). These arguments all suggest that market trading was illegal in North Korea during the late 2000s. Although the North Korean authorities appeared to encourage semi-legalised trading activities in designated areas such as general markets (jonghap shijang) from 2002 to 2004, the policy was reversed in 2005 to repress such activities.

The government imposed taxes to collect some revenue from individuals who participate in informal activities. Some of the revenues that firms collected from their '8·3 workers' could have been used to pay government taxes. The term '8·3 workers' was derived from the date when Kim Il-sung instructed managers and workers in firms to produce consumer goods using by-products and wastes from factories in a self-reliant manner (3 August 1984).Thus, some part of the revenue of the North Korean government was derived from informal economic activities.

2.3.d Income of North Koreans

The extent of household activities in the informal economy can be understood if we estimate the share of income from the economy in the total income. We derived the annual household income by aggregating the components of total income for the reference years, that is, from 2006 to 2009. The questionnaire asked respondents to report their official income, including official wages, wages-in-kind, government transfers, income from informal economic activities, income from other family members, financial aid from other people and other income. We compared the household income derived by aggregating the components of income with the total income that was reported by the respondents and then checked the discrepancies between these two groups of income. Any inconsistencies were subsequently corrected, if possible. Table 2.13 shows the household income and the share of each component of total income for the reference years.

Given the non-random nature of the sample, annual household income should not be considered to represent the North Korean household income in each year.[50] In particular, the sample size for 2006 and 2008 only had two digits, which might be insufficient to generate any reliable conclusion. Therefore, the findings from the table should be considered with caution.

Table 2.13 shows that the total household income ranged from KPW 2 to 3.3 million, except in the year 2008. The amounts are equivalent to US$870 to US$1,450 if we apply the average exchange

Table 2.13 *Annual Nominal Household Income of North Korean Refugees and Share of the Income Components in North Korea, 2006–2009*

Year	2006	2007	2008	2009
Household total income (won)	2,111,361	3,273,708	1,179,036	2,942,876
Share of official income (%)	0.1	1.2	2.4	1.8
Share of informal income (%)	73.1	58.1	74.0	64.1
Share of income from other members (%)	22.9	16.2	0	17.2
Share of financial aid from other people (%)	3.8	20.8	17.5	14.4
Share of other income (%)	0.1	3.7	6.1	2.5
Number of observations	44	164	11	123

rate in the North Korean black market from 2006 to 2009. The table also reveals an extremely low percentage of official income in the total income, that is, less than 3 per cent during this period.[51] This finding may be attributed to the low participation rate of the official economy and, possibly, official wages that do not reflect inflation. By contrast, the percentage of household income from informal economic activities ranges between 58 and 74 per cent of total income, which suggests that households mostly rely on the informal economy for their economic living, as the official economy of the country fails to provide sufficient jobs. Table 2.13 shows the high percentage of financial aid in the total income. The financial aid percentage was mostly in double digits, and the average percentage of financial aid from 2006 to 2009 was 14.1 per cent. However, detailed information on the sources of financial aid is not available. Based on interviews with some of the refugees, financial aid primarily comes from family members or relatives living outside of North Korea, such as in South Korea and China.

Table 2.14 *Annual Average Income Per Capita of North Korean Refugees, 2006–2009 (KPW, US$)*

Year	2006	2007	2008	2009
Nominal income per capita (N. Korean won)	545,988	760,392	281,353	782,251
Price index	100	199.06	195.82	209.97
Real income per capita (in 2006 price)	545,988	381,991	143,682	372,548
Exchange rates in black markets (won equivalent to US$1)	2,500	3,000	3,317	3,670
Nominal income per capita (US$)	218	253	84	213
Gini coefficient (household income)	0.755	0.660	0.467	0.570
Number of observations	44	164	11	123

Sources: Table 2.13, the market (jangmadang) exchange rates (end-year) (Mun, 2008, for the years of 1996–2007; Goodfriends and Daily NK for the other years). The real income per capita in KPW for various years is expressed in the 2006 prices.

Note: We used the household income to compute Gini coefficient. We excluded households with zero income because most of these households were soldiers in the army.

To better understand the North Korean household economy, we derived the annual real income per capita from 2006 to 2009 using the number of family members from the four surveys. The household nominal income is presented in Table 2.13, and the price index is presented in the Appendix. We also converted nominal income per capita from North Korean currency into US dollars using the informal market (jangmadang) exchange rates for each year. The nominal household income for each year was used to measure the extent of income inequality according to the Gini coefficient.

Table 2.14 shows that the real income per capita of North Korea has fluctuated substantially across the years. Such a large fluctuation might have resulted from various factors, including measurement errors. In terms of income in US dollars, income per capita ranges from US$200 to US$260 except for 2008. However, the exchange rate between KPW and US$ is likely not to reflect the real value of won because of the repression of the informal market in foreign currency and perceived risks. The table also suggests that the income inequality measured by the Gini coefficient is extremely high in North Korea – higher than 0.6, which is far higher by international standards, in most years except 2008.[52] This high coefficient may have been caused in part by the state's failure to pay a sufficient amount of official wages and to redistribute income across households. Also it may have resulted from the prevalence of informal economic activities and the opportunities of foreign trade.

2.3.e   Channels for Obtaining Food and Consumer Goods

A socialist economy is based on central planning, which instructs firms on the type and quantity of consumer goods they are required to produce. These goods are sold to households through official channels, such as state retail shops. However, given the widespread informal economic activities in North Korea, the official distribution network might have significantly reduced. We examine the extent to which households rely on markets to obtain food and consumer goods.

It is necessary to weight data from the surveys of refugees because regional disparities in ration allocation are considered to be significant. For example, residents in Pyongyang are said to receive special treatment in the rationing system, so that most of the residents there receive rations more regularly than residents from other regions (Kim, 1997b). A number of the refugees support this claim.[53] Therefore, it was necessary to use data from a large sample of refugees, including those who came from Pyongyang; we use not just the data from the 2009 survey but also data from surveys conducted in 2004 and 2007.[54] Without these additional data, the small sample of Pyongyang residents included in the 2009 survey could not have provided reliable figures. We apply data on population distribution in North Korea from the 2008 census to the figures computed from the survey data. Specifically, we use the share of the total population living in Pyongyang, Pyongando, Hamkyungdo and other provinces (Jagangdo, Yanggangdo, Hwanghaedo and Gangwondo) as weights to allow the figures from the refugee sample to represent the North Korean population as a whole.

Households obtain their food and other consumer goods through a variety of channels, which we divide into three categories: official channels (consisting of rationing and state retail shops), self-production and purchasing from the markets. We ask the respondents about the channels through which they obtained food and consumer goods, ranking them from the most frequently used to the second, the third, and so on. Tables 2.15 and 2.16 show the extent to which North Koreans use each of the three channels in four different regions to obtain food (Table 2.15) and consumer goods (Table 2.16). The most frequently used channel for food is purchase from markets, at 59.1 and 58.6 per cent, unweighted and weighted by the population share, respectively. In other words, about 60 per cent of the North Korean population rely on markets to obtain food. Only 22.6 per cent of the population use official channels, including rationing, and 14.9 per cent rely on self-production as the most frequently used channel for obtaining food.

Another interesting finding is the significant difference between Pyongyang and other regions in terms of obtaining food through the official channel. As far as food is concerned, 40 per cent of the residents in Pyongyang use the official channel most frequently, followed by residents in Pyongando (28.0 per cent), Hamkungdo (19.8 per cent) and the other provinces (12.8 per cent). In addition, self-production and purchase from markets among the respondents from Pyongyang seem to be less important than they are among the respondents from other regions. However, even in Pyongyang, markets play a key role in providing accessible food. Moreover, markets are as important as the official channel, given that the differences in using these channels are statistically insignificant.

Table 2.15 *Share of Respondents Who Identified Each Channel as the Most Important for Obtaining Food*

	Share of the respondents who identified each channel as the most important in total respondents (%)	Share of the population in the total population (%)	Share of the respondents multiplied by share of the population (%)
Official channel			
Pyongyang	40.0	13.9	5.56
Pyongando	28.0	29.0	8.12
Hamkyungdo	19.8	23.1	4.57
Jagangdo, Yanggangdo, Hwanghaedo and Gangwondo	12.8	34.0	4.35
Total/average	19.8	100.0	22.6
Self-production			
Pyongyang	0	13.9	0
Pyongando	16.0	29.0	4.64
Hamkyungdo	23.5	23.1	5.43
Jagangdo, Yanggangdo, Hwanghaedo and Gangwondo	14.2	34.0	4.83
Total/average	21.3	100.0	14.9

Table 2.15 (cont.)

	Share of the respondents who identified each channel as the most important in total respondents (%)	Share of the population in the total population (%)	Share of the respondents multiplied by share of the population (%)
Purchasing from markets			
Pyongyang	46.7	13.9	6.49
Pyongando	57.3	29.0	16.62
Hamkyungdo	58.5	23.1	13.51
Jagangdo, Yanggangdo, Hwanghaedo and Gangwondo	64.5	34.0	21.93
Total/average	59.1	100.0	58.6

Table 2.16 *Share of the Respondents Who Identified Each Channel as the Most Important for Obtaining Consumer Goods*

	Share of the respondents who identified each channel as the most important in total respondents (%)	Share of the population in the total population (%)	Share of the respondents multiplied by share of the population
Official channel			
Pyongyang	26.7	13.9	3.71
Pyongando	20.0	29.0	5.80
Hamkyungdo	17.8	23.1	4.11
Jagangdo, Yanggangdo, Hwanghaedo and Gangwondo	9.2	34.0	3.13
Total/average	16.9	100.0	16.8
Self-production			
Pyongyang	6.7	13.9	0.93
Pyongando	12.0	29.0	3.48
Hamkyungdo	21.1	23.1	4.87
Jagangdo, Yanggangdo, Hwanghaedo and Gangwondo	9.9	34.0	3.37
Total/average	18.7	100.0	12.7

Table 2.16 (cont.)

	Share of the respondents who identified each channel as the most important in total respondents (%)	Share of the population in the total population (%)	Share of the respondents multiplied by share of the population
Purchasing from markets			
Pyongyang	46.7	13.9	6.49
Pyongando	66.7	29.0	19.34
Hamkyungdo	66.2	23.1	15.29
Jagangdo, Yanggangdo, Hwanghaedo and Gangwondo	69.5	34.0	23.63
Total/average	66.4	100.0	64.8

Table 2.16 shows the results in the case of consumer goods. Generally, the dominance of the markets is confirmed. Two-thirds of North Koreans rely on markets for acquisition of consumer goods, a higher share than for acquisition of food. The official channel and self-production are used most frequently by 16.8 and 12.7 per cent of the total population, respectively. However, even in Pyongyang, people rely more heavily on the market channel than on the official channel, given that 46.7 per cent of the residents in Pyongyang purchase consumer goods from the markets. At the same time, the market channel distributes 64.8 per cent of consumer goods to the North Korean population, followed by the official channel (16.8 per cent) and self-production (12.7 per cent).

The respondents were also asked to give the share of food and consumer goods they had obtained through the most frequently used channel. The method for estimating the use of different channels for obtaining food and consumer goods is as follows. First, we identify both the most and second-most frequently used channels, together with the share of food and consumer goods obtained through the former. For the most frequently used channel, we make the sum of the share of the respondents multiplied by share of the population in each of the three channels to be equal to 100 per cent by weighting the figures (total/average) in accordance with the respective share in the sum.[55] Second, we aggregate the share of food and consumer goods obtained through each of the three channels used most frequently. Third, we assume that the remaining share of food and consumer goods was fully acquired through the second-most frequently used channel and that the share of food and consumer goods obtained through each channel is equivalent to the share of consumption through each channel.[56] Lastly, we add the share of consumption of food and consumer goods through the most frequently used channels to that of the second-most frequently used channel.

Tables 2.17 and 2.18 show the importance of each channel in terms of its share in the supplying of food (Table 2.17) and consumer goods (Table 2.18). Approximately 59.7 per cent of food and

Table 2.17 *Importance of Channels for Obtaining Food*

	Share of the respondents who identified this channel as the most important (1)	Average share of food obtained through this channel (2)	Consumption through the first channel [(3)=(1)*(2)]	Consumption through the second channel (4)	Share of consumption through this channel (5)=[(3)+(4)]
Official channel (%)	23.5	70.9	16.7	7.7	24.4
Self-production (%)	15.5	70.6	10.9	5.0	15.9
Purchasing from markets (%)	61.0	85.9	52.4	7.3	59.7
Total	100.0	–	80.0	20.0	100.0
Total respondents	1,017				

Notes: (1) Share refers to the percentage of the respondents to whom the channel is the most important in obtaining food or consumer goods, in number of total respondents. (2) Other channels such as purchases from Soomae sangjeom (repurchasing shops) are excluded from the calculation because only four respondents identified such channels as the most important for obtaining food.

Table 2.18 *Importance of Channels for Obtaining Consumer Goods*

	Share of the respondents who identified this channel as the most important (1)	Average share of goods obtained through this channel (2)	Consumption through the first channel [(3) =(1)*(2)]	Consumption through the second channel (4)	Share of consumption through this channel (5)=[(3)+(4)]
Official channel (%)	17.8	61.9	11.0	2.0	13.0
Self-production (%)	13.5	87.5	11.8	7.8	19.6
Purchasing from markets (%)	68.7	89.5	61.5	5.9	67.4
Total	100.0	–	84.3	15.7	100.0
Total respondents	1,017				

Notes: (1) Share refers to the percentage of respondents to whom the channel is the most important in obtaining food or consumer goods. (2) Other channels such as purchasing from Soomae sangieom (repurchasing shops) are excluded from the calculation because only nine respondents identified such channels as the most important for obtaining consumer goods.

67.4 per cent of consumer goods are distributed in the markets, a finding that indicates the virtual breakdown of the official retail network. The distribution of food and consumer goods through rationing and state retail shops accounts for only 24.4 per cent of food and 13 per cent of consumer goods. Households also rely on self-production to obtain food and consumer goods: 15.9 and 19.6 per cent of food and consumer goods, respectively, are produced by the households themselves.

2.3.f Conclusion

The North Korean household sector experienced a dramatic change in the early and mid-1990s, as well as a deviation from the conventional socialist system. Household economic activities occurred mainly in markets rather than in official workplaces. Households derived higher income from markets than from their official jobs, and spent most of their income on markets rather than through official retail networks. Specifically, North Koreans earned 62.7 per cent of their individual total income in the informal economy, whereas official income accounted for only 1.3 per cent. They also tended to work more informally than officially, as 71.2 per cent of North Korean households participated in the informal economy and only 50.6 per cent of the total workforce participated in the official economy. Furthermore, only 24.4 per cent of food was distributed through official channels, including food rationing and the state retail network, and 13.0 per cent of consumer goods were delivered to households through the official channel. By contrast, 59.7 per cent of food and 67.4 per cent of consumer goods were purchased in markets.

Increases in the informal market changed the behaviour not only of households but also of firms. In fact, informalisation, led by households, induced firms to make revenue in the informal economy. As we will discuss in the next section, it provided firms with opportunities for making revenue by allowing 8·3 workers.

In addition, they used informal markets for purchasing inputs and for selling outputs.

The market activities of North Korean households may have transformed the various features of not only the economy but also the society. Tension may exist between the authorities and the market participants in North Korea, as reflected by the changes in policy of the authorities toward the markets. This situation indicates the authorities' concerns about the negative effects of market activities on the stability of the socialist regime. The expansion of the informal economy may be associated with corruption, changes in social norms and incentive problems for government officials. These issues are addressed in the last section of this chapter.

Appendix: Consumer Prices in North Korea

Data on the prices of goods and services are not published by the North Korean authorities. Hence, it is necessary for us to construct a price index before we can compare the purchasing power of North Korean households across different years. We use a simple approach to estimate the consumer price index of North Korea from 1996 to 2009, using the replies of survey respondents to three questions that pertain to market prices of selected goods. These questions were presented in the three surveys conducted in 2004–2005, 2007 and 2009. We also use other data on prices that were provided by various organisations, including non-governmental organisations (NGO).[57] We check for consistency between data from our surveys and data provided by these organisations for periods when both data are available. We use the former data when both sources provide similar figures or when the latter are unavailable, but use the latter when the differences between the two data sets are substantial. More specifically, we use market prices from our surveys for 1996 and 1997 because no data on prices exist in the other sources. As regards the period from 1998 to 2001, South Korean government data provided by Lee (2005) are used because we found some substantial discrepancies between the data from our surveys and from the government source. The data from our survey are utilised for the period from 2002 to 2007, given that there are few differences in the data on prices between those two sources. Lastly, the weekly and bi-weekly prices in 2008 and 2009 were obtained from Daily NK, a South Korean NGO, and were averaged for the respective year.

Corn and rice are the most important food items for North Korean households. However, constructing a consumer price index for North Korea according to the market prices of these items may yield inaccurate estimates, as the prices for such goods are directly affected by international aid. In other words, a consumer price index constructed according to both prices will underestimate a true price index because rice and corn are supplied partially by foreign governments and international aid organisations. In fact, the pork price increased relatively quickly compared to the other two prices from 1996 to 2009, indicating that the rice and corn prices might be affected by international aid. Therefore, we use the pork price to represent the prices of other goods and services that are unaffected by international aid.

Our surveys reported that the North Korean refugees had spent about 65 per cent of their income on rice, corn, potatoes, vegetables and cooking oil. The annual consumption of corn was similar to that of rice. Therefore, we assume that North Korean households spend 32.5 per cent of their income on rice, 32.5 per cent on corn, and 35 per cent on other goods and services. The price of these goods and services is represented by the pork price. The following table shows our figures for the consumer price index from 1996 to 2009 and the associated inflation rate from 1997 to 2009.

Table A.2.1 shows that consumer prices increased more than 36-fold from 1996 to 2009. The average annual inflation rate from 1997 to 2009 was 44.3 per cent. Substantial fluctuations were also observed in the estimated inflation rates, which might reflect

Table A.2.1 *Estimated Consumer Price Index and Inflation Rates in North Korea*

Year	1996	1997	1998	1999	2000	2001	2002
CPI	100.00	109.73	110.75	153.25	108.55	126.89	184.60
Inflation (%)	–	9.73	0.93	38.37	–29.17	16.90	45.48
Year	2003	2004	2005	2006	2007	2008	2009
CPI	561.42	1,503.98	1,530.54	1,766.27	3,515.93	3,458.67	3,708.63
Inflation (%)	204.14	167.89	1.77	15.40	99.06	–1.63	7.23

Sources: Surveys conducted in 2004, 2007, 2009 and 2011; Lee (2005); Daily NK

highly volatile economic conditions in North Korea. For example, inflation rates from 1997 to 2001 were relatively small, which may have been influenced by aid from South Korea and the United States that increased from US$53.6 million in 1996 to US$325.4 million in 2001. The sharp increase in inflation in 2002 and 2003 may have been caused by July 1st Measures, which increased the official prices of consumer goods and services as well as official wages and salaries. The increased autonomy of enterprises as well as decreased aid from South Korea and the United States (falling from US$446.7 million in 2002 to US$313.4 million in 2004) may have increased the inflation rates in 2003 and 2004. The stable inflation rates in 2005 and 2006 may be due to increases in crop harvest. The Korean Rural Economic Institute (KREI) found that the North Korean crop harvest increased from 4.31 million tons in 2004 to 4.54 million tons in 2005 and to 4.48 million tons in 2006. However, the crop harvest decreased by 10.7 per cent the following year, which may have resulted in the large increase in the inflation rate seen in 2007. The inflation rate decreased again in 2008 after the crop harvest reached the same level in 2004, according to estimates from KREI.

2.4   FIRMS: SURVIVING WITH MARKETS AND FOREIGN TRADE

2.4.a   Decentralisation in the Enterprise Sector

The traditional central planning system comprises plans for firms' activities. Detailed planning of output, input and finance is performed at the national level, and the plans are then imposed on firms by command. The central planning board devises plans to maintain the balance between supply and demand, both of which depend on firms' fulfilling their output targets. However, these plans are never perfect, and this produces a number of inconsistencies. North Korea has emphasised detailed and consistent planning throughout its history of socialism. The main purpose of the Daean management system was to instil the Party leadership in firm activities. However, this objective can hardly address the shortages of inputs in a socialist system (Park, 2002).

North Korean firms are classified into several categories (i.e. Special, 1st, 2nd, 3rd, etc.) in terms of their size and their importance in the national economy (Academy of Social Sciences, 1985). For instance, firms in the Special category typically have a strategic importance and employ more than 10,000 workers. Examples include firms that operate in the defence industry. Furthermore, the authorities classify these firms into two groups: national firms and regional ones. The firms belonging to Special, 1st, 2nd and 3rd categories are classified as national firms. These firms are directly controlled and supported by the central planning body, and resources at the national level are principally allocated to them. The other firms are classified as regional. Resource allocation for firms belonging to regional governments is lower in priority than allocation for national firms, and the regional firms are usually instructed to seek their resources at the regional level.

Significant changes were observed in the enterprise sector during the late 1970s and the early 1980s. First, as previously discussed, a group of North Korean firms began to be integrated into 'combined firms' (Yeonhap Giupso). These combined firms aimed to improve management efficiency by integrating a group of related firms. Second, the authorities decentralised foreign trade in response to the country's increasing foreign debt and poor economic conditions. North Korea managed to import machinery and technology from the West in the 1970s by incurring foreign debts. However, these debts were not paid, partly because of the oil shocks during the same period. This first phase of decentralisation allowed several large firms, provincial governments and cabinet institutions to trade with foreign companies (Yang, 2008). However, the Ministry of Foreign Trade directly controlled this trade, both by determining the price to be applied to exports and imports and by controlling whether the firms had permission to import products. This meant that the North Korean authorities remained the backbone of the central planning system, while at the same time giving other institutions the initiative to engage in foreign trade.

The second phase of decentralisation occurred in 1991 when the Soviet Union was on the verge of disintegration. A source from North Korea explained the so-called 'New System of Foreign Trade' as 'the system in which, under the guidance of central plans of the State, not only Committee for External Economy but also other committees, Ministries and provincial governments are allowed to establish trading firms and engage trade directly with foreign countries in various forms and methods' (Lee, 1992, p. 30). This system allowed the designated institutions to plan and execute foreign trade for themselves on the basis of their output capacity and economic conditions.

Similar to the first phase, the second phase of decentralisation can be regarded as an attempt to mitigate the shock caused by the collapse of the CMEA (Council for Mutual Economic Assistance), that is, the communist trade bloc. North Korean authorities realised that they could no longer supply inputs and consumer goods to all firms, regions and institutions, and for this reason asked these organisations to seek their own means of survival, allowing them to engage in foreign trade. For example, a provincial government could purchase inputs from abroad to supply the firms in that province. The province was then required to export the firms' output in order to earn hard currency to pay for the imports.

The third decentralisation occurred in 2002 after the implementation of the July 1st Measures. Cities, counties and firms were given the right to engage in foreign trade, and trading companies were allowed to sell their imported goods directly to consumers. The decentralisation of foreign trade meant the *de facto* destruction of the central planning system. The autonomy of various institutions and firms to engage in foreign trade implied that central planning could no longer control all the activities of these bodies. Instead, the North Korean authorities confined the scope of central planning to some firms that belonged to the Special category. Firms in the Special category are given inputs in accordance with central planning, whereas the other firms are not, and must seek their own means of survival. As a result, a majority of these non-Special firms have ceased to trade normally, as the extent of their operations largely depends on their access to foreign economic relations.[58]

The disintegration of the economy into four state institutions occurred simultaneously with the decentralisation of the enterprise sector. These four state institutions can be classified as the army, the Workers' Party, the cabinet and the regional governments. Because of the difficulty of providing resources for state institutions, the army and the Party became independent from the central planning mechanism that was directed by the cabinet. The Party created its own trading company (Daesung Trading Company), established the Party Office 39 in 1974 and founded Daesung Bank under its control. The Party continued to expand its territory to its own firms and trading companies. The major role of these firms was to supply resources to Party organisations by engaging in business with foreign companies. A similar process can be observed in the army economy. The Second Economy Committee, which was in charge of the economy relating to the army, was established in the mid-1970s and was independent of the cabinet. This committee merged several organisations in the defence industry into a single organisation and established its own mechanism to plan, produce, distribute and export products, including weapons. In the mid-1990s, the Ministry of the People's Army began to establish its own trading companies and took some firms, mines and farms away from the cabinet to feed the soldiers and strengthen the army. As a result, the army and Party economies currently control a large share of the resources produced in North Korea, and engage with foreign businesses as well. Regional governments control a relatively small number of firms in their respective areas. By engaging in foreign trade and investing in their own firms, regional governments are attempting to generate resources to support their own institutions.

Informal markets are also utilised by firms to generate revenue. When national authorities failed to provide inputs in accordance with central planning, many firms likely turned to informal markets as a way to fill the void. The informal economy, which initially emerged from household activities, gradually became larger and required inputs for informal production and outputs transacted at the markets. In response to these circumstances, firms began to allow workers to engage in the informal economy on the condition that they contribute to generating revenue for the firm. Firms were also able to sell outputs in the markets, and in that way could earn money that they could in turn use to buy inputs from the markets.

In this manner, central planning has been virtually destroyed in North Korea. From the outset, central planning was not implemented consistently, because of the arbitrary intervention of the leader in making economic decisions. Such inconsistency induced several bottlenecks, shortages and forced substitutions. The disintegration of the economy into different sectors of the state institutions intensified over time. As a result, central planning is now confined to a certain sector of the economy, while the rest of the economy suffers a coordination vacuum. The firms that are no longer covered by central planning need to seek their own means of survival. Some of them rely heavily on foreign business and market activities.

2.4.b   Firms and Informal Markets

We now investigate the extent to which firms relied on markets rather than on plans in terms of markets for labour, inputs and outputs. The data we use on markets for labour, inputs and outputs come from surveys of North Korean refugees conducted in 2009 and 2011, as we discussed in the previous section. We will measure the extent to which firms used informal labour markets, using data on '8·3 workers'.[59] Firm managers allowed some of their workers to be absent and to make money outside of their firms, particularly in the markets. However, these workers were required to pay an 8·3 fund (8·3 jageum) to their firms, and this amount provided an important source of revenue for firms.

The surveys in 2009 and 2011 asked the respondents whether 8·3 workers existed in their firms in North Korea, the proportion of these 8·3 workers in their total workforce and the ratio of the wages of these 8·3 workers to the official wages. The existence of 8·3 workers is well known among North Koreans, and some respondents also reported observing such practices themselves. Approximately 58.7 per cent of the respondents confirmed the existence of 8·3 workers in their firms, 30.5 per cent did not report any 8·3 workers in their firms and 10.8 per cent had no idea about the existence of such workers. Overall, at least 58.7 per cent of the firms in North Korea had 8·3 workers. These workers also made up a weighted average of 23.2 per cent in the total workforce[60] and they paid an 8·3 fund to their firms, an amount seven times higher than the official wages. This finding suggests that by using the funds paid by 8·3 workers, firms are able to pay salaries to non-8·3 workers. In other words, North Korean firms earn more revenue by allowing some of their workers to work informally and then collecting part of their earnings in return for this privilege. This finding tells us that the informal economy boosts the official economy by supplying the latter with substantial financial resources.

Official firms also use the goods market aside from the labour market. These firms purchase some inputs from the markets and then

Table 2.19 *Reliance of State Firms on Markets*

	Share of workers/inputs/outputs that rely on markets	Details
Informal labour market	23.2%	8·3 workers pay on average 7 times as much as official wages
Informal input market	27.1% – 67.4%	Use of central planning: 32.6% Use of managers' personal connections: 18.1% Purchase from markets: 27.1% Contribution by workers: 15.3% Others: 6.9%
Informal output market	16.1% – 54.5%	Use of central planning: 45.5% Managers' personal connections: 19.6% Selling at markets: 16.1% To workers in lieu of wages: 8.1% Others: 10.7%

sell their outputs in the markets. The respondents were asked what channels their inputs were supplied through and where the outputs of their firms were delivered or used.

Table 2.19 summarises the results. The labour, input and output markets occupy significant portions of the sample. Central planning allocates 32.6 per cent of the inputs, 27.1 per cent of the inputs are purchased from markets and 18.1 and 15.3 per cent are supplied using the personal connections of firm managers and contributed by workers. These connections of firm managers may include barter exchanges with input-producing firms and indirect purchase of inputs using supply agents. Workers may purchase inputs from markets. Therefore, 27.1 to 67.4 per cent of the inputs use the market mechanism to acquire inputs. The table also shows that fewer than half of the outputs are allocated by central planning. Roughly 19.6 per cent of the outputs are disposed of using the personal connections of firm managers and 16.1 and 8.1 per cent of the outputs are sold in markets and paid in lieu of wages, respectively. Those who obtained outputs using personal connections and received them in lieu of wages could sell them in the markets. Therefore, 16.1 to 54.5 per cent of the outputs are either directly or indirectly disposed of in the markets.

2.4.c   Firms and Foreign Trade

Given the virtual collapse of the inter-firm supply chain for a large number of North Korean firms, these firms rely heavily on the external sector to obtain inputs and consumer goods. In order to pay for imports, firms must seek items to be exported, such as natural resources, clothes, agricultural products and fish. In this way, foreign trade becomes a lifeline for North Korean firms, which are affiliated to state institutions. In effect, North Korean institutions, and thus the regime itself, depend on trade for their operation. In response to decentralisation in the external sector, the authorities have implemented special approaches for controlling such firms by issuing trading licences, implementing a quota and collecting the Revolutionary Fund.

Aside from the central government, the trading companies that belong to various state institutions also engage in foreign trade. For example, the oil that is imported from China through the pipeline between China and North Korea is allocated to the national government, which then allocates it to various sectors, firms and institutions. The import of cereals also includes the produce demanded by the central government. Minerals are exported by trading companies with a trading licence, and the materials for apparel and clothes are imported by trading companies with a licence, or without a licence but in possession of a leasing agreement.[61]

Decentralisation in foreign trade can weaken the control of the state over the economy. To prevent this, the North Korean authorities utilise a control mechanism that is based on 'waku',[62] a licence for foreign trade. Trading companies must obtain a waku before conducting business with foreign companies.[63] A waku also specifies an allowable amount of goods to be traded (Yang, 2008; Lim et al., 2011).[64] For example, a certain trading company possesses a waku that allows coal exports of up to 10,000 tons. In this manner, the state can control the volume of exports and imports of the country.

A waku is not tradable, but can be lent to another unlicensed trading firm (Yang, 2008). In exchange, the lending firm obtains a certain amount of commission from the unlicensed firm, which can help them fulfil the specified amount of trade in the waku.[65] Trading firms with a waku can obtain financial resources by exporting certain goods to foreign countries. These exports allow the firms to import food and consumer goods for their workers or to sell in North Korean markets, which subsequently generate inputs to help them run their businesses. In addition, they offer a part of these resources to the leader, as we will discuss below.

A waku can be regarded as a privilege provided by the state. Because of this, North Korean trading companies face severe competition from one another to obtain a waku. State institutions also compete with one another for additional waku.[66] Given that powerful state institutions or individuals can easily obtain a waku, the army and the Party enlarge their foreign businesses by obtaining more waku. The bodies to be given a waku are ultimately selected by the leader of the state, who can decide which state institution will be strengthened or empowered, and how the power of these state institutions will be balanced.

Controlling waku gives power, but not financial resources, to the leader. The leader realises some financial gain from the activities of the state institutions, including those that generate hard currency. He collects foreign currency in the form of the so-called 'Revolutionary Fund', foreign currency that is presented to the leader by various institutions and companies when they earn foreign currency though their business activities. The Revolutionary Fund was introduced in the 1970s when North Korea faced a foreign currency crisis, but it was emphasised more strongly from the 1990s. These funds can be collected in several ways. For example, an army organisation may dispatch a businessperson to conduct business with companies in China. This businessperson, who is called 'foreign currency earner' (oihwabeoligun), is required to send a certain amount of foreign currency to the state institution, which then gives part of this currency to the leader. Another example is when trading companies, or institutions to which such companies belong, offer a part of their foreign currency earnings to the leader. The state leader can use Revolutionary Fund monies for various purposes, such as to strengthen the leader's power, to import luxury goods from foreign countries and present them to elites, to provide foreign currency to a firm in which the leader conducts a Spot Guidance and to run state institutions and firms. Lim et al. (2011) argue that the Revolutionary Fund partially plays the role that had been played by the Juseok Fond before the economic crisis of the 1990s. One major difference between these two funds is that the Revolutionary Fund comprises foreign currency, whereas the Juseok Fond mainly comprises commodities but also includes currencies. Moreover, the Juseok Fond could only be collected when the economy was in normal operation, whereas the Revolutionary Fund could be funded when the economy relied on foreign trade for its survival. The Revolutionary Fund was established because the North Korean authorities needed to control the economy and maintain the power of their leader during the near-collapse of the North Korean socialist economy.

The control exercised over waku and the Revolutionary Fund is not compatible with that of the central planning mechanism. The central planning mechanism is designed to control all firms' activities, including finance, meaning that central planners have the means to understand the financial status of firms. By contrast, waku and the Revolutionary Fund cannot monitor the financial accounts of institutions, firms or individuals. Strict monitoring of such activities and the collection of most of the financial resources from firms' foreign activities are undesirable because they undermine the firms' incentives to generate additional hard currency.

Therefore, some institutions, firms and individuals may become richer and come to possess a large amount of foreign currencies because they are able to keep any financial resources that remain after they have paid the Revolutionary Fund. Some North Korean refugees we surveyed have said that, 'Now in North Korea, the government is poor but a large amount of money lies in the non-government sectors'.[67]

Foreign trade can influence the governance of North Korean firms. A manager who excels over the managers of other firms in terms of trade performance is recognised as a competent manager. A Korean-Chinese businessperson interviewed by the author reported the following:

> Two North Korean firms, one large and the other relatively small, were merged into one firm. The manager of the large firm was old yet less competent in managing the firm, especially in terms of foreign trade, than the young manager of the small firm. Contrary to expectations, the young manager was appointed as the manager of the merged firm. This situation was unthinkable in North Korea before the country began to engage in foreign trade.

2.4.d   Firms and External Relations: Firm-Level Investigation[68]

Surveys and Data Description

We conducted on-site surveys of the firms in Dandong that were involved in North Korean businesses. Dandong is a Chinese city of 2.4 million residents, located alongside the Yalu river (Aprokgang, in Korean), which divides China and North Korea. The North Korean city facing Dandong across the Yalu is Shineujoo; it has 350,000 residents, making it the sixth city in North Korea in terms of population. The strategic importance of Dandong in North Korean trade lies in its geographical proximity to the major North Korean city and the availability of all four means of transportation (i.e. port, railway, road and pipeline). As a result, more than 60 per cent of trade between

North Korea and China takes place through Dandong (Kim and Jung, 2015).[69]

The survey in Dandong was conducted from February 2012 to August 2013, with an interval from August 2012 to June 2013. The owners or managers of the firms in the survey, or those who had full knowledge of their business with North Korea, were selected as the main respondents. A total of 176 firms participated in the survey, of which 138 were engaged in trade, 54 were engaged in investment and 16 were engaged in both trade and investment. Although the firms were not selected randomly, we aimed to select participants that represented the whole sample of firms in Dandong as fully as possible. In more detail, we took the size of the firms, the type of owners and type of businesses into account when we contacted firms for a possible survey. Furthermore, the size of the sample is large, in that it covers about 10 to 20 per cent of all registered firms in Dandong doing business with North Korea (Kim and Jung, 2015).

We identified the owners of the firms in terms of their ethnicity, citizenship and residence. Four major groups of businesspersons in Dandong have been conducting transactions with North Korea. The *Chinese* (Hanjok) group involved businesspersons who were Chinese in terms of their citizenship, ethnicity and residence. The *Korean-Chinese* (Chosunjok) group refers to businesspersons who are Korean in ethnicity, but Chinese in terms of citizenship and residence. The *Chinese-North Korean* (Chosun Hwagyo) group comprises those who are Chinese in ethnicity and citizenship, but are permanent residents of North Korea. The *South Korean* group refers to ethnic Koreans who are citizens of South Korea.

Each of these groups utilises its advantages in conducting its business. The Chinese group is able to take advantage of a strong marketing capability within China and a relatively stable political relationship between China and North Korea. The Chinese group can also benefit from geographical proximity, the possibility of visits to North Korea, the settlement of claims through institutional arrangements between China and North Korea and networking with

Chinese local government and banks. Most of the Korean-Chinese have the advantage of speaking both Korean and Chinese, and thus are good at networking with both South Korean and Chinese companies. They also find it easier to visit North Korea than do South Koreans. Most of the Chinese-North Koreans were born and raised in North Korea, have a full command of both Chinese and Korean languages and are familiar with North Korean local conditions. The South Korean group can take advantage of networking with South Korean companies in receiving orders and selling goods in South Korea. To reflect the heterogeneous characteristics of these groups, we selected a sufficient number of samples from each to participate in our survey. Of the 176 participating firms, 76 were owned by Chinese, 40 were owned by Korean-Chinese, 35 were owned by Chinese-North Koreans, 23 were owned by South Koreans or their associates and 2 were owned by neither Chinese nor Koreans.[70]

The surveys had a twofold purpose. First, these surveys aimed to understand the business relationships between China and North Korea at the firm level. The survey results are expected to shed light on the prospects of such relationships as well as the performance of the firms. Second, the surveys aimed to uncover the economic situations in North Korea, according to the experiences of the participating businesspersons who possess sufficient knowledge of the firms and industries in North Korea, considering their transactions and contacts with such firms. Their evaluations can be regarded as expert opinions, especially if their businesses were conducted for a sufficiently long time. Such assessments were deemed reliable because these businesspersons could either earn or lose money, depending on the accuracy of their assessments. Therefore, their perceptions and opinions provide a prism through which we are able to examine economic circumstances in North Korea.

Table 2.20 shows the distribution of firms in terms of business type. Of the trading firms, 55.8 per cent were involved in exports or imports. The major export items included machinery, electronics,

Table 2.20 *Business Types of Firms*

Trading firms (number of firms: 138)		Investment firms (number of firms: 54)	
Types	Share (%)	Types	Share (%)
Export	31.2	Joint management	13.0
Import	24.6	Joint investment	13.0
Outsourcing	31.2	Equipment investment in light manufacturing	22.2
Wholesale/retail trade	11.6	Equipment investment in extractive industry	33.3
Others	1.4	Investment in hiring workers	18.5
Total	100.0	Total	100.0

Source: Surveys of the firms in Dandong.

Notes: (1) Sixteen firms that are involved in both trade and investment are included in both categories. (2) Joint management refers to management by both foreign and North Korean managers in a firm, for which investment is made by foreigners and North Koreans. (3) Equipment investment refers to equipment provided by Chinese or elsewhere and delivered to the North Korean firm, which is considered a type of investment. Generally, the return from such investment is obtained in the form of products, such as minerals and clothes, which are produced by the firm. (4) Investment in hiring workers refers to the hiring of North Korean workers who are working in a firm that is located in China.

electric appliances, second-hand cars, cosmetics, medicines and food (flour, cooking oils, etc.). Goods imported from North Korea to China mostly comprised minerals (coal, iron, gold, lead, etc.), agricultural products (mushrooms, perilla, bellflower roots, etc.) and fish. Approximately one-third of the firms (31.2 per cent) used North Korea as an outsourcing destination. The majority of the outsourcing firms

were engaged in clothes manufacturing and were using cheap yet relatively skilled labour from North Korea. Roughly a third of the investment firms were firms in the extractive industry engaged in equipment
investment, 22.2 per cent were in light manufacturing and involved in
equipment investment, 18.5 per cent were Chinese firms that hired
North Korean labour, 13 per cent were operating under joint management and 13 per cent were operating under joint investment.[71]

The majority of the firms started their businesses with North
Korea in the early 2000s, whereas only 8.5 per cent of the 176 firms
began to trade or invest in North Korea before 2000.[72] The business
relationships between the surveyed firms and the North Korean firms
lasted for an average of 5.9 years, with a maximum of 20 years.
The number of firms that started doing businesses with North Korea
remained at one digit per annum until 2003, and then increased to
a two-digit number from 2004. This trend might be affected by the
economic measures undertaken by the North Korean government
during the same period as well as by the Sunshine Policy of South
Korea toward North Korea.[73] However, the number of these firms
declined beginning in 2010. A total of 22 firms opened new North
Korean businesses in 2008 and again in 2009, but these figures
decreased to 17 and 15 firms in 2010 and 2011, respectively.
The decline may be attributable to economic sanctions that South
Korea imposed on North Korea in 2010. This demonstrates that firms
are exposed to large risks associated with the changes in the policies of
North Korea and other countries.

Table 2.21 shows the institutions to which North Korean firms
belong as well as the owner types of these firms. As explained before,
the North Korean authorities permitted different state institutions –
namely, the army, the Workers' Party, the cabinet (central government) and the regional governments – to establish trading firms
through which they could engage in trading activities with foreign
countries. This is clearly seen in Table 2.21, which shows that most of
the North Korean firms are affiliated with one of the four state
institutions.

Table 2.21 *Number of Trading Firms Doing Business with North Korea by Institution and Type of Owner*

	Chinese (Hanjok)	Korean-Chinese (Chosunjok)	Chinese-North Korean (Chosun Hwagyo)	South Korean associates	Others	Total
Party	19	11	10	3	0	43
Army	18	6	7	2	1	34
Cabinet	12	7	2	5	2	28
Regional governmen-s	19	16	8	2	0	45
Individuals	8	0	8	10	0	26
Total	76	40	35	22	3	176

Source: Surveys of the firms in Dandong (2012 to 2013); Kim and Jung (2015)

Regional governments owned the largest number of North Korean trading and investment firms (45 firms), followed by the Workers' Party (43 firms), the army (34 firms) and the cabinet (28 firms). Among the 43 Party-controlled firms doing business with North Korea, 19 were Chinese, 11 were Korean-Chinese and 10 were Chinese-North Korean. A similar pattern is observed for the firms controlled by the army, of which the Chinese firms outnumbered the other types. In contrast, firms affiliated with South Korean associates are less likely to trade with North Korean firms belonging to the Workers' Party or the army. Instead, 45 per cent of firms associated with South Koreans engage in business with North Korean individuals who work on behalf of official firms or state institutions. The firms for which these individuals work are mostly small-scale, and are leased or spun off from the official firms. This might be caused by the large risk attached to business between South Korean and North Korean firms.

Determinants of Firm Performance

Using the data from the surveys of the Chinese firms, we analyse the performance of firms that are engaged in business with North Korea and estimate its determinants. Two groups of measures are used for firm performance. First, current profitability, which is measured using the profitability of firms in 2011, is used as a proxy for firm performance. Second, future profitability is measured using the changes in expected profits within the next year. Table 2.22 shows characteristics of the firms in connection with the performance measures.

Table 2.22 shows a typical firm that started doing business with North Korea about six years ago (that is, in 2006 or 2007). The annual revenue and profitability amounted to US$4.83 million and 16.18 per cent, respectively. Revenue per employee was US$277,000. It also suggests that the average revenue of trading firms is larger than that of investment firms, but the imbalance is caused by one extremely large trading firm. When this firm is excluded, the average revenue of trading firms amounts to US$1.87 million, which is less

Table 2.22 *Characteristics and Performance of Firms Doing Business with North Korea*

	Types and affiliations of firms	Revenue (US$1,000)	Duration of business (years)	Profitability[1] (per cent)	Revenue per worker (US$1,000)	Increase in expected profits in one year[2]	Increase in expected profits in three years[2]
Business types	Trading firms	5,548	5.6	16.14	277	0.56	0.78
	Investment firms	2,946	6.0	16.21	209	0.79	0.85
	Trading/ investment firms	3,843	7.6	16.40	443	0.79	0.71
Ownership	Chinese	7,929	5.1	17.38	278	0.62	0.85
	Korean- Chinese	4,385	6.6	11.02	339	0.46	0.69
	Chinese-North Korean	645	6.8	19.53	220	0.90	1.00
	South Korean associates	1,502	6.1	12.62	283	0.64	0.58
	Others	5,573	4.0	40.33	42	1.00	1.00

Table 2.22 (cont.)

Types and affiliations of firms		Revenue (US$1,000)	Duration of business (years)	Profitability[1] (per cent)	Revenue per worker (US$1,000)	Increase in expected profits in one year[2]	Increase in expected profits in three years[2]
Affiliation	Army	16,400	7.5	21.26	481	0.70	0.69
	Party	1,584	5.5	14.10	216	0.78	0.86
	Cabinet	5,792	5.5	16.07	178	0.52	0.73
	Regional governments	922	5.3	14.29	306	0.58	0.88
	Individuals	767	5.7	16.34	168	0.58	0.71
Average		4,832	5.9	16.18	277	0.63	0.79

Source: Surveys of the firms in Dandong (2012 to 2013)

Notes: (1) Profitability for trading firms refers to the ratio of profit to total revenue (margin), whereas profitability for investment firms refers to the return on assets (total investment). The average of profitability that is weighted by the share of trading or investment firms in the total number firms is used for those categories that include both trading and investment firms. (2) Three answers to the question, 'Do you think that your expected profits will increase within one year and three years?' are possible: 'yes', 'no' and 'I do not know'. The figures in the last two columns refer to the average of the answers from trading and investment firms that are weighted by the share of these firms in the total number of firms. A value of '1' is assigned to 'yes', whereas a value of '0' is assigned to 'no'.

than the average revenues of either investment or trading/investment firms. The differences in profitability across the three business types are insignificant. In contrast, in terms of expected profits, the trading firms are less optimistic than either the investment or the investment/trading firms.

A high level of heterogeneity in performance is observable, depending on the type of ownership. Chinese firms outrank all of the other firms in terms of revenue, while Chinese-North Korean firms have the lowest revenue as they are typically involved in small-scale wholesale and retail businesses on the basis of their network advantage inside North Korea. However, Chinese-North Korean firms performed better than all of the other firms in terms of profitability. Firms owned by South Korean associates and by Korean-Chinese record the lowest profitability, perhaps because economic sanctions against North Korea have significantly affected their main business, which is to deal with demand from South Korea. Such difficulties are also reflected in these firms' more negative perceptions of their future profit potential, compared to the firms owned by Chinese and Chinese-North Koreans.

Those firms engaging in businesses with army-affiliated North Korean firms perform best in all of the performance indicators. Both the size of the revenue and revenue per worker are the largest, and profitability is the highest, although its difference from that of cabinet-affiliated firms is not statistically significant. This finding may be attributed to the North Korean policy emphasising the importance of the army in the country. The longest duration of business relations with army-affiliated firms indicates its dominance in keeping waku, compared with other state institutions. Nevertheless, those firms that are engaged in businesses with Workers' Party-affiliated firms hold the most optimistic views of future profits. Overall, those firms that are engaged in businesses with army- and Workers' Party-affiliated firms either record higher profitability in the current year or expect their profits to increase in the next year more commonly than other firms.

We use regressions on firm performance to get a fuller under-standing of its determinants. We employ three groups of variables as explanatory factors. The first group is related to firm-specific factors that include the size of the revenue, the number of workers involved in North Korean business, the duration of doing business with North Korea, the main industrial sector of the business and the types of firms (e.g. trading, investment and both trading and investment). The second group is related to North Korean factors, which include the affiliation of the counterpart North Korean firm, the predictability of changes in North Korean laws, regulations and policies, and the advantages and constraints of doing business with North Korea.[74] Advantages are classified into four groups: namely, size of markets, abundance of natural resources, low wages and production cost and 'others'. Similarly, we divide the constraints into three groups: namely, the risks associated with changes in the policies of North Korea and those of other countries, the problems related to North Korean firms (i.e. failure to meet the delivery date and difficulty in controlling product quality) and 'others', which includes the problems caused by inadequate infrastructure. The third group refers to the ownership types of the firms. The Chinese, Korean-Chinese, Chinese-North Korean, and South Korean firms each have their own advantages and disadvantages, as discussed before.

Table 2.23 shows the estimations of the determinants of current profitability. Model (2) is different from Model (1) in that the former includes additional regressors, including advantages and constraints in doing business with North Korea. No statistical differences are observed among trading, investment and trading/investment firms. Moreover, the duration of doing business with North Korean firms does not affect the current profitability of firms. The coefficient of the industry of natural resources is positive yet marginally insignificant.

In terms of affiliation, among all of the four state institutions, only those firms that do business with army-affiliated firms in North Korea have a higher profitability than those that do business with Workers' Party-affiliated firms, whereas the coefficients of the

Table 2.23 *Determinants of the Current Profitability of Firms Doing Business with North Korea*

Groups of variables	Variables		Model (1)	Model (2)
Types of firms	Trading firms		Reference category	
	Investment firms		−5.38 (0.56)	−5.93 (0.60)
	Trading/Investment firms		−0.45 (0.08)	−0.91 (0.15)
Size of revenue (divided by US$1 million)			−0.02 (0.35)	−0.02 (0.42)
Number of workers			0.03 (1.24)	0.03 (1.22)
The starting year of North Korean business	Before 1998		Reference category	
	1998 to 2007		3.08 (0.53)	2.37 (0.40)
	After 2007		4.13 (0.63)	3.02 (0.48)
Industrial sector of business	Trade		1.49 (0.15)	1.46 (0.14)
	Natural resources		8.04 (1.16)	10.07 (1.34)
	Wholesale/retail		5.49 (0.47)	4.42 (0.37)
	Others		Reference category	
Possibility to visit North Korea (without problem = 1; otherwise = 0)			8.81 (2.44)**	8.10 (2.19)**
Affiliation of the North Korean firm	Army		9.22 (1.88)*	8.64 (1.72)*
	Party		Reference category	
	Cabinet		−0.14 (0.17)	0.19 (0.04)
	Regional governments		0.68 (0.16)	0.15 (0.24)

Table 2.23 (cont.)

Groups of variables	Variables	Model (1)	Model (2)
	Others	0.77 (0.13)	1.14 (0.19)
Ownership of the firm	Chinese	Reference category	
	Korean-Chinese	−7.54 (1.86)*	−7.96 (1.88)*
	Chinese-North Korean	0.08 (0.02)	−0.49 (0.11)
	South Korean associates	0.17 (0.03)	−0.71 (0.28)
	Others	7.25 (0.44)	9.15 (0.55)
Attractiveness	Low wages and cost		−0.56 (0.12)
	Natural resources		−0.58 (0.10)
	Others		Reference category
Constraints	Firm factors		1.66 (0.29)
	Policy changes		4.90 (1.25)
	Others		Reference category
No. of samples		175	175
R^2		0.14	0.15

Note: Absolute t-value is provided in parentheses. The significance at the 10 and 5 per cent significance level is indicated by * and **, respectively.

performance of the firms affiliated with the other institutions are not statistically significant. This suggests that engaging in business with an army-affiliated firm is more profitable than engaging in businesses with firms that are affiliated to other institutions. This result may be attributable to the fact that the army has had superior power over the other institutions in North Korea, particularly during the period of Kim Jong-il, in which the Military-First (Songun) Policy dominated the direction of government policies.[75] This enabled the army to obtain more lucrative business opportunities and to keep such opportunities for a relatively long period, compared with the other state institutions.

The possibility of visiting North Korea without a problem is positively associated with the profitability of firms in both Models (1) and (2). The ability to visit North Korea facilitates communication between firms and enables them to check the production processes of both firms, which can help them control the quality of their outputs. Visiting the plant or the firm is also essential for investment firms. Chinese, Korean-Chinese and Chinese-North Koreans can visit North Korea much more easily than South Koreans. South Korean citizens are required to obtain permission, from both the North Korean and South Korean governments, before they can visit North Korea, and such visits have become virtually impossible since the introduction of sanctions in 2010.[76]

In terms of ownership, Korean-Chinese ownership is negatively correlated with the profitability. This finding can be understood from the perspective of network advantage. Korean-Chinese firms can easily use their ethnic background and connections to access South Korean markets. However, North Korean products are no longer allowed legal access to South Korean markets, pursuant to sanctions imposed by South Korea in 2010. Therefore, those firms that are owned either by South Koreans or by Korean-Chinese have lost their competitiveness in accessing South Korean markets. South Korean firms might have closed down their businesses and returned to South Korea, whereas Korean-Chinese firms have continued with their businesses. A different interpretation is that the low profitability of South Korean firms can be accounted for in terms of the difficulty those firms' owners have visiting North Korea.

Table 2.24 shows the binary probit estimations on the expected profit of firms. The firm type, the year of starting the North Korean business and the industrial sectors of businesses do not affect the expected profit. Similarly, as a result from current profitability, Korean-Chinese ownership is negatively correlated with expected profits. In other words, the Korean-Chinese view the future of their businesses with North Korea more pessimistically than the other ethnic groups. By contrast, North Korean-Chinese believe that their profits will increase more than those of Chinese firms. One interpretation is that North Korean-Chinese regard their advantages of understanding and networking with locals in North Korea as not easily replaced by any other group, but Korean-Chinese businesspersons think that they do not possess unique advantages compared to any other groups of businesspersons.

Companies doing business with firms that belong either to the cabinet or to individuals view their future less favourably than those whose North Korean partners belong to the army, the Workers' Party, or the regional governments. This can be interpreted as indicating that cabinet-affiliated firms do not provide a favourable business environment for their counterparts in China because the cabinet is less powerful than the army and the Workers' Party at the national level, and has less information and fewer networks than the regional governments at the regional level.

The perception that firm factors are the most important constraints on doing business with North Korea is positively associated with the expected profit of firms. This implies that the perception that the reference category (i.e. electricity shortages and difficulty in logistics) is more important than firm factors. The same finding is obtained for changes in the policies of North Korea and other countries. In other words, businesspersons trading with North Korea expect that firm factors and policy changes will not be as important as infrastructure

Table 2.24 *Determinants of the Expected Profit of Firms Doing Business with North Korea*

Groups of variables	Variables	Model (1)	Model (2)
Types of firms	Trading firms	Reference category	0.26 (0.33)
	Investment firms	0.11 (0.15)	0.52 (0.89)
	Trading/Investment firms	0.51 (0.96)	0.01 (0.74)
Size of revenue (US$1 million)		0.005 (0.86)	-0.01 (1.63)
Number of workers		-0.01 (1.15)	
The starting year of North Korean business	Before 1998	Reference category	-0.86 (1.30)
	1998 to 2007	-0.40 (0.70)	-0.40 (0.58)
	After 2007	0.16 (0.27)	-0.93 (1.13)
Industrial sector of business	Trade	-0.72 (0.94)	0.75 (1.08)
	Natural resources	0.20 (0.32)	0.38 (0.32)
	Wholesale/retail	0.68 (0.62)	
	Others	Reference category	0.39 (1.18)
Possibility to visit North Korea (without problem = 1; otherwise = 0)		0.47 (1.46)	-0.56 (1.16)
Affiliation of the North Korean firm	Army	-0.54 (1.15)	-1.06 (2.20)**
	Party	Reference category	-0.48 (1.14)
	Cabinet	-1.02 (2.30)**	
	Regional governments	-0.61 (1.60)	

Table 2.24 (cont.)

Groups of variables	Variables	Model (1)	Model (2)
	Others	−2.08 (2.62)***	−2.01 (2.41)**
Ownership of the firm	Chinese	Reference category	
	Korean-Chinese	−0.56 (1.80)*	−0.80 (2.32)**
	Chinese-North Korean	1.04 (2.07)**	0.70 (1.30)
	South Korean associates	1.04 (1.91)*	0.76 (1.37)
Attractiveness	Low wages and cost		−0.39 (1.00)
	Natural resources		0.10 (0.19)
	Others		Reference category
Constraints	Firm factors		1.02 (2.05)**
	Policy changes		0.95 (2.43)**
	Others		Reference category
No. of samples		130	130
Pseudo R²		0.22	0.26

Note: Absolute t-value is provided in parentheses. The significance at the 10 and 5 per cent significance level is indicated by
* and **, respectively.

problems. These businesspersons are interpreted as believing that firm factors will improve and policies will become more predictable in the future, whereas the inadequacy of infrastructure will become the most important constraint on doing business with North Korea.

Perceptions of Businesspersons of the North Korean Economy
The survey asked questions not only about the performance of the firms but also about their perceptions of the North Korean economy. The latter questions include those about the predictability of North Korean laws, regulations and institutions, the extent of adherence to the contract of a counterpart North Korean firm, the future of the North Korean economy, the expected profits from trade, the major advantages and constraints in their business activity and the intention to change the volume of trade or investment. We look at the replies of the businesspersons to these questions one by one. Table 2.25 summarises the answers to the question on the future of the North Korean economy.[77]

Table 2.25 shows a generally positive evaluation of the future of the North Korean economy. This might be related to the decisions of firms to engage in business with North Korea based on these views. As seen from the bottom row of the table, fewer than 3 per cent of the total respondents replied that the North Korean economy would grow worse or much worse in the future, 41 per cent replied that the economic conditions of North Korea would be unchanged, 37 per cent believed that the economy would become better and 19 per cent believed that the economy would become much better. No substantial differences were found between each business type, as trading firms were slightly less positive about the future of the North Korean economy than the investment firms or those engaging in both types of business. In terms of ownership, the Chinese-North Korean-owned firms evaluated the future of the North Korean economy less positively than the Chinese- and the Korean-Chinese-owned firms. In terms of affiliation, those dealing with firms affiliated with the cabinet and the regional governments were more positive in their

Table 2.25 *Future of the North Korean Economy (Per Cent)*

		Much worse	Worse	Same	Better	Much better	Total
Business types	Trading firms	0.82	2.46	41.80	38.52	16.39	100.0
	Investment firms	0.00	2.63	36.84	39.48	21.05	100.0
	Trading/investment firms	0.00	0.00	43.75	25.00	31.25	100.0
Ownership	Chinese	1.32	1.32	34.21	43.41	19.74	100.0
	Korean-Chinese	0.00	5.00	22.50	45.00	27.50	100.0
	Chinese-North Korean	0.00	0.00	68.57	20.00	11.43	100.0
	South Korean associates	0.00	0.00	59.09	31.82	9.09	100.0
	Others	0.00	33.33	0.00	33.33	33.33	100.0
Affiliation	Army	0.00	2.94	52.94	26.47	17.65	100.0
	Party	2.44	2.44	43.90	31.71	19.51	100.0
	Cabinet	0.00	0.00	28.57	46.43	25.00	100.0
	Regional governments	0.00	4.44	26.67	48.89	20.00	100.0
	Individuals	0.00	0.00	56.00	32.00	12.00	100.0
Average		0.57	2.27	40.91	37.50	18.75	100.0

Source: Surveys of the firms in Dandong (2012 to 2013)

evaluations of the future of the North Korean economy than those working with firms affiliated with the army, the Workers' Party and individuals. This view may be related to the possibility that reforms in North Korea will reduce entry barriers and thus privileges enjoyed by the army and the Workers' Party.

The respondents were also asked about the predictability of the laws, policies and regulations that could affect their businesses.[78] The responses are summarised in Table 2.26. The majority of the respondents perceived the changes in North Korean laws, policies and regulations as unpredictable. Specifically, 43.75 and 26.14 per cent of the respondents replied that foreseeing such changes was, respectively, absolutely and somewhat impossible. Therefore, conducting business with North Korea entails a large perceived risk. In terms of business type, firms that invested in North Korea and those that invested in and traded with the country argued that such changes were more predictable than those firms that only traded with North Korea. This difference could be partly attributable to information that was possessed by these particular firms. For instance, investment firms were more likely than trading firms to possess a larger amount of information on business environments. Such differences could also be caused by the self-selection of these firms: investment firms carry a larger risk, so they are likely to perceive the business environment more positively than those that only trade with North Korea.

Ownership has a little influence on the firms' perceptions toward changes in the laws, policies and regulations of North Korea, except for Chinese-North Koreans, who believe these are more predictable than the other groups of owners. In terms of affiliation, those engaged in business with army-, Workers' Party- and cabinet-affiliated North Korean firms argued more that such changes were predictable than the other groups. However, whether this heterogeneity resulted from a sample bias or from the different attitudes and approaches of North Korean firms in doing business with foreigners remains uncertain.

Table 2.26 *Predictability of Laws, Policies and Regulations (Per Cent)*

		Perfectly possible	Somewhat possible	Somewhat impossible	Absolutely impossible	Total
Business types	Trading firms	0.00	24.59	22.13	53.28	100.0
	Investment firms	5.26	34.21	36.84	23.68	100.0
	Trading/investment firms	6.25	43.75	31.25	18.75	100.0
Ownership	Chinese	1.32	26.32	22.37	50.00	100.0
	Korean-Chinese	5.00	30.00	22.50	42.50	100.0
	Chinese-North Korean	0.00	25.71	48.57	25.71	100.0
	South Korean associates	0.00	36.36	13.64	50.00	100.0
	Others	0.00	33.33	0.00	66.67	100.0
Affiliation	Army	5.88	29.41	38.24	26.47	100.0
	Party	0.00	19.51	41.46	39.02	100.0
	Cabinet	3.57	67.86	3.57	25.00	100.0
	Regional governments	0.00	22.22	20.00	57.78	100.0
	Individuals	0.00	8.00	24.00	68.00	100.0
Average		1.70	28.41	26.14	43.75	100.0

Source: Surveys of the firms in Dandong (2012 to 2013)

The respondents were asked to evaluate the extent of the adherence of North Korean firms to the terms of the contract during the past five years.[79] According to the bottom row of Table 2.27, 62.5 per cent of the firms argued that the extent of such adherence had improved over the past five years, whereas fewer than 2 per cent argued that such adherence had deteriorated. The investment firms perceived the adherence of North Korean firms more positively than did the trading firms. In terms of ownership, about 72 per cent of Korean-Chinese firms replied that North Korean firms had improved their adherence to the terms of the contract, whereas more than 30 per cent of South Korean firms argued that North Korean firms had substantially improved their keeping the terms of the contract. No substantial differences were observed across the perceptions of the firms of each affiliation type, except those of firms doing business with individuals.

This positive evaluation of the adherence of North Korean firms to the terms of the contract contrasted with negative perceptions of the predictability of the laws, policies and regulations in North Korea. In other words, companies engaged in business with North Korean firms argued that such firms improved their business practices in terms of contract adherence, despite the large risk brought about by government-initiated changes in their business environments. This evaluation is also reflected in Table 2.28, which shows the advantages and constraints associated with doing business with North Korea.

Foreign firms do business with North Korea for various reasons, such as the large size of consumer markets for North Korean goods, the low wages of North Korean workers and the low production cost in the country. All of this gives North Korea competitive export prices and demand from other countries. However, trading with North Korea is often constrained by frequent changes in the policies of North Korean authorities. Of the respondents engaging in trade with North Korea, 44.5 per cent identified the policies undertaken by North Korea and other countries as the most important constraint in trading with North Korea, whereas 29.2 per cent of the respondents identified the failure of North Korean firms to meet the delivery date or to control

Table 2.27 *Adherence to the Terms of the Contract (Per Cent)*

	Types and affiliation of firms	Substantially improved	Improved	No change	Deteriorated	Substantially deteriorated	Total
Business	Trading firms	8.20	49.18	41.80	0.82	0.00	100.0
	Investment firms	23.68	47.37	23.68	2.63	2.63	100.0
	Trading/investment firms	25.00	56.25	18.75	0.00	0.00	100.0
Ownership	Chinese	5.26	51.32	42.11	1.32	0.00	100.0
	Korean-Chinese	20.00	52.50	22.50	2.50	2.50	100.0
	Chinese-North Korean	8.57	54.29	37.14	0.00	0.00	100.0
	South Korean associates	31.82	27.27	40.91	0.00	0.00	100.0
	Others	33.33	66.67	0.00	0.00	0.00	100.0
Affiliation	Army	14.71	50.00	35.29	0.00	0.00	100.0
	Party	14.63	53.66	26.83	4.88	0.00	100.0
	Cabinet	14.29	50.00	32.14	3.57	0.00	100.0
	Regional governments	11.11	62.22	26.67	0.00	0.00	100.0
	Individuals	7.69	19.23	73.08	0.00	0.00	100.0
Average		13.07	49.43	35.80	1.14	0.57	100.0

Source: Surveys of the firms in Dandong (2012 to 2013)

Table 2.28 *Advantages and Constraints in Doing Business with North Korea*

Trading firms				Investment firms			
Advantages		Constraints		Advantages		Constraints	
Factors	Share (%)	Factors	Share (%)	Factors	Share (%)	Factors	Share (%)
Market size in other countries	32.6	Frequent changes in policies	29.2	Abundance of natural resources	48.2	Frequent changes in policies	35.2
Low wages	23.2	Failure to meet the delivery date	17.5	Low wages	29.6	Implementation of policies in other countries	14.8
Abundance of natural resources	15.2	Implementation of policies in other countries	15.3	Stable labour supply	18.5	Difficulty in communicating with or visiting North Korea	9.3
Low production cost	13.8	Difficulty in communicating with or visiting North Korea	15.3	Market size in other countries	3.7	Shortage of electricity	7.4

Table 2.28 (cont.)

| | Trading firms | | | | Investment firms | | | |
| | Advantages | | Constraints | | Advantages | | Constraints | |
Factors	Share (%)	Factors	Share (%)	Factors	Share (%)	Factors	Share (%)	Factors	Share (%)
Government support (low tariff/VAT refund)	8.0	Difficulty in controlling quality	11.7			Insufficient protection of investment	7.4
Stable labour supply	3.6	Government corruption	8.0			Government corruption	7.4
Others	3.6	Difficulty in settling claims	2.2			Difficulty in logistics	5.6
		Others	0.7			Others	13.0
Total	100	Total	100	Total	100	Total	100

Source: Surveys of the firms in Dandong (2012 to 2013); Kim and Jung (2015).

Note: The survey included 138 and 54 trading and investment firms, respectively. Sixteen firms that are involved in both trade and investment are included in both categories.

the quality of their products as the largest constraint. The difficulty of communicating with and visiting the country, as well as corruption in the government institution that oversaw the trading activities of North Korea, were also identified as major constraints.

Investment firms identify the abundance of natural resources as the most important incentive to invest in North Korea, followed by low wages and a stable supply of labour. In terms of constraints, 35.2 per cent of the respondents from investment firms identified the frequent changes in policies by North Korean authorities as the most important constraint, followed by the implementation of policies in other countries. This means that, as in the case of trading firms, country risk was identified as the most important constraint on doing business with North Korea. Institutional problems, such as difficulty in communicating with and visiting the country, insufficient protection of investment and government corruption, as well as infrastructural inadequacies such as electricity shortages and logistical difficulties, were also regarded as important constraints.

The respondents were also asked about their intention to change the volume of their business with North Korea.[80] The results are presented in Table 2.29.

The responses from firms are divided into two categories: expand (46.0 per cent) and no change (43.7 per cent). Most of the firms that engage in businesses with North Korea were at least neutral about their future business with North Korea. Only 6.9 per cent of the firms planned to curtail their business with North Korea, whereas 3.4 per cent intended to terminate their contracts with North Korean firms. A relatively high percentage of South Korean firms intended to reduce the volume of their trade or investment in North Korean firms or eliminate it altogether, which might be attributable to the sanctions imposed by South Korea against North Korea in 2010.

About half of the surviving firms demonstrated fairly optimistic views about the future of the North Korean economy and their businesses with North Korea.[81] They argued that North Korean firms had

Table 2.29 *Intention to Change the Volume of Business with North Korea (Per Cent)*

Types and affiliation of firms		Expand	No change	Decrease	Stop	Total
Business	Trading firms	47.9	43.8	5.8	2.5	100.0
	Investment firms	43.2	40.6	8.1	8.1	100.0
	Trading/investment firms	37.5	50.0	12.5	0.0	100.0
Ownership	Chinese	52.6	42.1	4.0	1.3	100.0
	Korean-Chinese	55.0	25.0	15.0	5.0	100.0
	North Korean-Chinese	23.5	76.5	0.0	0.0	100.0
	South Korean	38.1	33.3	14.3	14.3	100.0
	Others	66.7	33.3	0.00	0.0	100.0
Affiliation	Army	40.0	50.0	7.5	2.5	100.0
	Party	36.4	57.6	3.0	3.0	100.0
	Cabinet	57.1	32.2	3.6	7.1	100.0
	Regional governments	57.8	33.3	6.7	2.2	100.0
	Individuals	36.0	48.0	16.0	0.0	100.0
Total		46.0	43.7	6.9	3.4	100.0

Source: Surveys of the firms in Dandong (2012 to 2013).

improved their adherence to contracts, but the country risk was still perceived as a major constraint in their trading activities. Therefore, trade and investment in North Korea could increase as long as the country risk did not substantially increase. Many participating firms largely benefited from their business with North Korean firms in terms of natural resource supply and low wages. These benefits could also offset risks from the unpredictability of changes in North Korean laws, policies and regulations.

2.4.e   Conclusion

This section first studies the reliance of firms on informal markets and foreign trade. Foreign trade, markets and firms are interlinked in socialist North Korea in a way that causes the survival of firms to depend heavily on external trade and markets. The breakdown of central planning, and with it the supply chain in the domestic economy, which started in the late 1970s and intensified in the 1990s, forced firms involved in trade to make hard currency, which was in turn used to purchase energy, inputs and food from abroad. This development was the result of a series of decentralisations of foreign trade by the North Korean authorities, which regarded the earning of foreign currency as the utmost priority in managing the North Korean economy.

The unplanned market sector is intertwined with the planned or controlled state sector. Specifically, the informal economy is interconnected with the official economy in terms of the labour, input and output markets. The 8·3 workers seek permission to be absent from their official work so they can participate in the informal economy, and they then pay a part of their earnings to their official firms. These payments have also become an important source of revenue for the official firms. Moreover, official firms can use this 8·3 fund to pay for wages, taxes and inputs. A significant part of firm activities takes place informally, as only 32.6 and 45.5 per cent of a firm's inputs and outputs are allocated by central planners, respectively. Rather, such firms use the informal economy as a main source for their revenue, selling at least 16.1 per cent of their outputs in the markets. They also rely on the informal economy for inputs: the share of inputs bought at the markets exceeds 17.1 per cent. In this way, North Korea has been experiencing an unprecedented informalisation of a previously rigid socialist economy.

The North Korean authorities control foreign trade with waku, a trade licence. Because firms are only able to engage in foreign trade if they have this licence, there is severe competition to acquire waku. The ability to informally lend waku in return for a substantial commission increases such competition. The execution of Jang Sung-taek in 2013 is believed to have been related to competition for waku. The North Korean leader uses waku to elicit loyalty from the elites and to maintain the balance of power among competing state institutions such as the army, the Workers' Party and the cabinet. Individuals and institutions engaging in external economic activities are required to donate to the Revolutionary Fund, which is under regime control. The leader may use Revolutionary Fund monies to finance Spot Guidance, national construction projects and imported luxury goods for himself and the elites. In this way, the effects of increasing external economic activities on the regime's stability are, supposedly, controlled by the North Korean leader.

The firm-level investigation using data from a survey of firms in China reveals active commercial transactions between China and North Korea. It also confirms that North Korean firms are affiliated with the four state institutions: the army, the Workers' Party, the cabinet and regional governments. Firms that have trading or investment relationships with an army-affiliated North Korean firm perform the best. This might be explained by North Korea's Military-First policy, which allows the army to obtain more lucrative and more stable business opportunities thorough the waku system. Results from an empirical investigation suggest that firms owned by the Chinese and Chinese-North Koreans have tended to perform better in business with North Korea than either South Korean- or Korean-Chinese-owned firms, after the 2010 imposition of sanctions by South

Korea on North Korea. The results also show that businesspersons in China regard country risk as the biggest obstacle in doing business with North Korea, whereas they consider that North Korean firms have tended to improve the quality control of their products and the extent to which they are able to meet delivery dates. Although they have positive perceptions of the future of the North Korean economy, they believe that changes in policies and regulations affecting their business are largely unpredictable.

Appendix: North Korean Foreign Trade[82]

There has been heightened interest in North Korea's trade statistics during recent years. 'Mirror statistics' that can be accessed through trading partner countries are among the few available long-term statistics on North Korea. In addition, it is believed that these statistics are relatively reliable because they are provided not by North Korea but by its trading partners, which have interests neither in understating nor in overstating the volume of trade with North Korea. Using these data, several works have assessed the North Korean economy (Choi, 1991; Eberstadt, 2009; Lee and Lee, 2012; Lee et al., 2013; Jung, 2014).

Despite assumptions about their reliability, existing studies find that differences in the volume of exports and imports are not negligible, depending upon the source of the statistics. There are three main sources of trade statistics: United Nations Commodity Trade Statistics Database (UN Comtrade), the International Monetary Fund's Direction of Trade (IMF DoT) Statistics and the Korea Trade-Investment Promotion Agency's (KOTRA) North Korean Trade Statistics. However, researchers find a number of errors in the UN Comtrade and IMF data on North Korean trade, partly because some trade partner countries confuse South Korean with North Korean trade. The KOTRA collects North Korean trade statistics reported by trading partner countries, but confines such countries to those it considers likely to trade with North Korea. It subsequently checks the details of reported trade statistics and constructs the final data. Hence, both the number of trade partner countries and the volume of trade are smaller in the KOTRA statistics than in those of UN Comtrade and the IMF DoT.[83] For example, the KOTRA reports the number of North Korea's trading partners as about 60 to 70 countries, whereas the UN and the IMF put these numbers at 90 to 140 (Kim, 2014c). In addition, the KOTRA estimates that the volume of North Korean trade in 2008 amounted to US$3.815 billion, whereas the UN and the IMF estimate it at US$6.543 and US$8.225 billion, respectively (Kim, 2014c).

Lee et al. (2010) assess the reliability of different trade statistics by classifying trade commodities into four groups: Class 1, the commodities that are traded at least once with the three major trade partner countries (that is, South Korea, China and Japan, the reference group of commodities) and whose trade volume should not exceed the maximum amount of trade between North Korea and one of the three main trading partners; Class 2, the commodities that belong to the reference group but whose amount of trade exceeds the maximum amount; Class 3, the commodities that do not belong to the reference group of commodities; and Class 4, the commodities whose HS code starts with 9999 and that are traded, in a given year, with a country which appears only in one of the statistics sets provided by the UN and the IMF but not by KOTRA. They find that the volume of trade satisfying the Class 1 category has been always smaller than that estimated by the KOTRA. For instance, Class 1 category trade amounted to US$2.17 billion in 2005, while the KOTRA estimate for the same year is US$2.98 US billion. Discrepancies become much wider when these figures are compared with those of the UN and the IMF, which show the volume of trade in 2005 at US$3.85 and US$4.30 US billion, respectively (Kim, 2014c). The addition of Class 2 trade to that of Class 1 increases the total to US$3.08 billion in 2005, which is slightly higher than the KOTRA's estimate for the same year. Reviewing such evidence, Kim (2014c) concludes that the KOTRA estimates are more accurate than the other two, although none of the three is free from biases. We use the data provided by the

KOTRA regarding North Korean trade with other countries except for South Korea. As for inter-Korean trade, we use the data reported by Korea International Trade Associations (KITA) of the Republic of Korea.

Figure A.2.1 shows the trend of North Korean exports and imports from 1990 to 2014. The general trend of North Korea's trade follows a U-shape. Before the collapse of the Soviet bloc, North Korea's trade volume amounted to US$4.18 billion. However, the dissolution of the Soviet bloc, and thus the CMEA, shrank North Korean trade by 45 per cent from 1990 to 1994. It further decreased to US$1.66 billion in 1998 because of the severe economic crisis. However, the decreasing trend turned around in the late 1990s when North Korea opened its doors to other countries including China and South Korea. That is, the North Korean authorities had to purchase grain and energy from abroad to overcome the economic crisis, but needed foreign currency to pay for imports. Policy emphasising the earning of foreign currency also contributed to the increase in trade. In addition, decentralisation of trade allowed many firms and institutions to access foreign trade for survival. As a consequence, in 2006 the volume of trade surpassed 1990 levels. The increasing trend in trade accelerated beginning in 2010 as a result of a surge in both exports and imports. In particular, North Korea was able to substantially increase the export of anthracite in response to a large demand from China and its high price (Lee, 2015).

One conclusion from these trade statistics is that North Korea is not a closed economy any more. According to Table 2.6, North Korea's GDP per capita was US$749 in 2013, when its population was 24.525 million. These figures yield a North Korean GDP of US$18.38 billion dollars for 2013. Hence, the ratio of trade to GDP, which is regarded as an indicator of the openness of a country, stands at 46.2 per cent. This is lower than 56.3 per cent, the average openness of the member countries of the OECD in the same year, but the gap is not too large.[84] This suggests that North Korea, which had emphasised Juche and autarky, has been transformed fundamentally since the 1990s.

billion US$

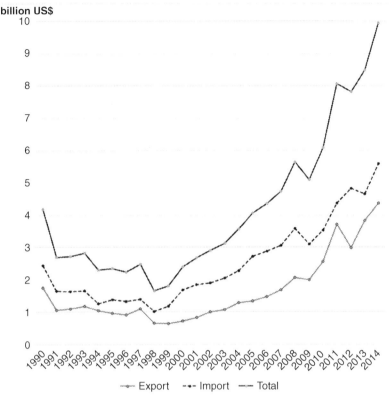

FIGURE A.2.1 Export, Import and Total Trade of North Korea, 1990–2014
Sources: KOTRA, Ministry of Unification, Statistics Korea (http://kosis
.kr/bukhan/index.jsp)
Notes: The imports of North Korea include not only imports from foreign
countries, but also carried-in products from South Korea. According to
the South Korean official classification, trade between South Korea and
North Korea is regarded as intra-country trade and not as inter-country
trade. However, we include imports from South Korea as part of North
Korean imports in order to understand the overall pattern in the trade of
the country.

Some studies claim that the North Korean trade deficit causes
a decrease in the foreign currency revenue of the North Korean authorities (Graham, 2007). However, one should be aware that a calculation
of the trade deficit based on our trade statistics may be

misleading. Putting aside unofficial trade and inaccurate trade statistics, there appears to be some form of commission attached to trade, which is taken by the North Koreans. During our firm surveys in Dandong, several businesspersons in China suggested that they pay a commission when they trade with North Koreans: they make a deal that goods exported from North Korea will be sold at a lower price than the prevailing world market price. Part of the difference between the two prices is given to the North Korean exporter in the form of a commission. A blog written by a North Korean refugee journalist working for Dongailbo, a South Korean newspaper, reports this practice and suggests that one main reason for Jang Sung-taek's death was a large commission he received from his Chinese trading partners.[85] In addition, a blogger at the Peterson Institute for International Economics argues that the prices of corn and wheat exported from China to North Korea were higher than world market prices (Haggard et al., 2013).[86] This practice can be associated with commissions paid by Chinese exporters to North Korean importers. Surveys of firms in China doing business with North Korea reveal that Chinese firms tend to pay 'extra costs' to their North Korean counterparts. In more detail, more than half of the firms pay these 'extra costs', which are on average 7 per cent of their sales, indicating that North Korean firms and institutions obtain financial resources not only by exporting commodities but also by taking trade-related commissions.[87]

Figure A.2.2 presents the trends of the main export items in terms of amount and proportion of total trade. We selected the export items whose average share of total exports from 1993 to 2012 exceeds 8 per cent.[88] These include the following items: mineral fuels, mineral oils and products of their distillation (HS code 27); articles of apparel and clothing accessories, not knitted or crocheted (HS code 62); fish, crustaceans and molluscs (HS code 3); and electrical machinery, equipment and parts (HS code 85). The figure suggests that the recent increase in exports from the late 2000s is driven by substantial rises in these items except for fish, crustaceans and molluscs, especially

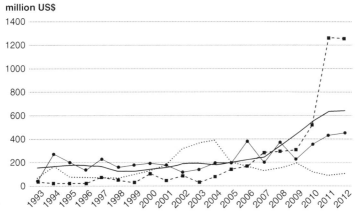

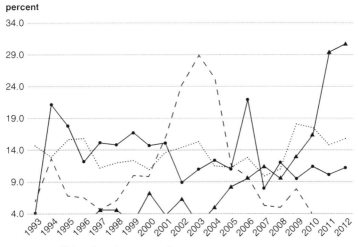

FIGURE A.2.2 The Amount of Main Export Items of North Korea and their Shares in Total Export

Source: UN Comtrade database, KITA database

Notes: The exports of North Korea not only include those to foreign countries, but also those products that go to South Korea. According to the South Korean official classification, the trade between South Korea and North Korea is regarded as intra-country, not inter-country trade. However, we include exports from North Korea to South Korea as part of North Korean exports to understand the overall trade pattern of the country.

mineral fuels, mineral oils and products of their distillation. The export of fish, crustaceans and molluscs peaked in the early 2000s and then fell substantially. This was caused by an increase in these exports to Japan in the early 2000s, which were subsequently hit by Japanese sanctions.

As Figure A.2.2 shows, the major export items of North Korea from 2010 include apparel and clothing, mineral fuels (mostly coal) and electrical equipment (e.g. electrical transformers and cables). The other major export items related to mineral resources include iron and steel (HS code 72), ores, slag and ash (HS code 26) and zinc (HS code 79). Apparel and clothing include knitted or crocheted items (HS code 61). Exports of apparel and clothing include carried-out products from the KIC and outsourcing products.[89] Orders of apparel and clothing are typically made in China, South Korea and European countries and are then transferred to trade agents in China who make the outsourcing orders to North Korea. Overall, the two major export items of North Korea are related to minerals (32 to 44 per cent of the total exports from 2010 to 2012, when we include commodities belonging to HS 27, 72, 26 and 79) and apparel (18 to 22 per cent of total exports if we include commodities belonging to HS 61 and 62) from 2010 to 2012.

Some changes were observed in the share of major export items between 2010 and 2012. For example, apparel and clothing (HS codes 61 and 62) made up 21.7 per cent of total exports for 2010. The share of such commodities was reduced to 18.6 per cent in 2011, but rebounded to 20.6 per cent in 2012. This trend can be partly attributed to South Korean sanctions against North Korean exports and imports other than trading that involves the KIC.[90] In contrast to clothing and apparel's relatively stable share of total exports, the share of natural resources, including coal, iron and steel, substantially increased from 27 per cent in 2010 to 45.4 per cent in 2011 and to 43.4 per cent in 2012. Such a sharp increase in the export of natural resources may be the result of a number of factors. First, increased Chinese demand, in addition to soaring prices, made exports of natural resources from

North Korea more lucrative during this period (Kim, 2013). Second, the South Korean sanctions, which were enforced on 24 May 2010, shifted the direction of North Korean exports to China (Lee and Lee, 2012; Jung, 2016). North Korean authorities attempted to compensate for the trade loss caused by these sanctions by exporting more natural resources to China. Jung (2016) reported that North Korean exports to China increased by 63.7 per cent as a result of the South Korean sanctions. Third, by trial and error, Chinese and North Korean firms devised a less risky business model that combined equipment investment with return-in-kind. Lack of equipment used to be a major hindrance in the extraction of natural resources in North Korea. Now, Chinese firms provided machinery to North Korean firms and received natural resources in return (Kim and Jung, 2015), encouraging more firms to follow their example over recent years. These three explanations are not mutually exclusive but complementary.

Figure A.2.3 shows the main items of North Korea's imports from 1993 to 2012. We have selected commodities whose average share of total imports exceeds 6 per cent for the above period. They include the following items: mineral fuels, mineral oils and products of their distillation (HS code 27); nuclear reactors, boilers, machinery and mechanical appliances (HS code 84); electrical machinery, equipment and parts (HS code 85); and cereals (HS code 10). The largest proportion of mineral fuels, mineral oils and products of their distillation consists of crude oil imported from China. The main import items belonging to HS code 84 are computers, machines for mining and those used for construction. Cables, transformers and mobile phones are included under HS code 85. Corn, wheat and rice are the main agricultural products belonging to the cereals category, most of which are imported from China.

Like exports, imports have been increasing, particularly since the mid-2000s. The sharp increase in the mineral fuels, mineral oils and products of their distillation category reflects rises in the price of oil. In fact, the amount of Chinese oil supply has been fairly constant since 1997 at about 0.5 million tonnes per year (Statistics Korea,

million US$

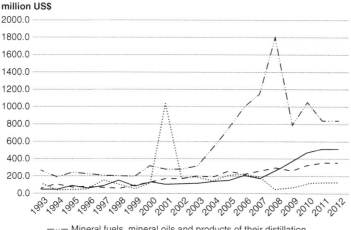

—··— Mineral fuels, mineral oils and products of their distillation
— — Nuclear reactors, boilers, machinery and mechanical appliances
—— Electrical machinary and equipment and parts
······· Cereal

Percent

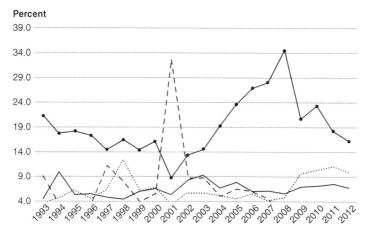

—•— Mineral fuels, mineral oils and products of their distillation
—— Nuclear reactors, boilers, machinery and mechanical appliances
······· Electrical machinary and equipment and parts
— — · Cereal

FIGURE A.2.3 The Amount of Main Import Items of North Korea and their Shares in Total Import

Source: UN Comtrade database, KITA database

Notes: The imports of North Korea not only include imports from foreign countries, but also those products that originate from South Korea. According to the South Korean official classification, the trade between South Korea and North Korea is regarded as intra-country, not inter-country trade. However, we include imports of South Korean products by North Korea as part of North Korean imports to understand the overall trade pattern of the country.

various years). Increases in the amount of items in categories HS 84 and 85 are related to North Korean authorities' emphasis on construction and IT technology. The spread of mobile phone use among North Koreans contributed to this increase.[91] One notable change in the late 2000s is the share of the import of cereals of total imports, which did not exceed 4 per cent from 2008 to 2012.[92] The main reason for this change is aid from South Korea and international organisations from 2008 to 2009. Although such aid decreased substantially after 2010, cereals did not rise above 2.5 per cent of total imports.[93] An increase in agricultural production is a likely cause of this trend. According to the KREI in South Korea, North Korean grain production increased from 4.1 million tonnes in 2010 to 4.68 million tonnes in 2012 (Statistics Korea, various years). For the same period, WFP and FAO, which dispatched a team of monitors to North Korea to collect information on the country's grain production, estimate that it increased from 4.5 million to 4.66 million tonnes.

Figure A.2.4 shows the major trading partners of North Korea's exports from 2002 to 2013 in terms of the shares of export of each country in total exports. As of 2013, North Korea's biggest export partner is China. In 2013, the share of exports to China was 76 per cent of total exports. The amount of North Korean exports to China had increased more than ten-fold from 2002 to 2013, rising from US$0.27 billion in 2002 to 2.91 billion in 2013. North Korea's exports to South Korea made up 16 per cent of total North Korean exports in 2013, the lowest share since 1999. The main reason for the decline was that the South Korean government forbade any trade and investment in North Korea, except trade relating to the KIC, on 24 May 2010 in response to the sinking of a South Korean naval ship *Cheonanham*. These sanctions changed South Korea from the biggest export destination for North Korean goods (from 2006 to 2009) to the second-biggest destination.[94]

While China and South Korea are the most important trading partners of North Korea, other countries accounted for at most

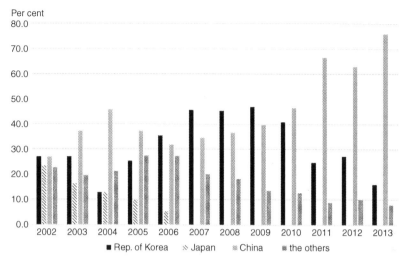

FIGURE A.2.4 The Shares of North Korean Export by Major Trading
Partners
Source: KOTRA

10 per cent of its total trade from 2011 to 2013. North Korea's exports
to Japan amounted to 23.3 per cent of its total trade in 2002, but since
then have fallen to negligible levels. This resulted from economic
sanctions imposed by the Japanese government against North Korea
after North Korean authorities acknowledged in September 2002, the
kidnapping of Japanese citizens.

Figure A.2.5 presents the major trading partners of North
Korea's imports from 2002 to 2013 in terms of the shares of import
from each country in total imports. China has been the biggest exporter to North Korea since 2005. North Korea's imports from China
rose sharply, from US$0.47 billion in 2002 to 3.6 billion in 2013.
The Chinese share of total North Korean imports in 2013 was
78.2 per cent. These very high proportions of both exports to and
imports from China, both of which exceeded 75 per cent in 2013,
underscore China's dominant position as a trade partner for North
Korea. South Korea is the second-largest exporter of goods to North
Korea. However, the South Korean share of North Korean imports

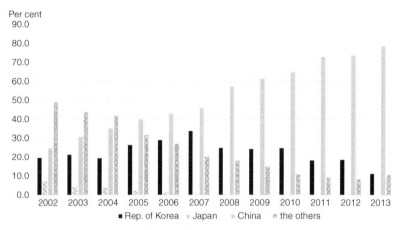

FIGURE A.2.5 The Shares of North Korean Import by Major Trading
Partners
Source: KOTRA

declined from 33.7 per cent in 2007 to 18.3 per cent in 2011, and
further, to 11.2 per cent in 2013. The decrease in share in 2011
resulted from the May 24 Measures of the South Korean government,
as discussed above. A further shrinkage in the share in 2013 was
mainly due to the temporary closure of the KIC: North Korean authorities withdrew all North Korean workers from the complex in April
2013. Although the complex reopened in September 2013, trade
between South Korea and North Korea decreased significantly
that year. As in the case of exports, the share of imports from the
other countries (excluding China and South Korea) was not high: it
ranged from 8 to 11 per cent during 2011–2013. The pattern of imports
from Japan is also similar to that of exports: imports from Japan fell
substantially from 2002 and descended to negligible levels beginning
in the late 2000s.

In sum, the collapse of the Soviet bloc and the dissolution of the
CMEA in the early 1990s came as a heavy blow to the already-
weakened North Korean economy. The amount of foreign trade
decreased from US$4.18 billion in 1990 to US$2.69 billion in 1991.
The severe economic crisis called the 'Arduous March' in the mid- and

late 1990s further decreased foreign trade, which fell to US$1.66 billion in 1998. In response to this, North Korean authorities further decentralised foreign trade in 2002 by allowing trading firms and state institutions, including regional governments, to engage in foreign trade. The amount of trade, which began to recover steadily beginning in 1998, has accelerated since the early 2000s and soared rapidly from the late 2000s to 2013, at least partly because of increases in the prices of natural resources and a large demand for anthracite from China. North Korea's main export items include natural resources such as anthracite and iron, apparel and clothes, and fish. The main import items include crude oil, machines for mining and construction, and cereals. In 2013, the share of foreign trade volume as a percentage of GDP in North Korea stood at 46 per cent. Hence, North Korea can be regarded as an open economy in terms of share, though there are still institutional impediments and heavy restrictions on foreign trade.

2.5 REGIME STABILITY IN NORTH KOREA: CORRUPTION AND MARKETS[95]

2.5.a Introduction

Section 1.5 of Chapter 1 suggested that the causes of the collapse of the socialist economy include coordination failure, informalisation, the quantity and the quality of corruption and the forced surrender of a dictator. One can argue that coordination failure has been taking place in North Korea because of the coexistence of central planning and markets without a clear division (Haggard and Noland, 2010; Yang, 2010a; Kim and Yang, 2012).[96] The other four explanations are directly or indirectly related to corruption. In this section, we discuss North Korea's regime stability as affected by market activities and corruption. In particular, we pay attention to the quality of corruption in the way that corruption affects the socialist economy – that is, whether the socialist economy is strengthened or weakened by corruption.

One of the striking features of the current North Korean economy is the prevalence of bribery. According to the 2013 Worldwide Governance Indicators compiled by the World Bank, North Korea is one of the most corrupt countries in the world: among 210 countries, North Korea ranked at 8th from the bottom. This status is in line with numerous testimonies from North Korean refugees. They report that bribes are necessary whenever one takes even one small step, and they provided anecdotal evidence on bribes in connection with market activities, travel, college admissions and even in connection with escaping from North Korea.

Corruption is defined as the abuse of entrusted powers for private gains (Bardhan, 1997; Shleifer and Vishny, 1993). Corruption can be classified into various categories in terms of its type such as bribery, embezzlement, fraud and extortion (Andvig, et al., 2000). Some scholars classify corruption in terms of degree. Grand corruption, which typically involves high-ranking bureaucrats and politicians, refers to large-scale corruption, and the value of corrupt transfers is high and often tied to one-time exchanges. In contrast, petty corruption takes place at lower levels of the administrative hierarchy and is more pervasive, involving transfers of smaller value. Petty corruption is closely related to people's day-to-day life experiences, such as the 'street-level extortion' of policemen and 'speed-money' at lower administrative levels involving bribes to facilitate bureaucratic action such as the speedy processing of an application. Rose-Ackerman (1978) denotes grand corruption as legislative corruption and petty corruption as bureaucratic corruption.

There are two contrasting arguments on the effect of corruption on a society. One group of scholars argues that corruption affects the economic performance of a country negatively by preventing businesses from being started and grown and by distorting the allocation of talent (Murphy, Shleifer and Vishny, 1991; Mauro, 1995; Rock and Bonnett, 2004).[97] Furthermore, corruption endangers the stability of a society by causing a deterioration of credibility in formal and informal institutions, not only in market economies but also in socialist ones. Treml and Alexeev (1994) and Grossman (1998) maintain that corruption related to the informal economy caused the disintegration of the Soviet economy. According to these authors, the expansion of the informal economy, which increased corruption and rent-seeking activities, distorted the information required for efficient planning and undermined the ideological foundations of the society. Socialist countries are also arguably more vulnerable to corruption because it undermines the fundamental values of socialism, based on equity and institutional control over society (Grossman, 1998).

In contrast, many other studies suggest that corruption can be regarded as 'greasing the wheels' of an economy that suffers from hold-ups by bureaucrats and the grabbing hand of the government (Leff, 1964; Huntington, 1968; Rock and Bonnett, 2004). According to this perspective, corruption, which can act as the second-best option in helping economic agents to bypass such institutional deficiencies, contributes to improving efficiency in the economy. In the context of the Soviet economy, some form of corruption was used to increase output as the tight requirements of plans 'forced' managers to break rules in order to achieve plan-fulfilment goals (Heinzen, 2007). More specifically, the managers of firms used secret money to purchase raw materials and spare parts that were not always delivered in accordance with the plan (Harrison and Kim, 2006).

The above discussion suggests that the relationship between corruption and the stability of a socialist regime is not clear-cut. Corruption appears to be a double-edged sword for the stability of a socialist regime. Corruption may contribute to the stability of a socialist regime by allowing the purchase of much-needed inputs of production to fulfil the planned output target. However, members of the public, who believe that the socialist system is neither credible nor fair, are likely to mistrust it all the more. In addition, information needed for planning is distorted if firm managers rely not on the plan but on other means of production, which may lead to a weakening of control for the firms' central planners. Moreover, corruption is likely to destabilise a socialist regime if it is tied not to the fulfilment of the planned output target but to informal market activities.

What are the relationships among bribery, markets and regime stability in North Korea? This analysis first presents several hypotheses on the characteristics of bribery and the behavioural patterns of the dictator, officials and market participants in connection with bribery, markets and regime stability. In more detail, we will ask the following questions: Does bribery in North Korea contribute to the stability of the regime? Is there any possible equilibrium among the three actors (namely, the dictator, officials and market participants) in North Korea today? What does this equilibrium tell us about the extent and trending of bribery? These questions are important not only for evaluation of the current situation faced by the North Korean authorities but also for comprehending the future of the North Korean regime. Following the presentation of our hypotheses, we will test them empirically using data from surveys of North Korean refugees.

In order to conduct empirical exercises, we needed data that enable measurement of the extent of bribery in North Korea. Obviously, data on bribery are hard to come by, because the revelation of bribe-giving or bribe-taking is likely to present an individual or firm with difficulties in most countries. In this regard, data from surveys of North Korean refugees who have settled in South Korea offer a unique opportunity to understand the nature and the extent of bribery in North Korea. The refugees are relatively free to reveal their bribe-giving practices from the time they were living in North Korea. Although it must be remembered that our samples of North Korean refugees are not drawn randomly from the North Korean population, an increasing number of refugees from the various strata of society indicates that the survey data can provide useful information on the extent and the nature of bribery there.

2.5.b Policies toward Markets

From 2002 to 2004, the North Korean authorities appeared to ratify the process of marketisation from below through some changes in institutions and policies. The July 1st Measures in 2002 introduced some form of material incentives for firms and workers, and overhauled administered prices and wages. General markets were introduced in 2003 to facilitate market transactions. At the same time, the authorities levied taxes on markets in the form of market usage fees paid by traders in the markets and taxes paid by firms that were involved in market transactions.

Beginning in 2005, the state began to reverse earlier reforms, repressing market activities and abolishing general markets. There were reports that the North Korean authorities tried to forbid market trading conducted particularly by women under a certain age. This policy appeared intended to target relatively young women who were most active in street vending or sales in markets. In 2009, the authorities launched 'the 150 days' warfare', mobilising labour to collective farms and construction sites, with particular focus on participants in market activities. The objective of the currency reform announced in late November 2009, which forced the population to convert their old currency to new currency at a 100:1 conversion ratio with a moderate ceiling, was in line with the purposes of a series of such policies: namely, to reduce market activities and reassert control over the ruined socialist economy.

However, the currency reform turned out to be a failure. First, serious complaints from the people and negative shocks to the economy led the Prime Minister to apologise publicly for the policy mistake. A minister-level official in the Workers' Party was reportedly shot dead because of his responsibility for the currency reform (Yonhap News, 18 March 2010). Of the 134 refugees who escaped from North Korea after the currency reform, whom we surveyed in 2011, 94.8 per cent replied that the policy was wrong. Furthermore, 88 per cent of the respondents believed that the currency reform contributed to the instability of the regime. Second, the currency reform effort deteriorated economic performance without achieving its intended effect of macroeconomic stabilisation.

According to our estimates, annual growth rates in 2009 and 2010 were –3.39 per cent and –0.25 per cent, respectively, in spite of the fact that rates in 2008 and 2011 were positive. Bank of Korea's estimates also suggest that GDP in 2009 and 2010 declined by 0.9 per cent and 0.5 per cent, respectively. Furthermore, a decrease in money supply due to the currency reform did not result in lowered inflation. In informal markets (jangmadang) in Pyongyang, US$1 was transacted with KPW 3,845 in November 2009, before currency reform, but fell to KPW 134 in December 2009 because of the currency reform (Daily NK).[98] However, won depreciated substantially afterward and, as a result, US$1 was exchanged with KPW 4,000 to 5,000 in November and December 2010. This suggests that hyperinflation took place from November 2009 to November 2010, and the reform failed to bring down inflation rates.

Realising the failure of the currency reform and the discontent among the people, the North Korean authorities took a more lenient approach toward market activities. Markets reopened in various places, and most transactions were allowed as long as sellers paid a certain amount in fees and abided by regulations. This policy continues in Kim Jong-un's regime.

The North Korean economy from the 1990s on can be described as the coexistence of a socialist system and marketisation from below. The authorities have attempted to control the direction of the economy, but without much success. Sometimes they appeared to worry that seemingly unfettered market activities went too far. Market transactions were allowed in order for households to survive, but the economy's heavy reliance on markets was believed to be dangerous to the stability of the regime. This attitude of the authorities toward markets accounts for the zigzag nature of state policy efforts.

To control the process of marketisation, the North Korean authorities developed the penal system that began to play an important role in repressing market activities (Haggard and Noland, 2009). During the famine, the state established low-level disciplinary facilities called rodongdanryeondae, which can be translated literally as 'labour training camps'. The legal reform in 2004 regularised these facilities and stated that individuals who committed various crimes, including participation in illegal market activities, would be detained in these facilities for up to two years (Han, 2006). Police officers called anjeonwon are responsible for dealing with the day-to-day life of the people, including controlling and repressing market activities.[99] However, some crimes related to markets are treated as more serious and thus are dealt with by the National Security Agency (NSA, Bowibu). For example, the NSA has reportedly established a special task force to identify 'criminals' who trade in illegal items such as state property and goods made in South Korea.[100] The involvement of the NSA in controlling market activities is considered to be evidence that the authorities regard informal markets as an important threat to the stability of the regime.

2.5.c Analysis and Hypotheses

We will test two groups of hypotheses related with North Korea's regime stability. The first group concerns the characteristics of bribery in North Korea. There are possibly two types of bribery in this group that differ in terms of their effect on the stability of the regime. One criterion for distinguishing 'good' from 'bad' bribery is related to its domain, namely, the planned formal sector or the informal market sector. In a socialist economic system, bribery related to economic activities is normally tied to the planning mechanism (Kim, 2002; Harrison and Kim, 2006; Heinzen, 2007). Understanding that there is a bonus mechanism based on the difference between planned output and actual output, the manager of a firm has an incentive to reduce the planned target even if he or she has to pay bribes. One of the necessary steps is to bribe an input supplier. For this, the firm manager needs secret money that can be used to purchase raw material and spare parts that are not always delivered in accordance with the plan. In theory, the central plan should guarantee the delivery of inputs needed by firms, but it fails to do so, partly because the plan is not perfect and operates with many problems. Hence, the manager is left without the necessary inputs but is still required to fulfil the output target. Without a secret fund, the manager will not be able to meet the target, which could have a negative effect on the welfare of the managers and workers in the firm. Hence, a secret fund is necessary, and the manager may rely on several tactics to generate such a fund. For example, the manager may transfer passive money in the enterprise account to active money that can be used to purchase goods and services. In other words, according to the socialist planning system, the income received by a supplying firm cannot be spent at the manager's discretion as cash, but should be put in the account at the monobank. Yet firms find ways to channel this money into cash. In addition, firms may sell scarce goods and services that they produce at higher prices. In order for this to happen, the manager needs to bribe the monitoring organisation so that it will turn a blind eye to these illegal activities. This form of bribery is interpreted as 'economic crime in the interest of the enterprise' and 'greasing the wheels'. It does not cause an incentive misalignment between the dictator and the managers, because both of them have incentives to keep the socialist system in operation; in other words, neither of them wants to destroy the 'wheels'.

Corruption related to market activities is harmful for the socialist system, because markets, as a new wheel, are able to replace the old wheel of socialism. Bureaucrats receiving bribes from market participants are less likely to follow the rules dictated by the socialist system. More specifically, participants in market-related activities bribe officials who are responsible for monitoring, controlling and cracking down on such activities. In return for bribes, officials impose less severe penalties and sometimes turn a blind eye to illegal activities. The effect of this form of corruption on the welfare of the public is likely to be positive, while such an effect on the total volume of production is ambiguous (Wellisz and Findlay, 1986).[101] However, officials are incentivised to deviate from the interests of the dictator, who wants to keep the planned system. Thus, an incentive misalignment between the dictator and officials may arise when market-related bribery is widespread, and corruption that reinforces market activities rather than formal activities is more dangerous to the stability of the socialist regime.[102] Hence, an important question to look at is whether bribes are related to the formal socialist sector or to the informal market one.

Hypothesis 1 Bribery in North Korea is related mainly to informal markets rather than to the formal sector.

Another criterion to distinguish 'good' corruption from 'bad' concerns the effect of corruption on production. Grossman (1977) maintains that corruption involving the diversion of state property for private businesses reduced shortages of consumer goods and thus decreased the disincentive effects of shortages. Harrison and Kim (2006) focus on a change in the quality of corruption in reaction to a reduction in plan tautness, and suggest that the partial liberalisation of the Soviet economy was accompanied by a change in the quality of corruption from 'good' to 'bad'; in other words, from 'production-oriented corruption' to the corruption of simply 'lining one's pocket'. Similarly, good corruption may contribute to the stability of the regime because it adds to the aggregate supply of goods and services, while bad corruption does not.

Hypothesis 2 Bribery in North Korea is related to redistribution rather than facilitation of production.

The second group of hypotheses refers to the possibility of equilibrium among the three actors in the North Korean economy – the dictator, government officials and market participants – and the stability of such equilibrium. Each of the three actors has its own objectives and the ability to pursue its own preferences. We approach the analysis of bribery using a game framework involving three actors.

The objective of the dictator is to maintain power. The prevalence of bribery is dangerous to the dictator, especially if bribes are received in return for forgiving illegal market activities. Thus, the dictator prefers to order the abolition of such activities in order to strengthen his or her power. The question of why the dictator tolerates bribe-taking by officials then arises. Given well-developed information-gathering and repressive police machinery, it is difficult to believe that the dictator could be unaware of the prevalence of bribe-taking activities among the representatives of the state. He is also capable of punishing government officials if he wishes. At the same time, however, he understands that the loyalty of government officials is a key variable in maintaining power. If he orders government officials to abolish markets, officials are unlikely to implement that order as precisely as he would like because the abolition of markets will pose a severe difficulty for the officials' lifestyle. Given that the dictator does not possess sufficient resources to compensate officials for the loss of their bribes, he compromises by tolerating the bribe-taking practices of officials and implicitly allows them to live on bribes. If the dictator believes the markets are becoming big enough to challenge his power, he can order the repression of market activities. This order works, but only partially, because officials are only partially loyal to the dictator. This may not be ideal for the dictator but may be optimal, given the constraints under which the dictator must work.

The objectives of a government official are to survive and to enrich himself. To accomplish his goals, he can decide whether to take bribes from market participants or whether to remain loyal to the dictator. A strong form of disloyalty for the official is to strike against the dictator with a view to maximising his bribes from market participants. However, this possibility is limited, partly because such behaviour is currently too risky and the end of the dictator's power may mean the end of the official's power as well. Weak forms of disloyalty range from sabotage to slow implementation of the dictator's orders and more lenient treatment of rule-breakers. Complete loyalty means punishing participants in market activities in accordance with laws and orders from above. Hence, an official decides whether he will refrain from punishing market participants by receiving bribes or will punish them according to the law. An optimal response, given the North Korean political and economic circumstances, is to be partially loyal to the dictator but at the same time to receive bribes. The former is necessary for political survival, while the latter is necessary for economic survival. Is it possible to choose both of them simultaneously? Probably so, as long as the dictator decides to tolerate the corrupt practices of his officials. In other words, unless a certain official is too greedy or betrays the dictator, he can assume he is fairly safe, though corrupt. Being partially loyal but corrupt becomes the norm for typical officials.

Market participants have the same objectives as government officials: that is, survival and self-enrichment. They need to make decisions on whether they will bribe officials to avoid punishment or whether they will strike against officials. It is theoretically possible that market participants might directly challenge the dictator. However, this possibility can be ruled out at present, because it is difficult to believe it could happen under the current North Korean regime. We assume that it is possible to challenge officials, but it poses too high a risk. Hence, an optimal response of market participants is to bribe government officials so they will be able to continue to participate in market activities.

Given the objectives and the preferences of the three actors, equilibrium can take place. The dictator condones the actions of bribe-taking officials if they remain loyal to him. The dictator is not able to control the economy fully because officials are only partially loyal, and his preference that the markets be abolished is not realised. He compromises on this because it is currently the only way for him to stay in power. Government officials choose to be corrupt but still partially loyal to the dictator. Lastly, market participants, who are incapable of striking against government officials, pay bribes to officials and keep working in markets. Optimal responses of the three actors suggest a possibility of equilibrium in which a high degree of bribery takes place. An increase in bribery, however, is unlikely over the short and medium terms because the three actors do not want to significantly change their behaviour. Here we limit the time span to the short or medium term, because the nature of markets and bribery may affect the behaviour of the three actors in the long run. Hence the following hypotheses can be presented.

Hypothesis 3 The extent of bribery is high in North Korea.

Hypothesis 4 The trend of bribery in North Korea did not increase over the past decade.

2.5.d   Empirical Evidence

This study mainly uses survey data collected from North Korean refugees who escaped mainly in 2007–2009.[103] This survey in 2009 (the 2009 survey) focuses on income, expenditure, labour and informal economic activities while the respondents were living in North Korea, more specifically during the year before they left North Korea. The survey questionnaire is designed to include detailed questions on bribery in North Korea, including the amount of bribes, bribe-takers, bribe-givers and the reasons for giving bribes. These 2009 survey data were also merged with data from a survey of 675 North Korean refugees conducted in 2004 (the 2004 survey) and data from a survey of 134 conducted in 2011 (the 2011 survey). The results from these surveys are also used when we examine trends over time.

Hypothesis 1 can be tested by using the survey of North Korean refugees conducted in the three surveys, and looking at the relationship between bribery and informal markets. These surveys asked the following question: Please tell me 'For what purposes do you believe that people gave bribes?' Respondents were allowed to choose a multiple number of suggested answers. The results from the respondents' answers are summarised in Table 2.30.

Table 2.30 suggests that a prime reason for bribe-giving is related to market activities. It is notable, in all three surveys, that the most important reason for bribe-giving is related to working in informal markets, followed by avoidance of punishment. The share of the respondents choosing this answer ranged from 31 to 51 per cent. The answer 'avoiding punishment' does not provide further information on whether this is related to markets or other factors. Yet a correlation exercise suggests that most respondents who chose this answer also selected the answer 'to continue to work in informal markets', suggesting that people paid

Table 2.30 *Reasons for Giving Bribes*

Reasons for giving bribes	2004 survey	2009 survey	2011 survey
	Percentage share (per cent)		
To be promoted	11.30	12.96	11.36
To continue to work in informal markets	41.74	31.75	50.76
To start a new business	16.52	11.66	2.27
To avoid punishment	20.87	28.94	31.06
To avoid working in the formal sector	5.22	13.82	3.79
Other reasons	4.35	0.86	0.76
Total cases	100.0	100.0	100.0

Sources: The 2004, 2009 and 2011 surveys

Notes: Unlike the other surveys, which asked respondents to choose only one reason, the 2009 survey allowed multiple choices. Hence, the share of each reason was calculated as a proportion of the number of choices of the respective reason in the sum of total cases.

bribes to avoid punishments related to market activities.[104] Although the shares of the respondents choosing 'to avoid working in the formal economy' vary considerably, from 3 per cent in the 2011 survey to 5–14 per cent in the 2004 and 2009 surveys, respondents reported that a bribe was necessary because people preferred not to work in the formal sector. Instead, a majority of them are believed to have preferred working in markets, since income from such activities far exceeded that available from the formal sector. These cases appear to be related to the so called '8.3 workers', who paid money to enterprise managers in return for being allowed to be absent from their official work.[105]

The only answer that is clearly related to the formal sector is 'to be promoted', but the share of this response is only 11–13 per cent. In contrast, 43–58 per cent of total cases that include 'to continue to work in informal markets' and 'to start new business' are specifically concerned with market activities. In addition, 26–42 per cent of the cases choosing 'to avoid punishment' and 'to avoid working in the formal economy' are likely to be associated with such activities. This suggests that bribe-givers want to derive income from market activities, a portion of which are illegal and subject to punishment. There are also a number of cases in which work in markets requires that a worker have permission to be absent from his or her official workplace, and thus he or she is required to pay bribes, perhaps to the manager of the enterprise or to the person responsible for granting such permission.[106]

The 2009 survey also includes a question, 'Who do you believe are main bribe-takers?' Respondents were asked to choose from the following list: firm or collective farm managers, National Security Agents, police officers, surveillants of the community, high-ranking government officials and others. According to the data in Table 2.31, respondents believe the main bribe-takers in North Korea to be police officers. More than half (54.7 per cent) of the respondents replied that police officers are the main bribe-takers, followed by National Security Agents. Police officers and National Security Agents are responsible for monitoring and controlling markets. In particular, in everyday life, police officers are the first level of authority to deal with market participants, and that proximity appears to be a prime reason why they are the main bribe-takers. On the other hand, only 10.8 and 9.8 per cent of respondents identified high-ranking government officials and firm or collective farm managers as main bribe-takers, respectively. In sum, among various types of officials and firm or farm managers, those who control the informal sector directly were found to be especially active in receiving bribes. The 'others' category, which was chosen by 1.9 per cent of the respondents, included judges, prosecutors, border guards, university deans and soldiers.

The findings in Table 2.31 are corroborated by responses to the question, 'What groups of people do you think are the main bribe-givers?' The questionnaire lists four possible choices: official workers or collective farmers, traders in North Korean markets, international

Table 2.31 *Main Bribe-Takers*

Bribe-takers	Share of total
Police officers	54.7%
National Security Agents	22.4%
High-ranked government officials	10.8%
Farm or factory managers	9.8%
Surveillants of community	0.4%
Others	1.9%
Total	100.0%

Source: The 2009 survey

traders including shuttle traders and those who engage in home production. The shares of respondents who replied 'Yes' to this question for each group are 30.6 per cent (official workers or collective farmers), 72.1 per cent (traders in North Korean markets), 42.6 per cent (international traders including shuttle traders) and 19.4 per cent (those who engage in home production). The data indicate that North Koreans believe that those who conduct market-related activities are the primary bribe-givers.[107]

The findings from the reasons for bribe-giving and the status of main bribe-givers suggest that North Korean bribery can be categorised as 'bad' corruption in terms of the domain of bribery. Such bribery is associated with informal market activities rather than with the formal economy. Bribery and informal markets are likely to reinforce each other, which could lead to the destabilisation of the socialist system. In other words, the two factors of the collapse of the socialist regime, as we discussed in Section 1.5 of Chapter 1, have been undermining the North Korean socialist system.

As regards Hypothesis 2 on the relationship between bribery and production, we rely on data on the types of informal economic activities as a main domain of bribery. According to Table 2.11, the most popular types of informal economic activities are trading, smuggling, repair and other services. About half of workers in the informal economy participate in the above activities when a multiple choice is allowed for choice of informal work. The second-most popular type is cultivating kitchen yard or private plots: one-third of informal workers engage in these activities. Although about 30 per cent of informal economic activities involve the production of goods, they appear not to be highly value-added: the items that include food, alcohol, and footwear and clothes account for 85.5 per cent of informal production. This finding suggests that informal production concentrates in the areas that require simple work, and thus it cannot add a high value.

Most production activities are undertaken on a small scale: 47.2 per cent and 41.5 per cent of such activities were conducted alone or with at most two other people, respectively, according to the 2009 survey. These figures did not change substantially in the 2011 survey: 57.8 and 33.7 per cent of respondents among those who engaged in informal production replied that informal production activities were undertaken alone and with another person, respectively.

The above findings suggest that trading is the most important informal economic activity. In addition, relatively few households participate in production activities, which tend to produce simple goods and be conducted on a small scale. In other words, the informal economy in North Korea in which bribe-giving and bribe-taking take place most frequently fails to substantially increase economic value. This characteristic of bribery is regarded as 'bad' corruption in that it fails to substantially increase the supply of goods and services.

As regards Hypotheses 3 and 4, Kim and Yang (2012) used the surveys of North Korean refugees conducted in 2004 and in 2009, which asked questions on the share of bribes in the total expenditure of North Korean households. The surveys include data from North Korean refugees who left North Korea in different years, and thus allow one to look at the trend of bribes as a percentage of total expenditures from 1996 to 2007, with the exception of 2004 and 2005.[108]

Table 2.32 shows the trend of the share of household spending on bribes as a proportion of total expenditures. The unweighted

Table 2.32 *Trends in the Share of Spending on Bribes as a Proportion of Total Expenditures*

Year	1996	1997	1998	1999	2000	2001	2002	2003	2006	2007
Share (%)	8.8	10.7	9.2	7.6	5.2	9.3	8.7	10.0	10.1	9.9

Source: Kim and Yang (2012)

average share of bribes is 8.95 per cent. The minimum and maximum shares are 5.2 and 10.7 per cent, respectively, although we should consider these estimates to be only rough figures. This high share of bribes is surprising, even when compared with the late Soviet period before the collapse of the Soviet Union. Kim (2003) estimates the share of bribes in the GDP in the late perestroika period to be about 2 per cent. If the share of bribes in household expenditures is converted to bribes' share in the GDP, it is estimated that spending on bribes is about 6–7 per cent of North Korean GDP.[109] This suggests that, in terms of the share of bribes in North Korea's GDP, bribes are much more prevalent in North Korea than they were in the late Soviet period just before that regime's collapse.

Most of the respondents in the 2009 survey replied that bribes are widespread in North Korea. To the question, 'To what degree are bribes prevalent?', 54.7 and 43.0 per cent of respondents replied 'very prevalent' and 'prevalent', respectively. In addition, 73 per cent of respondents reported that they themselves had paid a bribe at least once. Multiple instances of bribe-giving were frequently found among the respondents: 38 per cent replied that they had given bribes multiple times on an irregular basis and 25 per cent reported having given bribes multiple times and regularly. These findings suggest that the rate of bribery in North Korea is high, confirming Hypothesis 3.[110]

North Korea has a legal system that calls for punishment of bribe-taking officials. The original law against bribe-taking is found in the law made in December 1946. The criminal code, which was drawn up in 1995 and revised in 2004, contains Chapter 7, according to which officials involved in either bribe-taking or bribe-giving are subject to punishment with labour training for up to two years. If they received the bribe through extortion or if the amount of bribe is excessively high, the officials are to be punished with re-education (kyohwa) for up to four years. However, the stipulations of the criminal code regarding bribes do not appear to be effective in reducing bribery in North Korea.

We test Hypothesis 4 by looking at whether there is any increase in bribery from 1996 to 2007. During the period under investigation, there were two important changes in policies toward markets or the economy as a whole. First, North Korea implemented a major economic reform in 2002, called 'the July 1st Measures'. This reform was based on the principle of a less-centralised decision-making structure, allowing some autonomy of enterprises in planning targets, setting prices, selling goods in markets and purchasing inputs and spare parts. Second, repression of markets began in 2005. The North Korean authorities applied age restrictions to market traders and the opening hours of markets. Furthermore, they attempted to abolish markets in some cities. We investigated whether these policy changes had a significant effect on the proportion of bribes. The timing of these two policy changes suggests some possible break in the trend, either between pre-2002 and post-2002 or between pre-2005 and post-2005. We use t-tests to check whether there was any significant gap between the mean of the share of average spending on bribes in total household expenditures during the period before (pre-2002 or pre-2005) and after policy changes (post-2002 or post-2005). The test results suggest that there was no significant difference in mean of the share of the average spending on bribes in total household expenditures between the two periods.[111] Empirical evidence confirms Hypothesis 4.

The finding that the share of bribes in household expenditures has not increased for about 10 years suggests that political control over bureaucrats and market traders has not weakened, despite the economic crisis and the prevalence of informal economic activities. Two factors may account for the success of this control. First, the police machinery is largely intact in North Korea, as it was not in the late perestroika period in the Soviet Union. Entities within the police machinery such as the NSA and the People's Security Agency (anjeonbu) are still powerful organisations, and the system of peer monitoring including inminbanjang (head of the neighbourhood units) is well developed and still maintained in North Korea.

In addition, the authorities tend to apply tougher measures to economic crimes related to market activities (Haggard and Noland, 2009). Such harsh and arbitrary punishment has deterred bureaucrats and market traders from bolder and more aggressive exploitation of bribery opportunities. Second, there is some evidence that informal market activities have not increased substantially from 1996 to 2007, suggesting limited opportunities to increase bribery (Kim, 2009b).

2.5.e   Effects of Markets and Corruption on the Stability of the Regime

The fact that the share of spending on bribes in total household expenditures has not changed significantly for the last 10 years implies the existence of an equilibrium concerning bribery, at least in the short or medium term. This equilibrium formed because the three actors prefer high, but non-increasing bribery as their optimal strategy. The dictator, who is unable to pay government officials wages sufficient for a normal lifestyle, condones their corrupt behaviour as long as they remain loyal to him. Haggard and Noland (2009) suggest that the dictator increased the discretion of government officials such as National Security Agents and police officers when they deal with informal market activities. They can exercise much discretion regarding whether to arrest, detain and terrorise those who participate in such activities. This can be interpreted as an intention by the dictator to repress market activities, but at the same time to let National Security Agents and police officers find a way to survive. An effective way to achieve these two goals is to increase the discretion of those who are responsible for controlling (and repressing, if necessary) market activities. Market traders understand that the police have real power with much discretion and thus are incentivised to bribe the agents in order to avoid arrest and harsh punishment.

An equilibrium is established between government officials and market participants as bribe-takers and bribe-givers, respectively, and strong collusion may even develop. Especially when a certain bribe-giver repeatedly bribes an official, they can make acquaintance and develop a mutual understanding between themselves. This may result in ineffectiveness or reduced effectiveness in the enforcement of government policies restricting market activities. Yang (2010a) reports the following testimony of one North Korean refugee.

> Once I was arrested, I paid some amount of bribe and was released subsequently. Then I was not arrested because I got acquainted with police officers. Those who paid bribe appear in markets without being afraid of police officers at least for some period. Police officers do not arrest traders who have paid bribe recently and let them keep trading, say, for about 15 days. After about 15 days, police officers demand bribe again.[112]

As regards the stability of such equilibrium in the long term, we need to understand the nature of bribery in North Korea. Bribery represents a particular type of unofficial exchange between the representatives of the state and the population. Such interactions illustrate the deficiencies of central planning, which fails to operate in an ideal way. Bribe-givers believe that the state is not living up to its promises to the population. The failure of the state to fulfil its basic obligations is sufficient to make the public believe that bribing a state official is not a crime at all. Furthermore, mere survival is a prime motive for a number of market participants. These conditions can easily justify bribe-giving. Similarly, officials may take bribes without feeling guilty because the salaries they receive are much below the level of subsistence, and they regard bribe-taking as their self-help mechanism in response to government failure. A culture of bribery emerges from this sort of justification of both bribe-giving and bribe-taking, and becomes a norm in the society. Indeed, bribery is a kind of survival strategy amid economic crisis and state failure. This type of survival-oriented bribery is difficult to crack down on unless there is an alternative way of providing the income necessary for normal living.

Bribery is epidemic in its nature. If bribery is regarded as both necessary and tolerated, more people want to take part in such practices. Detection and punishment are more difficult because there are too many people involved. Bribery is a form of reciprocity, in that both bribe-givers and bribe-takers can be mutually benefitted. This leads to the strong possibility of collusion. Unless bribe-takers are unusually greedy or do not keep promises, they are hard to detect. These arguments imply that the dictator has to exercise harsher rules against market activities to keep the magnitude of such activities in check. The application of softer, or even similar rules as before to market activities will result in a significant growth of market activities associated with more bribery. This implies that, from a longer-term perspective, the dictator has to face an uphill battle to protect his power from being shaken by market participants and bribe-taking officials.

The possibility of a negative shock can make such equilibrium fragile. Shleifer and Vishny (1993) suggest that the partial liberalisation of dictatorship can make corruption rampant as one individual's corruption or a dictator's corruption is transformed into corruption involving a number of agents who have administrative power. These authors illustrate their point by using the example of the collapse of the Soviet Union: Gorbachev's attempt to partially liberalise the economy contributed to a substantial increase in corruption during perestroika, which helped lead to the eventual collapse of the Soviet system. More recent literature also emphasises the relaxation of political control over the economy as an important cause for the disintegration of the Soviet Union. Harrison (2002) claims that the Soviet authorities were forced to stop monitoring the activities of firms because the cost of monitoring increased and political control became softer over time. In particular, he argues that the regime of a dictatorship is more stable when dictatorial rule is cruel and secret. According to him, glasnost and perestroika contributed to a radical change in the nature of political control in the Soviet Union, from random and cruel punishment to expected, more-transparent and less-harsh punishment. As a result, the public as well as firms were able to strike against the authorities without fear that they would suffer overly harsh consequences. Harrison and Kim's (2006) argument that the partial liberalisation of the Soviet economy was accompanied by a change in the quality of corruption from 'good' to 'bad' is also in line with the findings of this study.

There are three possible reasons why this equilibrium may break down in the long run. First, both markets and bribes have a tendency to expand. They are based on human nature and encourage the pursuit of both survival and self-enrichment. Unless strong factors such as institutions and policies deter markets and bribes from expanding, they tend to become larger and larger. If a norm of bribery is established, there develops a path dependency that makes reversal more difficult and forward movement along the path easier. Actors regard the current situation as a norm, and consider what they have to do, taking the current situation as a given. Over time, bureaucrats and traders enriched from bribe-taking or illegal businesses may find that there is no alternative except to strike against the dictator in order to keep their accumulated wealth safe. This implies that government policies should get tougher against informal markets and bribery over time. Otherwise, the expansionary nature of markets and bribery will destabilise up to the point that they will collapse the socialist regime. This may explain why the North Korean authorities attempted to repress market activities from 2005 to 2009. Nevertheless, despite such attempts at repression, the share of bribe expenditure as a percentage of total expenditure has not decreased.

Second, in the long run, market activities are likely to change North Koreans' support for socialism and the regime based on it. Through experiences of working in markets, North Koreans may realise that the socialist economy fails to work properly and socialist ideology prohibits increases in their welfare and economic growth. There is some evidence of the effects of market activities on support for a market economy. The 2011 survey includes the questions on the following five topics respecting the elements of a market economy: support for performance-based salary, support for private ownership, support for society with competition, support for growth through competition and support for reward based on effort. We tested whether informal activities affect these market elements. Among three types

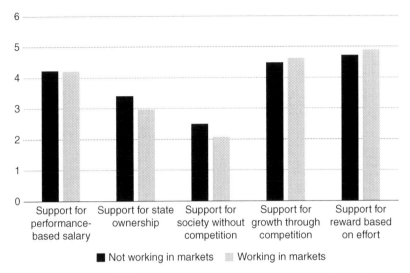

FIGURE 2.3 Differences in Support for a Market Economy Depending on Market Activities
Source: The 2011 survey
Notes: In each question, the respondents were asked to choose one among the following five choices: (1) strongly disagree; (2) somewhat disagree; (3) neither agree nor disagree; (4) somewhat agree; (5) strongly agree.
We derived weighted average by multiplying figures from 1 to 5 to each choice from 'strongly disagree' to 'strongly agree'.

of informal activities – private-plot activities, cattle-breeding activities and market trading – we find that market trading affects two of these elements significantly. Figure 2.3 shows the results. Except for supporting performance-based salary, those who participate in market activities tend to support the elements of a market economy more strongly than those who do not participate in them. Among these, the differences in three elements turn out to be statistically significant: disapproval of state ownership, disapproval of society without competition and support for rewards based on effort, which are significant, at least at the 10-per-cent significance level.[113] This finding indicates that North Koreans' ideological support for socialism shrinks as they become involved in market activities.

Third, external shocks can affect the stability of the equilibrium. A key factor in maintaining the stability of the regime is fear. Officials should fear dismissal and punishment by the dictator. Participants in markets should be afraid of being detected, arrested and punished by officials. If the extent of societal fear is somehow diminished, the regime is likely to destabilise. When fear drops to a nominal level, the regime may suddenly collapse. The extent of fear is a function of the dictator's character, his choices, the learning curve of officials and market participants and other political, economic and external conditions. If the dictator's behaviour is predictable, officials and market traders will prefer to challenge him up to a certain limit. The cruelty of the dictator can deter the other actors from betraying him. Such randomness and cruelty are dependent not only on the dictator's character but also on his choice variables. Yet, if the dictator chooses to be random and cruel, he should be able to enforce such choices or risk losing credibility and encouraging the other actors to challenge him. The learning curve of officials and market participants is also an important consideration. Over time they will learn more clearly what benefits them most. Their exposure to money-making can affect their thinking, preferences and behaviour. Hence, when they regard the dictator as less cruel and more predictable, they will want to expand the areas in which they can make money. In addition, a further substantial decline in economic conditions can trigger actions of the public against the dictator, particularly when political control over the society becomes less strict.

This may be one reason the North Korean authorities implemented currency reform in November 2009. Repression over markets began in 2005, but relatively moderate forms of repression such as forbidding market trading on the part of women under a certain age were found to be largely ineffective in reversing the trend of marketisation. Strong collusion between officials and market participants may have accounted for this policy failure. Although repressive policy was able to check or slow the pace of marketisation, the dictator might have wished to go further and actually reverse the trend. In 2009 he might have wanted to implement policy that would bypass the collusion and instead affect market participants directly. Currency reform, unlike previous measures against markets, seemed to serve the dictator's desires well, because it did not require perfectly loyal officials.

However, the authorities appear to have underestimated the role of markets in feeding both participants and extorters. Due to rising discontent with repression of markets, information suggests that the dictator allowed one of the key figures in the design and implementation of currency reform to be shot dead, and reinstalled markets. The experience of the currency reform and the dictator's setback may have led people to reevaluate of the robustness of the regime. As a result, both officials and the public may believe that the regime is not as strong as they previously thought. This belief could be a starting point for the derailment of the North Korean regime.

The discussion above sheds lights on why Kim Jong-un uses fear. In 2013 he ordered the murder of Jang Sung-taek, his uncle-in-law, who was regarded *de facto* as the most powerful leader. In addition, Hyun Yong-chul, the Minister of People's Armed Forces, was purged and executed in 2015. Under Kim Jong-un's regime, multiple senior army officials have been demoted and key military figures frequently replaced. Fear can be a powerful instrument in controlling the elites and government officials who are corrupt and perhaps only partially loyal. Markets and foreign trade have installed objectives which differ from those of the dictator in the mind-sets of ordinary North Koreans and top elites and government officials alike. Hence, fear is being used to counter-balance the growing influence of markets and foreign trade over North Koreans.

2.5.f Conclusion

The relationship between markets, bribery, and regime stability in North Korea has been investigated using data from surveys of North Korean refugees. More specifically, four hypotheses about the characteristics of North Korean bribery and the size as well as trend of bribery have been tested. The findings can be summarised as follows.

First, bribery in North Korea can be characterised as 'bad' corruption because, unlike in other traditional socialist countries, it ties mostly to informal markets, not to the formal sector, and does not substantially increase the supply of goods and services. North Korean bribery reinforces informal markets where consumer goods imported or smuggled from China dominate but where production is not facilitated. Thus it has the potential for negative impacts on the stability of the regime.

In North Korea, bribery is widespread and household expenditures on bribes are exceedingly high. The average share of spending on bribes in total household expenditures from 1996 to 2007 was 8.95 per cent, which translates into 6–7 per cent of GDP. This proportion in North Korea is 200–250 per cent higher than was the comparable share of bribes in GDP during the late perestroika period of the Soviet Union, which is known to have experienced high levels of corruption and rent-seeking activities. In spite of the high level of bribes, however, the share of bribes in North Korean household expenditures did not significantly increase from 1996 to 2007. This implies that the authorities were still able to keep the level of bribes from expanding, even though they might have difficulty in making any substantial reductions.

These findings suggest that the current situation regarding the informal economy and bribery may be characterised as an equilibrium. It is an equilibrium in the sense that all three actors – the dictator, officials and market participants – do not currently want to change their behaviour significantly. Given resource constraints that make it difficult for the dictator to pay his officials appropriate salaries, he implicitly allows officials to receive money from market participants, unless they betray him. In other words, as long as officials remain loyal and do not cause severe problems among bribe-givers, the dictator condones a certain level of corrupt activities among his officials. Officials prefer to remain partially loyal to the dictator. Challenging him is too dangerous and does not provide much reward, even if such a challenge leads to success. A dictator who is too weak (or the end of the dictatorship) will mean a decline in or complete loss of officials' power. In contrast, complete loyalty that obeys the dictator's order to abolish markets is likely to make officials' economic survival difficult. Hence officials choose to be corrupt but partially loyal to the dictator. Following suit, participants in the informal economy, who have found bribery a costly but efficient way to escape arbitrary regulations and harsh punishments, decide to pay bribes.

However, such equilibrium among the three actors is fragile. Increased bribe-taking from participants in market activities can shift the interests of the police machine at least partially out of alignment with those of the dictator, suggesting possible damage to the regime's stability. The self-expanding nature of bribes and markets will put high pressure on the will and ability of officials to follow the dictator's interests. Both market participants and bureaucrats learn about markets and the dictator. Bureaucrats understand that bribes are a lucrative business, and market participants intensify their belief that money can buy anything. This situation may lead to a stronger collusion among market participants and bureaucrats to facilitate a marketisation of the socialist economy against the will of the dictator. A strong dictator can stagnate or even reverse the process of marketisation at the cost of being unpopular and even facing possible opposition. However, such action will carry a high risk.

The possibility of a sudden collapse does not currently appear to be high for the North Korean regime because the dictator is still capable of not only controlling government bureaucrats who are afraid of being punished but also avoiding a worsening economic crisis by partial opening-up of the economy and introducing some market activities that facilitate efficiency. However, the current equilibrium is unlikely to last for long. The above-mentioned learning curve, together with the pressure from bribery and markets on administrative bodies, will eventually destroy the socialist foundations of the society. The dictator may try to hit back, but will realise that the situation is getting worse for him. Instead, his setback will mean that more territory will be occupied by market traders and corrupt officials. Furthermore, market activities erode ideological support for socialism. The only solution will be a transition toward a market economy. Nevertheless, it is difficult for the current dictator to enact this option because it is likely to substantially decrease his power.

There is a possibility that the current equilibrium will end abruptly. A change in the character of leadership from strength to weakness would give officials and market participants a signal that there is no need to fear the dictator. This will lead to a rampant increase in bribery. The members of the police machinery may want to increase the amount of the bribes they receive because they will be less concerned about being punished by the dictator. It is also possible that petty corruption could evolve into grand corruption. Realising that there are large sums of money that might be made, key figures in the regime may be tempted to get involved in corrupt activities. In such a chaotic situation, market participants would be forced to pay higher and more numerous bribes because they would need protection from powerful organisations. This would increase public discontent against the dictator and the state. If the equilibrium were to end in this way, the sudden change could be the starting point of the abrupt collapse of the regime.

An important implication of this discussion is that time is not on Kim Jong-un's side. Although the probability of collapse is currently low, political control over society has already weakened due to informal markets and bribery. He is likely to face tougher challenges from government officials who have been exposed to markets and bribery. Unless he is perceived as strong, ruthless and charismatic, he might be contested by bureaucrats who want to maximise their income from bribes. This implies that significant changes can take place in his regime.

NOTES

1. This action is evident from Kim Il-sung's complaint about the inadequacy of their plans, during which he said: 'it is important for us to organise the

202 THE NORTH KOREAN ECONOMY

system of obtaining accurate calculation and statistics when implementing national plans. However, we tend to underestimate and neglect such tasks. As a result, the accurate information is not provided on time. For example [...] two completely different figures are presented in the reports by the Ministry of Heavy Industry: one reports that the inventory of coal is 700,000 tons at 1 October 1953, while another suggests a value of 16,000 tons for the same day. Many industries and departments violate the regulations on the procedure of reporting' (Kim Il-sung, 1983, Vol. 8, pp. 292–293). Based on the comparison between the Hungarian socialist statistical system and the North Korean system, Lee (2007a) concluded that North Korea substantially lagged behind other socialist countries in terms of quality and techniques for collecting and producing relevant statistical data.

2. Chullima refers to an imaginary horse that is able to run fast and for a long distance without stopping.

3. Kim Il-sung mentioned that the Daean management system reflected a managerial system in which seniors help their juniors with the Workers' Committee of a firm that directed and managed the activities of all firms by prioritising political agendas and mass motivating workers (Kim, 1983).

4. According to Qian et al. (2006), M-form organisation is defined as one that is broken down into self-contained multiple units in which complementary tasks were grouped together. By contrast, a U-form organisation is categorised into specialised units in which similar tasks are grouped together.

5. The first Yeonhap Giupso is reported to have been established in 1973 in accordance with Kim Il-sung's instruction. Since then, a number of Yeonhap Giupso were created in the 1970s (Nakagawa, 2003). However, Yeonhap Giupso was confined to key industries before the 1980s. It was only from the mid-1980s that Yeonhap Giupso expanded to all industries and its number increased substantially.

6. Yang (2001) suggested that Yeonhap Giupso represented both the elements of centralisation and decentralisation. Centralisation becomes more possible because the central planning body could concentrate on planning with a considerably smaller number of firms. Decentralisation occurred as many firms were controlled by a core firm that was combined with other firms, which subsequently acted as an agent on behalf of the central authorities.

7. Translated by the author from Kim Il-sung's New Year's Speech in 1979.

8. The North Korean Dictionary of Social Science defines the Juche method of agriculture as 'a scientific method of agricultural production which takes climates and biological and chemical characteristics into account in the intensive production of crops while using scientific findings and technology' (Academy of Social Sciences, 1985, p. 420). In practice, this method refers to an increase in productivity and expansion of land under cultivation.

9. The Soviet kolkhoz markets are called 'farmer's markets (Nongmin Shijang)' in North Korea. According to the North Korean Dictionary of Social Science, these markets are the remaining capitalist elements of commerce in the country and were inevitably used by households to purchase minor daily goods and secondary foodstuffs (e.g. vegetables) that were in insufficient supply in the public market (Academy of Social Sciences, 1970). Kim Il-sung ordered to move these markets from the city centre to the city outskirts as well as to allow only one market in every district. Refer to Chung and Jeon (2000) and Lim (2009) for accurate descriptions of such markets.

10. In January 2015, 125 South Korean companies employed about 53,700 North Korean workers. Most of these companies belonged to the textile industry (58 per cent of total companies), followed by machinery and metal (19 per cent) and electronics (10 per cent). However, the KIC closed down in early 2016 because of the response of the South Korean government against North Korea's tests of nuclear weapons and long-range missiles in the same year.

11. Zang (2009, 2013) presented the details of the various ways of making hard currency by North Koreans and the estimates of hard currency earned by such activities.

12. These debates are discussed in Kim (2005b) and Yoon and Yang (2009).

13. It is reported that the state takes 70 per cent of agricultural products and that the remainder goes to farmers who are allowed to dispose of it freely. This is a part of the June 28th measures in 2012 in which some measures increasing the autonomy of enterprises are also included (Joongang Daily, 21 December 2014).

14. Kim Il-sung published a document on 'Establishing Juche and Eliminating Dogmatism and Formalism in Ideological Projects' in December 1955 (Information Centre on North Korea, http://munibook.unikorea.go.kr/?s ub_name=information&cate=1&state=view&idx=71&page=1&stc= as of June 2016).

15. Control by won is the North Korean version of the Soviet 'control by ruble' (kontrol c rubl'nyam). This method controls the activities of all firms according to the central plans of the Central Bank. Self-accounting was introduced in the Soviet Union to increase the efficiency of firms by making the country accountable for the performance of a firm (e.g. by economising the use of resources).

16. Juche iron refers to the method of making iron with coal but without coke, which is not produced in North Korea. However, this method is unproductive, as previously claimed (Dong, 2010). The problem in the Juche method of agriculture was discussed in the previous section.

17. Kim Il-sung complained about the economic data in 1974 as follows: 'Economic data are not correct. There are no data on the waste of effort and the capacity of firms' (Kim, 1985, Vol. 29, p. 322).

18. Kimura (2001) identified two reasons to explain the reluctance of Kim Il-sung to establish 'scientific' socialist planning. First, such planning would weaken the power of Kim Il-sung because the Soviet planning system would give excessive power to bureaucrats. Second, North Korea was an agricultural society; hence, central planning was not an absolute necessity because this system would not generate large benefits.

19. The North Korean authorities did not yield to Soviet pressure to join the CMEA (Council for Mutual Economic Assistance), and then decided to push for heavy industry-based industrialisation amid opposition from the Soviet authorities.

20. Fond is the Russian term for 'fund'.

21. Juseok Fond has an unknown share in the total production of outputs. Based on an interview with a refugee from North Korea, Yang (2001) suggested that Juseok Fond had a one-digit or low two-digit percentage of total production.

22. Kornai (1992) called this phenomenon the chronic shortage of inputs. Various methods were adopted to solve such problems in the Soviet Union and Eastern Europe. Some firms traded with tolkachi (input suppliers), which unofficially sold inputs to firms. In response to shortages, firms hoarded more inputs and often had to substitute a similar input in place of a required input. Given the possibility of implementing inconsistent and taut planning in North Korea, the problems that were caused by the insufficient supply of inputs might become severe. Refer to Park (2002) for additional information on the problem of supplying inputs in North Korea.

23. The use of Spot Guidance for political propaganda in North Korea has been suggested as the official reason for the death of Kim Jong-il in 2011. The former president was reported to have suffered a heart attack while on a train ride to a power plant for Spot Guidance. In this manner, the North Korean authorities attempted to publicise Kim Jong-il as a diligent, caring and sacrificing leader.

24. In December 2013, Kim Jong-un visited an army unit that was responsible for feeding army personnel and gave them four fishing boats with which to catch 4,000 tons of fish. Within six months, the manager of the unit reported that they used to catch only 1,000 tons of fish every year, but were able to catch 4,000 tons of fish within six months after receiving the visit (http://news.mt.co.kr/mtview.php?no=2013121613514347967&VM N as of June 2016).

25. We used annual growth rates as a dependent variable, reported in Table 2.6.

26. These workers are called '8-3 workers', which is explained in more detail in Section 2.3.c.

27. This remark appeared in Kim Jong-il's speech on 18 June 2008 on 'Upholding the principles of socialism in economic businesses and enhancing the supremacy of the socialist economy'.

28. The maximum amount remains uncertain. Each household was initially allowed to exchange old money up to 100,000 won. However, some have reported that this amount increased from 200,000 won to 500,000 won per household because of severe public dissatisfaction (Korea Development Institute, 2009; Lee, 2013).

29. The army, the Workers' Party, the cabinet and the regional governments own those firms that are involved in export and import activities. Some part of their revenue is earned from these foreign businesses.

30. At the end of December 2013, the head of the South Korean National Intelligence Service reported to Congress that the execution of Jang Sung-taek was a result of the conflict between related groups for material gains involving foreign trade (Dongailbo, 26 December 2013).

31. For example, the Central Yearbook of Chosun (Chosun Joonang Yeongam) has statistical annexes that provide comprehensive statistical data. However, these statistical annexes have not been published since 1960.

32. This approach estimates the extent of Soviet hidden inflation by subtracting the CIA estimates of Soviet GNP growth rates from the

official NMP growth estimates. Assuming that the hidden inflation has been higher during the early stages of economic development, the hidden inflation is regressed on income per capita and income per capita squared. The coefficients that are obtained from this estimation are subsequently applied to North Korean data. Therefore, the actual industrial output growth rates represent those that are reported by North Korea minus those that are accounted for by hidden inflation.

33. They show that the GNP shares of the agriculture, manufacturing and services sectors in 1992 are equal to 22, 38 and 40 per cent, respectively.

34. For a more detailed discussion on this method, refer to Kim (2008).

35. Kim et al. (2007) and Kim (2014a) applied this method to estimate the North Korean growth rates from 1954 to 1989 and from 1954 to 2012, respectively. We use the most updated data and extend the estimation up to 2013. Kim (2014a) derives GDP per capita in PPP in 1990 US dollars, but that in market exchange rates in 2005 US dollars. This work applies the reference year consistently to both GDP per capita in PPP and in market exchange rate. Furthermore, the base year on which growth rates for other years are estimated is different: Kim (2014a) uses 1954 as a base year, but this work uses 2012 as a base year.

36. Appendix to this section explains in detail how to estimate GDP per capita in 2012, which is the base year of our estimations, and how to convert GDP per capita in PPP to that in nominal exchange rates.

37. Such change may be caused by the criticism that North Korean GDP per capita estimates from the Bank are extremely high, considering the dire economic conditions of the country.

38. It is not clear how the UN estimates North Korean GDP per capita. Some researchers indicate that raw data in North Korean won are provided by North Korea.

39. Such similarity is primarily caused by the fact that our estimates are based on agricultural production and the growth rates of the industrial and mining industries, which the Bank of Korea uses as well.

40. We use GNI and GDP interchangeably, given that the differences are not large.

41. The regression results are as follows: GDP per capita in nominal exchange rate = 141.99 + 0.3579 GDP per capita in current international US dollars. Both the coefficients are statistically significant.

42. The amount of grain rations decreased several times before the 1990s. The average amount of rationed grain decreased by 13 per cent in 1973; the amount was further reduced by 10 per cent in 1987 with the announcement of reserving grain for 'rice for patriotism' (Lee, 2004).

43. The informal economy can be defined as activities that are not reported to the authorities or those that are not included in the national statistics (Kim, 2005a). The second economy in the CPEs is closely related to the informal one. According to Grossman (1977), the second economy refers to activities that either violate the rules of the authorities or directly pursue one's personal interests. Most of the market activities in the CPEs are informal because such activities violate the rules. Therefore, these activities are suppressed and unreported. Informal economic activities largely overlap with market activities, but these are not the same in the North Korean context. For instance, the self-consumption of agricultural products grown in private plots is informal, but it is not considered a market activity. At the same time, several market activities (e.g. selling consumer goods in government-designated facilities) pay specific fees to the government. Therefore, these activities are not informal according to their first definition; they can be regarded as second economic activities because they directly pursue a person's interests. In our analysis, we use informal and market activities interchangeably, although one has to bear in mind the distinction between the two activities.

44. Yu et al. (2012) suggested that the dominance of female refugees was caused by a stricter monitoring of males. The increasing involvement of various non-government organisations and commercial businesses in the escape of these refugees also increased their chances of bringing their families, including their mothers and children, when fleeing North Korea.

45. Upon arrival in South Korea, North Korean refugees are interviewed by South Korean intelligence services for a certain period and afterwards transferred to Hanawon.

46. The most recent population census in North Korea was conducted by the Central Bureau of Statistics from 1 to 15 October 2008. The census was based on a house-to-house interview by enumerators using the census questionnaire. The population enumerated in the census included all of the North Korean citizens living in North Korea as of the date of the census. The report, containing a number of aggregated tables, is available at the following UN website: http://unstats.un.org/unsd/demographic/s

ources/census/2010_PHC/North_Korea/Final%20national%20census%
20report.pdf as of July 2015, but became unavailable as of June 2016.
Instead, the tables reported in the document appeared in the following
website: www.maxwell.syr.edu/moynihan/kpac/Datasets/2008_DPRK_
Census_Data/ (as of June 2016).

47. These surveys were conducted by Nielson Korea per the request of a group
of researchers, including the author. The numbers sampled in the surveys
conducted in 2014 and 2015 were 161 and 191, respectively. Unlike the
surveys we used in this chapter, the surveys conducted by Nielson Korea
recruited the refugee sample regardless of their year of departure from
North Korea.

48. The participation rates are based on the responses to the following
question: 'Did you have secondary work?' Subsequently, the
questionnaire determines the types of secondary work (e.g. private plot
activities, cattle-feeding and market-related activities). Therefore, the
respondents understand the definition of secondary work.

49. This finding tends to underestimate the economic effect of an official job
on household welfare, as receiving rationed food and goods at a cheap price
is often associated with working an official job (Lee, 2009). However,
Table 2.10 indicates that only 40.5 per cent of the respondents replied that
they received rationed food or consumer goods. These respondents
occasionally received a limited amount of food and goods, depending on
government regulations. Therefore, the informal economy has become
more important to North Korean households than the official one in terms
of purchasing power.

50. Biases have two sources. First, refugees opted to escape from North Korea,
and thus these samples were self-selected from the general population of
North Koreans. Second, the samples of the surveys were not randomly
drawn from the refugees who settled in South Korea.

51. The low share of official income may be caused by measurement errors.
That is, the market price of rationed food has not been properly considered
in the official wages. The respondents were not asked about the amount of
rationed food but were asked whether they received rationed food and
what type of food they received. However, including the market price of
rationed food did not largely increase the share of official wages. Our
survey data show that the share of households for those who received
rationed grain was 20.5 per cent of total households, and the median of

rationed corn was 18 kg per month. This value translates to 864 kg of corn per year on average for four members of a family. The total market value of such ration was found to be about KPW 190,000. This market value increased the share of official wages in the total income from 1.8 per cent in 2009 to 7.6 per cent in the same year.

52. Latin American countries are known for their relatively high income inequality. The Gini coefficients in these countries range from 0.4 to 0.6. For example, the Gini coefficients in Argentina, Brazil and Colombia are 0.453, 0.539 and 0.559 in 2009, respectively, according to World Bank data (http://data.worldbank.org/indicator/SI.POV.GINI?page=1) (as of June 2016).

53. A refugee commented that Pyongyang is a different world in many aspects, including food availability and rationing (www.mediapen.com/news/articleView.html?idxno=82264 as of June 2016).

54. The author and other researchers participated in these surveys in 2004 and 2007 (Jeehong Kim, Taejong Kim, together with the author for the survey in 2004 and Suk Lee and the author for the survey in 2007). The numbers of samples were 675 and 115, respectively. The former survey used face-to-face interviews and mailed surveys, whereas the latter used a gang survey in a designated place administered by Gallup Korea.

55. For example, the sum of the share of the respondents multiplied by share of the population in Table 2.16 is 16.8, 12.7 and 64.8 percent for official channel, self-production and purchasing from markets, respectively. The sum of these three shares is 94.8 per cent. Hence, we used weights in accordance with the share of each channel for obtaining food in the sum to make it 100 per cent. The same procedure applied to computing the share of each channel in obtaining consumer goods.

56. It was rare that the respondents used the third-most-frequently used channel.

57. These NGOs collect the data on the prices of these products in some big cities from North Koreans who are able to communicate with these organisations.

58. Several refugees report that their firms have failed to operate normally because of shortages in inputs and electricity. Inputs were sometimes provided to these firms to produce presents for their leader (i.e. for his birthday celebration) for a short duration only.

59. Kim Il-sung emphasised the self-reliance of firms in supplying consumer goods on 3 August 1984. These firms were instructed to produce consumer goods using available by-products, waste, and unused inputs in their regions. Since then, 8.3 (August 3) has been extensively used to refer to production or economic activities that are unrelated to central planning but are conducted independently.

60. This question was asked using the following categorical examples: (1) 0 to 5 per cent, (2) 5 to 10 per cent, (3) 10 to 20 per cent, (4) 20 to 30 per cent, (5) 30 to 40 per cent, (6) 40 to 50 per cent, (7) 50 to 60 per cent and (8) 60 per cent or above. We obtain the weighted average by multiplying the midpoint of each category, except for the eighth category, for which we multiply 70 per cent by the share of the respondents in each category.

61. The licence can be leased to companies or institutions that lack one for a commission of up to 10 per cent of sales, according to interviews with refugees from North Korea (Kim and Yang, 2012).

62. The origin of the term 'waku' is unknown because it is not part of the Korean language. The term was likely derived from the Japanese word 'waku', which means 'frame or boundary of discretion'.

63. According to the North Korean refugees, only foreign trading companies could possess a waku. Therefore, manufacturing firms in North Korea must export or import through foreign trading companies with waku. For example, Kimchaek Iron and Steel Company, the most famous and prestigious manufacturing company in North Korea, would collaborate with the Chosun Black Metal Export and Import Company, a foreign trading company. However, a recent report from South Korea found that large manufacturing firms in North Korea, such as Kimchaek Iron and Steel Company and Musan Iron Ore Mine, had obtained licences to engage in foreign trade (Yeonhap News, October 10, 2013). (www.yonhapnews.co.kr/politics/2013/10/10/051 1000000AKR20131010191500097.HTML as of June 2016).

64. In their interviews with North Korean refugees, Lim et al. (2011) found that waku specified the volume of goods to be imported or exported by a specific firm.

65. According to Yang (2008), the lending of waku is not certified as a legal activity.

66. One Chinese-Korean businessman mentioned that he intended to change the affiliation of a counterpart trading company in North Korea from the Workers' Party to the army. He explained that the waku obtained by

a trading company belonging to the army was more stable than the waku possessed by a trading company belonging to the Workers' Party. A trading firm in Dandong, a Chinese city bordering North Korea, was believed to have become very successful through its collaboration with Seungri Trading Company, which belonged to the army and had a waku that allowed 70 per cent of North Korean coal to be exported to other countries.

67. The currency reform in November 2009 can be viewed as a policy for taking money from the non-government sectors to the government sector. This reform may have also targeted the shrinkage of markets (Kim, 2010b).

68. A more detailed analysis using the data presented in this section was carried out in Kim and Jung (2015). In this publication in Korean, the detailed testimonies of firm owners and managers together with quantitative analysis are reported. Some parts of this section are similar to those in the Korean book.

69. This figure includes the export of oil through the pipeline which originates from Heilongjiang province but goes through Dandong.

70. South Koreans have been forbidden from doing business with North Korea, except for those firms that are located in the KIC, as a result of the South Korean sanctions against North Korea in 2010. Therefore, some South Koreans appoint non-South Koreans as representatives of their firms, but these firms are still owned *de facto* by South Koreans.

71. Equipment investment refers to investment in machinery, means of transportation and electric generators that are used to produce output in the firm. North Korea lacks such equipment, a condition that often constrains its production activities.

72. This figure must be used with caution because the sample was not randomly collected and because the firms started their business with North Korea earlier than other firms, hence increasing the probability that the former would go out of business.

73. The Sunshine Policy refers to the policy of engagement with North Korea undertaken by Kim Dae-jung, President of the Republic of Korea, who inaugurated his term in 1998. Under this policy, South Korea provided economic aid and South Korean businesses were allowed to make economic transactions with North Korea. This policy lasted until the end of the administration of Ro Moohyun in 2008. The term 'sunshine' derived from Aesop's fable in which sun instead of wind led a traveller to take off his cloak.

74. Some variables that were asked in the surveys are not used in these regressions. For example, the evaluation of the future of the North Korean economy may be correlated with the performance of the firm. However, considering possible reverse causality, these variables were not used as independent variables.

75. Songun refers to the North Korean policy in which the army is regarded as the most important sector in resource allocation and state policy-making. The policy appeared in 1998 in the North Korean newspaper Rodongsinmun and became the dominant ideology of Kim Jong-il for the governance of North Korea (Kim and Lee, 2007).

76. The following are the proportions of those who replied positively to the question of whether it was possible to visit North Korea: Chinese (59.2 per cent), Korean-Chinese (90 per cent), Chinese-North Koreans (80 per cent) and South Korean associates (13.6 per cent). South Korean associates who replied positively to this question may have been referring to circumstances before the sanctions of 2010, or to visits by non-South Korean managers or employees working for firms owned by South Korean associates.

77. The respondents were asked, 'What do you think about the North Korean economy in the long run?'

78. The respondents were asked, 'To what extent do you think the changes in the laws, policies and regulations of North Korea are predictable?'

79. The respondents were asked, 'In your opinion, how has the extent of the adherence of North Korean firms to the terms of the contract (i.e. meeting the delivery date and product quality requirements) changed in the last five years?'

80. The respondents were asked, 'What would you like to do about the volume of your business with North Korea in the future?'

81. These results must be interpreted with caution because the sample of the firms was not drawn randomly, and the absolute majority of the firms represents the surviving firms.

82. Eberstadt (2009) and Lee et al. (2013) provide a detailed account of North Korean trade. The former focuses on the trends of import of capital goods, food, energy and transport. The latter analyses the recent trends of North Korean trade with China using aggregate and Chinese provincial data.

83. A more detailed analysis of differences in these statistics can be found in Eberstadt (2009), Kim (2007), Lee et al. (2010) and Kim (2014c).

84. It is likely that the reported trade volume understates the actual volume because of unreported shuttle trade and smuggling in border areas. For example, North Korean ships transfer fish to Chinese vessels in the West Sea (Yellow Sea) without reporting it to customs. It is also believed that North Korean shuttle traders pay bribes to customs officials to bring in goods exceeding the quantity specified by regulations.

85. Joo Seong-ha's blog: http://blog.donga.com/nambukstory/archives/88013 (as of June 2016).

86. http://blogs.piie.com/nk/?p=10488 (as of June 2016).

87. To the question, 'Have you paid "extra costs" to North Korean counterparts when you do business with them?', 53.4 per cent replied 'Yes', 26.4 per cent 'No' and 20.2 per cent 'Do not know'.

88. The UN Comtrade data do not include trade with the Soviet Union, and thus the trade data from 1990 to 1992 are not consistent with those from 1993 to 2012. Taking this discontinuity into consideration, we present the items of exports and imports from 1993 to 2012.

89. In February 2013, 72 out of the 123 firms in the KIC produced apparel and clothing.

90. These sanctions were imposed on North Korean trade and investment after North Korea sank the *Cheonanham*, a South Korean navy ship, killing 46 seamen. However, the KIC was excluded from the list of sanctions. Since then, most outsourcing to North Korea has been performed from China. Nevertheless, the final destinations of these goods might include not only China but also South Korea and Europe.

91. Koryolink provides a mobile phone service in North Korea. The Egyptian-based Orascom Telecom and Media and Technology Holding and the North Korean Ministry of Post and Telecommunications hold 75 and 25 per cent of the shares of Koryolink, respectively. It is known that the number of registered users of mobile phones exceeded 3.7 million in October 2015, although the actual number may be lower than this (Kim, 2014d; http://news.mk.co.kr/newsRead.php?no=1200229&year=2015 as of June 2016).

92. The sharp rise in the import of cereals in terms of amount and share is caused by Japanese food aid. The amount of aid was evaluated at the food price in Japan, not the world market price.

93. The share of cereals among total imports has decreased several times since the early 2000s. In the mid-2000s, cereals used to make up a high share of

the total imports of North Korea, amounting to $140 million to
$220 million and comprising 4 to 9 per cent of total imports. However, the
absolute amount and share of cereals in the total imports have both
decreased since 2008. Cereal was not included among the top 10 imported
items from 2008 to 2010. Yet, this commodity reappeared as a top-10
imported item from 2011, but its absolute value and share in the total
import were lower than during the early and mid-2000s.

94. Several reports show that some products are still being imported to South
Korea through China after the implementation of sanctions. In other
words, some commodities produced in North Korea are initially exported
to China, from which these products are exported again to South Korea
after changing the origin of the products from North Korea to China.

95. An earlier version of this section appeared as a working paper at the East
Asia Institute (Kim, 2010a).

96. Frank (2005) provides an alternative interpretation: A hybrid North
Korean system is a way to stabilise the regime by combining market
efficiency with stability based on central planning, particularly in the area
of obtaining food. The experience of the Chinese dual-track approach can
be viewed as reinforcing this argument. However, a critical question
remains on the efficiency and competence of state institutions sustaining
such a hybrid system.

97. In more detail, corruption is argued to undermine economic performance
in three main ways. First, it increases transaction costs and thus reduces
value-added created by enterprises. Existing entrepreneurs, knowing that
part of their profits will be taken away through corruption, are
incentivised not to expand their businesses, and potential entrepreneurs
are less likely to start them. Second, corruption hurts allocative efficiency
in that more efficient firms that do not bribe corrupt officials may lose out
in competition with less efficient firms that do pay bribes. Third,
corruption distorts the efficient allocation of entrepreneurial skills. Firms
may devote their energy to obtaining licences and favourable market
access instead of improving efficiency in an economy where corruption is
widespread and institutionalised. As an extreme case, a potential
entrepreneur may stop producing goods and services in order to leave the
business sector and become a corrupt bureaucrat. However, this
discussion is more relevant to market economies where businesses start
freely and people change jobs without severe restrictions.

98. Daily NK, an NGO based in South Korea, has been monitoring exchange rates and prices in informal markets regularly in three cities of North Korea, that is, Pyongyang, Shineujoo and Hyesan, since August 2009. These data can be accessed at: www.dailynk.com/english/market.php? page=11&catald= (as of June 2016).

99. Anjeonwon is the abbreviation of Sahwoeanjeonwon (Society Security Officers). The name anjeonwon has been changed to inminboanwon (People's Security Officers), but the public still uses anjeonwon more frequently. The police institution in North Korea is called inminboanseong (People's Security Agency).

100. A more detailed report can be found at www.dailynk.com/korean/read .php?catald=nko4500&num=51402. (as of June 2016).

101. This type of corruption may facilitate the supply of consumer goods in shortages either through informal production or by importing them from other countries. However, because of its small scale and lack of legal protection, such informal production may be more inefficient than production in the formal sector.

102. Davis (1988) draws out the linkages between market transactions in the informal economy and the bribes necessary for the informal economy to function in a socialist economy with a dictatorial political system.

103. For more details of this survey, refer to Section 2.3 of this chapter.

104. In the 2009 survey, 64.2 per cent of respondents who chose the answer 'avoiding punishment' also chose the answer 'To continue to work in informal markets'.

105. According to the 2009 survey data, the average amount of money 8·3 workers needed to pay was 23,000 North Korean won per year, while the average wage of official workers was 2,500 North Korean won.

106. This type of bribe may be used to strengthen the formal sector, because the boss of the enterprise or organisation can use money from 8·3 workers to pay taxes to the government, wages to official workers, purchase necessary inputs and so on.

107. The above results from the tabulation analysis are only indicative, because they fail to control for other variables. For a more rigorous investigation, Kim and Koh (2011) employ an econometric analysis to understand whether or not bribery is related to informal market activities and find that the probability of paying a bribe is positively correlated with participation in the informal economy. In addition, it is

found that bribery reduces working hours in the formal economy by 9 hours per week.

108. The number of refugees in a given year ranges from 42 to 179.

109. These estimates are based on the assumption that the share of household expenditures (consumption) in total North Korean GDP is 65–80 per cent.

110. Bribery is found virtually everywhere in North Korea. Using the data from a survey of refugees, Chai et al. (2006) list a wide variety of kinds of bribery. Among bribes related to noneconomic activities, refugees reported their experience of bribe-giving for the issuing of travel documents or passports, being a member of the Workers' Party, allocation of workplace, admission of their children to university and so on. In addition, the stealing of state assets and smuggling goods from China are among the most frequently reported forms of corruption.

111. For example, the average share of bribes weighted by the number of respondents for the periods of 1996–2002 and 2003–2007 are 8.9 and 10.0 per cent, respectively. However, this difference is not significant (p-value is 0.247 with the null hypothesis of no difference in the share between the two periods).

112. Cited from Yang (2010a, p. 10) and translated by the author.

113. It is possible that those who support a market economy are self-selected into market activities. Considering this possible endogeneity, we used an instrument variable approach in which gender is used as an instrument for market activities. We recoded the responses in a dummy variable and implemented instrument probit regressions. Regressors included age, education, the experience of military service and Party membership. The results show that working in markets significantly increases the probability of support for performance-based salary, support for private ownership and support for rewards based on effort.

3 Transition of the North Korean Economy

3.1 AN OVERVIEW OF THE TRANSITION EXPERIENCE

3.1.a Transition Strategy, Policies and Institutions in Eastern Europe

When socialist economies started a transition into market economies in the late 1980s and the early 1990s, economists as well as policy-makers tended to regard the transitions as a simple transplantation of the elements of a market mechanism into FSEs. Furthermore, they believed these economies would recover quickly because the market system is more efficient than socialism. This expectation was not realised, however, as all of the Eastern European countries and the former Soviet republics experienced a severe recession during the early years of their transition. In fact, the transition to a market economy turned out to be a rather lengthy and thorny process of adjustment.

This natural, grand experiment in the transition of economic systems generated much interest among economists and a soaring increase in the number of academic papers published concerning the experiences of the transition economies. These academic debates constitute the economics of transition. Economic transition is concerned with changes in economic systems, such as from socialism to capitalism. In a similar vein, the economics of transition addresses how to transform one economic system into a different one in a way that will most efficiently produce the benefits of economic progress.

In this section, we will review the experiences of transition economies, focusing on economic policies. Among the issues related to transition economics, the debate surrounding 'big-bang' (versus gradualism) transitions has attracted significant attention from economic theorists. In contrast, more policy-related topics such as stabilisation, liberalisation, privatisation and sequencing of policies have been addressed, mostly by empirically oriented researchers. In addition, the importance of institutions as a determinant of transition performance has been emphasised in various empirical works. These six topic areas – big-bang versus gradualism, stabilisation, liberalisation, privatisation, sequencing of policies and institution building – will be examined one by one in this section.

This section focuses on the economies of Eastern Europe.[1] In addition, the Chinese process of transition will be discussed as a point of comparison with the Eastern European models. Rich experience with the diverse policies implemented in transition countries is expected to deepen our understanding of appropriate policies for North Korea's transition. Well-documented evidence on the outcomes of transition policies in these countries will also provide important lessons for North Korea.

Transition Strategy: Big-Bang versus Gradualism

Transition in Eastern Europe began suddenly, without a roadmap for the transformation of the economic system. Hence, transition policies were improvised, based largely on the knowledge on what constitutes market economies. A working market economy requires private property rights and market coordination, which should replace public ownership of productive assets and central planning, respectively. As a result, economists and policy-makers alike believed privatisation and liberalisation should be implemented to transform an economic system from socialism to capitalism. In addition, a growing economy needs stable economic conditions and, thus, stabilisation of the economy should be an important policy for transition. Scholars in the economics profession are unlikely to deny the importance of these three policies for transition.

The question remains, however, whether it is desirable for these three policies to be implemented simultaneously and within a short time span. Economists supporting a big-bang approach believed so.

In contrast, scholars preferring gradualism argued that these policies should be implemented sequentially, over a relatively longer period. The experiences of transition economies are also diverse. Some countries, such as East Germany and Poland, chose the big-bang approach to transition, whereas other countries, such as China and Hungary, implemented a gradualist approach.

Table 3.1 summarises the cases for big-bang and gradualism. The literature on this debate concerns not only the benefits and costs of each strategy but also the political economic aspects of transition, given the fact that transition of the economic systems affects the political supports for reform. As regards the aspect of efficiency, the literature agrees that big-bang is better than gradualism because it takes less time to transform the old economy into a more efficient one. Concerning the political economy aspect of transition, however, views are divided. Some studies claim that big-bang boosts the credibility of reform and prevents a costly search for a third way (Van Winjbergen, 1992; Sachs and Woo, 1994). By contrast, others maintain that gradualism allows transition to start with a reform that makes the majority better off, and thus has a higher probability of success (Rodrik, 1989; Little et al., 1970). Studies supporting big-bang point out problems of gradualism, such as the difficulty of drawing a detailed plan of sequencing, the possibility of coordination failure and the blocking of further reform by those who emerged as winners in the early stages of transition (Funke, 1993; Murphy et al., 1992; Martinelli and Tommassi, 1997). According to gradualism, however, a transition cannot be started using a big-bang approach because of political constraints, whereas gradualism can work around such difficulties (Dewatripont and Roland, 1995; Fernandez and Rodrik, 1991; Dewatripont and Roland, 1992; Rodrik, 1989).

Empirical tests suggest that accumulated progress with transition has a positive effect on economic performance (Kim and Pirtilla, 2006; Falcetti et al., 2006). In other words, countries that made faster transitions experienced a higher rate of economic growth. However, it

Table 3.1 *Pros and Cons of Big-Bang and Gradualism*

Cases and criticism	Big-bang	Gradualism
Efficiency/ costs	• The adjustment costs are lower because the economy will be more efficient after a shorter period of transition (Mussa, 1984). • Income will increase more substantially following a transition recession (Falcetti et al., 2006).	• The costs of the early reversal will be lower (Dewatripont and Roland, 1995).
Political support	• The credibility of the government increases by signalling its commitment to transition (Van Winjbergen, 1992). • The reversal or the search for the 'third way' becomes more difficult (Sachs and Woo, 1994).	• Political support for transition increases by first implementing policies affecting the majority positively (Rodrik, 1989). • The decrease in income is less severe and, thus, political support for transition can be maintained (Little et al., 1970).
Criticism on the alternative approach	• It is difficult to draw up a detailed plan for the sequencing of transition policies (Funke, 1993). • A vacuum in the coordination mechanism emerges as neither the plan nor the market operates (Murphy et al., 1992). • The winners from the early period of transition prevent	• It is more difficult to start and continue transition without sequencing transition policies (Dewatripont and Roland, 1995; Fernandez and Rodrik, 1991). • Dilemma between fiscal deficit and political support deepens because of higher unemployment

Table 3.1 (cont.)

Cases and criticism	Big-bang	Gradualism
	implementation of the remaining transition policies that would undermine the benefits they have already realised (Martinelli and Tommassi, 1997).	rates (Dewatripont and Roland, 1992). • A larger number of losers prevents further transition (Rodrik, 1989).

is also true that progress in transition is endogenously determined by factors such as initial conditions and social cohesion. Kim and Pirtilla (2006) find that income inequality and unemployment rates are negatively correlated with transition progress. According to Roberts and Kim (2011), democracy facilitates the transition progress. These findings indicate that a speedier transition helps economic growth as long as it does not undermine the social cohesion and institutional mechanisms that ensure that public preferences are reflected in the transition policies.

One related research strand in the literature studies the optimal speed of transition (OST). According to OST research, transition involves the reallocation of resources across sectors. The replacement of central planning with a market mechanism will lead to the bankruptcy of inefficient firms, notably large state-owned enterprises (SOEs). Simultaneously, the private sector will become the domain wherein new and possibly more efficient enterprises will be created by employing the workforce laid off by inefficient enterprises. Hence, the question arises: At what speed should sectoral reallocation between the state and the private sector take place? If the pace of reallocation from the state to the private sector is too fast, the fiscal burden will intensify, as the government will need to finance benefits for the unemployed. Conversely, if it is too slow, it will be difficult for the efficient private sector to grow (Aghion and Blanchard, 1994).

A substantial decrease in East German output during the uni-fication process can be understood within the OST literature. East German industrial output had fallen by nearly 50 per cent within a few months after unification and had fallen by two-thirds in 1991. During the same period, employment was nearly halved. This was mainly due to the introduction of minimum wages far higher than the level of productivity of East German workers, combined with the setting of exchange rates between the two German currencies at 1:1 for wages. The German unification case implies that the excessively fast destruc-tion of Eastern German SOEs led to a sub-optimal output level.

Stabilisation

Economic stabilisation can be regarded as a precondition for sustain-able growth. Stabilisation requires reductions in inflation and the fiscal deficit. Policy-makers were concerned about the impacts that monetary overhang accumulated during the socialist period would have on inflation when the transition began. That is, they believed that hyperinflation caused by monetary overhang would increase the already-expected inflation, generating an inflationary spiral. Although the inflation rate was very high in some countries, such as Russia, when prices were liberalised, the rate reduced fairly quickly in most transition economies, partially because of government policies.

Some countries, such as Poland and the Czech Republic, used a fixed exchange rate as a nominal anchor during the early period of transition. Economies that adopted a fixed exchange rate regime sta-bilised faster and grew more quickly than those that used a floating exchange rate regime (Fischer et al., 1996; Kim and Pirtilla, 2006). This can be interpreted as evidence that a fixed exchange rate signalled the government's commitment to stabilisation and decreased uncertainty around economic variables among households and firms.

However, some qualifications should be made. First, insuffi-cient foreign currency reserves make it difficult for a transition country to adopt a fixed exchange rate regime. Hence, financial support from international financial organisations or from foreign countries is necessary. Second, a substantial undervaluation of a domestic currency is required before it pegs with the foreign currency. In this way, the fixed exchange rate is not only more defensible but also more effective in promoting exports. Third, the fixed exchange rate regime tends to lead to the real appreciation of the domestic currency because the inflation rate in a transition country is likely to be higher than that in an advanced country to which the currency is pegged. Therefore, it is necessary to change the exchange rate regime from fixed to floating, over time, in order not to lose price competitiveness in the world market.

A reduction in the fiscal deficit was a difficult task. Social security demands on expenditures are likely to increase because of a transition recession, whereas tax revenue decreases due to the same reason. In addition, the large unofficial economy that is found in most transition economies undermines the tax base. There is no easy solution for this other than an economic recovery and institutional development, which is accompanied by a shrinking of unofficial economic activities.

Economic stabilisation during the transition period should be encouraged not only by liberalisation policies but also by installation of a proper mechanism for economic stabilisation. In a market economy, monetary and fiscal policy plays the role of stabilising the economy. However, the roles of fiscal policy in a traditional socialist economy are distinctly different from those in a market economy. Fiscal policy in a socialist economy, conducted by the state budget, allocates financial resources between the household sector and the enterprise sector, and among industries, in accordance with central planning. In addition, monetary policy was virtually non-existent in a traditional socialist economy.

Fiscal and monetary policy in a market economy are essential policy tools for economic stabilisation. In order for monetary policy to be used to manage aggregate demand, the system of two separate

monetary flows in socialism should be abolished. Instead, all economic transactions should be conducted with money. That is, the
monetisation of the economy should take place. Subsequently, the
central bank should be able to control the amount of the money supply
in response to economic circumstances. The establishment of fiscal
policy in accordance with a market economy principle requires
changes in the tax system, including the introduction of income
taxes and transformation of expenditure items.

Liberalisation
Economic liberalisation concerns pricing and trade that are free from
government intervention. Price liberalisation is essential for a market
economy, where the price mechanism based on supply and demand
efficiently allocates resources and properly coordinates economic
activities. Price liberalisation during the transition period means
that the government abandons price controls and stops providing
retail price subsidies. Furthermore, it lends an implication that central
planning will be replaced by a market mechanism. Hence, most of the
transition economies in Eastern Europe and the former Soviet republics implemented price liberalisation at the outset of their transition
by abandoning central planning and abolishing retail price subsidies.

    Most of the transition economies in Eastern Europe and the
former Soviet republics began their transition toward a market economy under macroeconomic crises. Hidden inflation was high and
shortages of goods were severe, which was reflected in the empty
shelves and long queues at official retail shops, caused by retail price
subsidies, monetary overhang and the monetisation of fiscal deficits
(Kim, 2002). SBC and the associated siphoning effect of socialist firms
(i.e. the purchase of consumer goods with passive money in the enterprise sector) reinforced this problem (Kornai, 1986a; Kim, 2002).
Hidden inflation in the socialist period would be transformed into
open inflation if the government abandoned price setting and eliminated the retail price subsidies it had previously employed to keep
retail prices artificially low.

Although price liberalisation is justified on economic grounds, its effects on transition are beyond economic consideration. It affects the process of transition in the following three ways. First, it can influence the political economic nature of transition because price liberalisation is not distribution-neutral (Sah, 1987; Kim, 1997a; Lau et al., 2000). For example, the poor can be worse off due to price liberalisation because they lose the opportunity to purchase consumer goods at low prices by queuing, while free market prices are out of their reach. Second, it can work as a signal of the success of transition, as price liberalisation tends to be implemented in the beginning of transition. Gradual price liberalisation can be viewed as failure of transition because the electorates still experience shortages of consumer goods (Van Wijnbergen, 1992). On the contrary, it is possible that hyperinflation caused by full price liberalisation will signal to the electorate that transition is a painful process and not worth trying. The failure of reforms led by Yegor Gaidar in Russia in the early 1990s suggests this possibility. Third, it not only improves the efficiency of resource allocation but also encourages the implementation of other reform measures. For instance, the benefits of privatisation can be realised fully only when it is combined with price liberalisation. Small-scale privatisation and the entry of new, small firms are facilitated by liberalised prices freely determined in markets. Furthermore, entrepreneurship is affected positively by market environments rather than by government intervention in price determination.

There are two approaches to price liberalisation. China liberalised its prices using a dual-track approach: it maintained a planned track with planned prices and planned deliveries, while all other prices were liberalised at the margin. Planned prices and contracts were gradually phased out. In contrast, Eastern European countries liberalised prices in a big-bang way. A main advantage associated with gradual price liberalisation is that it helps poorer consumers to avoid suffering from the real income shock caused by higher market prices, especially for basic foodstuffs (Lau et al., 2000). Under dual-track price liberalisation, consumers are able to purchase certain quantities of goods at planned prices, which are normally much lower than market prices.

Dual-track price liberalisation is not always transposable to other countries. Although the administrative burden for the implementation of dual-track price liberalisation is not high, compared to that of fully working central planning, the government should be able to enforce planned prices with planned delivery (Roland, 2008). The producers have incentive to sell their outputs at market prices rather than at planned prices. Hence, a question remains as to whether the state has the capacity to monitor producer behaviour and to enforce the contracts inherited from the socialist era. If institutions should become so weak that the government is unable even to impose forms of contract enforcement, dual-track price liberalisation would not work for the economy.

Trade liberalisation concerns elimination of unnecessary restrictions on exports and imports. The ideal socialist system was based on autarky – that is, a self-sufficient economic system. However, such a system did not exist in reality, and all of the socialist countries engaged in foreign trade, although mostly trade among socialist countries. These countries applied a state monopoly of foreign trade in which only designated state institutions were allowed to be involved in trade. There were also heavy restrictions applied on trade, ranging from exchange-rate restrictions to non-tariff barriers. These had to be dismantled in order to transform the economy to a market basis. In addition, any restrictions on trade partners should be abolished. For example, most of socialist-era trade took place in the form of intra-trade within the CMEA, which was formed to facilitate trade among socialist countries in Eastern Europe and the former Soviet Union. Trade liberalisation requires that the country trade with other countries without restrictions.

Trade liberalisation is necessary for promotion of domestic competition. Given a monopolistic or oligopolistic industrial structure, trade liberalisation effectively imports competition from abroad, reducing domestic price distortions and the possibility of monopolistic price setting. Moreover, foreign trade helps to improve international competitiveness, as shown by some other East Asian countries, notably South Korea and Taiwan, which succeeded in export-driven economic development following the opening-up of their economies.

Some concerns can be raised regarding the effects of trade liberalisation on the economy. First, the early liberalisation of trade causes firms to produce goods and services with negative value added (McKinnon, 1991). In particular, socialist firms employ more energy but less technology, taking advantage of the price structure in the socialist economic system. A sudden move to free trade can make some firms unable to compete with foreign firms because their energy prices would increase and converge to the world market price. Hence, McKinnon (1991) suggests the protection of domestic industries by applying tariffs that allow firms a certain period of time to adapt their structure of production. Second, as a result of the lower competitiveness of domestic firms relative to foreign firms, unemployment would increase as domestic firms would experience bankruptcy. This will lead to a fiscal deficit because the government needs to spend more on social safety nets during the transition. Furthermore, the unemployed may believe that the transition hurts their welfare, and may thus oppose the implementation of further transition policies. Such political constraints can be a significant obstacle to the completion of transition (Dewatripont and Roland, 1995; Kim and Pirtilla, 2006).

The introduction of an exchange rate regime in accordance with a market principle is a precondition to trade liberalisation. Exchange rates in a socialist economy do not have any bearing on market prices. Instead, they are set arbitrarily by the government and utilised for trade and currency conversion, etc. Often there will be multiple exchange rates, each of which is applied to a specific purpose. The transition to a market economy requires convertibility of the currency according to exchange rates determined by currency markets. Currencies in a market economy are purchased and sold in currency markets. The exchange rate in a market economy normally reflects the fair price of the domestic currency. Although there was a fixed exchange rate set by the government, it would be difficult to sustain if it were highly misaligned with the rate that was determined freely by the markets. This lays the economic foundation for external trade and foreign investment. For this to happen, foreign exchange markets need to be established.

There are two broadly defined exchange rate regimes: fixed and floating. The fixed exchange rate regime includes the currency board system, in which the central bank is permitted to maintain the domestic money supply up to the amount of an increase in hard currencies at fixed exchange rates. Convertible and market-determined exchange rates promote the flow of commodities and people. In addition, macroeconomic variables are integrated in a way that makes them coherent. For instance, exchange rates affect imports and exports as well as inflation. At the same time, trade and inflation influence exchange rates. Furthermore, macroeconomic stabilisation can be accomplished with a nominal exchange rate as an anchor. This is called 'exchange rate-based stabilisation'. As discussed earlier, evidence supports the concept that a fixed exchange rate regime, including a currency board system, during the early transition period is positively correlated with better economic performance.

Privatisation and New Entry of Firms

Privatisation is one of the most important policies for the transition to a market economy. Socialism is based on state ownership of productive assets such as firms and land. However, state ownership is not compatible with the market mechanism, where scarcity interacts with self-betterment motives (Hayek, 1944, 1948). Consumers maximise their own utilities while producers want to make the highest profits possible. Resources are allocated in the most efficient way through the interactions of consumers and producers in the market. In addition, privatisation is an instrument for de-politicisation and thus restructuring of firms (Boycko et al., 1996). Restructuring of firms involving the shedding of workforces is necessary to make firms more efficient. In particular, SOEs tended to employ excessive numbers of employees due to SBC and inconsistency in planning. The probability of restructuring increases when the preferences of firm managers deviate from those of politicians who are interested in keeping unemployment rates low – that is, when a firm is controlled by private shareholders and managers rather than by politicians. Hence, privatisation can be regarded as *prima facie* policy to be implemented if a country attempts a transition toward a market economy.

Privatisation may not be the only way to make firms competitive. Some argue that the Chinese experience demonstrates that what is needed is not privatisation but creation of environments that are supportive of competition (McMillan and Naughton, 1992). In other words, the new entry of non-state or private firms in China made it possible for SOEs to pursue profit maximisation without privatisation (Lin et al., 2003). The critical difference between the Chinese and East European experiences can be accounted for by the relative share of agriculture and manufacturing industries, which might be correlated with the countries' stage of economic development. The dominance of agriculture indicates that the newly created non-SOEs (*de facto* private firms) had opportunities to employ a sufficient number of workers who previously worked as farmers. The presence of these non-SOE firms subsequently caused the remaining SOEs to operate under competitive pressure. The SOEs were subsequently privatised, step-by-step, beginning in the 1990s. In contrast, a more developed country, which had a larger share of the manufacturing industry, needed to employ workers who had been released from the SOEs. Hence, the privatisation of SOEs had the potential not only to improve the efficiency of the firms involved in privatisation but also to provide workers for newly created private firms. Nevertheless, the common element in both China and Eastern Europe was an increase in the share of output produced by private enterprises in the economy, which caused the supply of goods and services to rise. The difference was the way by which this goal was achieved: either by direct privatisation of SOEs (Eastern Europe) or by allowing the entry of new private firms, and thus putting SOEs under competitive pressure (China).

The objects of privatisation include firms, farms, land and houses. Ways to privatise these can differ depending on what is to be privatised. For example, in Eastern Europe and the former Soviet republics, collective farms were privatised primarily by transferring ownership rights to the members of the farms, and of houses to the tenants – that is, granting individuals the right to control the means of their livelihood. Methods of land privatisation varied substantially, depending on the characteristics of the land. For example, agricultural land and land occupied by houses tended to be privatised through the transfer of rights to those who possessed the farm or house. Land utilised by a plant was privatised together with the plant. Other land tended to be sold to outsiders.

The most challenging privatisation in the former Soviet Union and Eastern Europe proved to be that of large SOEs, for which various methods of privatisation were utilised. A number of studies assessing the effects of privatisation on firm performance are now available, and some consensus has been emerging (Boycko et al., 1994; Fyrdman et al., 1999; Havrylyshyn and McGettigan, 1999; Megginson and Netter, 2001; Djankov and Murrell, 2002; Nellis, 2002; Estrin et al., 2009). Diverse methods, from mass-voucher privatisation to spontaneous privatisation, were used to privatise large SOEs. For example, the Czech Republic and Poland used mass-voucher privatisation, while Hungary relied mainly on spontaneous privatisation or privatisation from below, that is, privatisation initiated by individual firms. Although it privatised SOEs using the voucher scheme, Russia's privatisation ended up with insider privatisation because concessions were given to managers and workers who wanted to purchase their firms before voucher privatisation took place. In East Germany, firms were sold to outsiders based on informal negotiation between the Truehandanstalt (Trust Agency), which was in charge of privatising East German assets, and potentially interested buyers.

At the outset of the transition in Eastern Europe, sales to out-siders were regarded as the default option for privatising large SOEs. However, it did not take much time for it to become apparent that this option was hard to apply to transition economies, for the following reasons. First, it was difficult to evaluate the value of the firms. The 'book value' of a socialist firm was useless, since central planning had dictated its input costs, output price and sales. Capital markets were either absent or underdeveloped, and so were unable to provide reliable information on a firm's value. Second, domestic savings were insufficient to permit purchase of the firms on sale. In particular, high inflation in the beginning of transition caused substantial shrinkage in the amount of domestic savings. Third, sale of firms to outsiders was viewed by the public as unfair. Those who were able to finance such purchases were likely to be either nomenklatura in the old regime or foreigners, and ownership by either of these groups would be viewed unfavourably by the public. In addition, insiders (managers and work-ers) of a firm were afraid that foreign ownership might lead to the grand-scale lay-off of workers. Fourth, given the difficulty associated with the valuation problem and shortage of capital, it would take a substantial amount of time to complete mass privatisation.

Realising the above difficulties associated with sales to outsi-ders, policy-makers in transition countries sought an alternative method of privatisation that could be implemented rapidly and would be regarded as fair. Equal-access voucher privatisation turned out to be a popular choice. Czechoslovakia first implemented voucher privatisation in 1992, followed by a number of other transition coun-tries, with some variations. The main variations included the follow-ing: whether the involvement of investment privatisation funds (IPFs) was encouraged or even made compulsory; whether a voucher was transferable to another person; and whether the auctions to exchange vouchers for shares of companies occurred continuously or in waves (Estrin and Stone, 1997).[2]

Current assessments of equal-access voucher privatisation are divided (Kenway and Chlumsky, 1997; Murrell, 1995; Djankov,

1999; Bennett et al., 2007). For example, Kenway and Chlumsky (1997) argued that IPFs in the Czech Republic were passive in terms of initiating positive changes in the management of a firm.[3] Djankov (1999) found that the extent of restructuring in firms that were privatised by the voucher scheme was similar to that in SOEs. However, Bennett et al. (2007) claim that voucher privatisation is positively associated with firm growth and ascribe this positive correlation to the speed of privatisation, to which they maintain voucher privatisation contributed. Megginson and Netter (2001) note that although it was the least productive, voucher privatisation was employed in many transition countries when there was no other feasible way of accomplishing privatisation, given the political and economic context.

During the early period of transition, a predominant piece of advice from economists from both academia and international financial organisations was to privatise large SOEs as soon as possible. However, such advice is now regarded as having been misguided (Nellis, 2002). For example, the Czech Republic implemented mass voucher privatisation within a few years after the start of transition, whereas Poland began voucher privatisation only in the late 1990s because of strong opposition from insiders and trade unions. There is little evidence that the economic benefits obtained from the Czech Republic's rapid privatisation are greater than those obtained through Poland's delayed action. In fact, East German privatisation (another example of a rapid privatisation) has been heavily criticised for its failures.

There is now a consensus that what matters for privatisation is not the speed but the proper establishment of ownership or creation of an appropriate type of corporate governance. Studies on the effects of privatisation methods on firm performance agree that privatisation works in transition economies (Megginson and Netter, 2001; Djankov and Murrell, 2002; Estrin et al., 2009). That is, the performance of privatised firms is better than that of SOEs. Nevertheless, the effects of privatisation vary substantially depending on which method of privatisation was employed. Privatisation to outsiders is regarded as the best way to accomplish privatisation, in terms of improving firm performance. In particular, concentration of ownership is found to improve firm performance. For instance, Djankov and Murrell (2002) found that the benefits of privatisation to funds and block holders are five and three times larger, respectively, than those of privatisation to insiders. In spite of some heterogeneity, foreign ownership also enhances firm productivity. Among insider privatisation, management buyouts are positively correlated with firm performance; employee buyouts have insignificant or even negative impacts on performance. These findings suggest that the privatisation method is more important than privatisation *per se* in terms of efficiency improvement. Core outsider ownership, which resulted in the largest improvement in firm performance, should be pursued by policy-makers. In this regard, some argue that the Estonian model of privatisation – that is, direct sales of firms to core outsiders while limiting the exchange of vouchers to a minority of stakeholders – is the best option to consider (Nellis, 2002).

The experiences of privatisation in transition economies demonstrate the importance of political considerations in privatising SOEs. Hence, the balance between economic efficiency and political legitimacy should be considered when policy-makers design a method for privatisation. In this regard, the advantages of voucher privatisation cannot easily be ignored. In addition to the fact that it is speedy, voucher privatisation is fair because it is distributed to all citizens at a marginal price. Furthermore, it provides the opportunity for citizens to learn about financial instruments, such as shares, and to contribute to the development of capital markets.

Restructuring is a key to improving firm efficiency. It takes various forms, including labour shedding, the development of a major new product line, upgrading an existing product line, obtaining a new product licensing, outsourcing a major production activity, exporting products to a new country and acquiring new production technologies. In spite of its importance, the determinants of restructuring have not been fully explored. Existing studies generally look at the relationships between privatisation and restructuring. For example, Carlin et al. (2001) found that private ownership is positively correlated with restructuring. Some studies suggest that restructuring can be facilitated by product market competition and hardening budget constraints (Claessens and Peters, 1997; Djankov and Murrell, 2002). In addition, Kim and Park (2016) investigated the effects of financing sources on firm restructuring, finding that bank financing (especially local bank financing) increases the probability of various forms of restructuring. This effect is enlarged when the size of the firm is small. In contrast, other forms of financing, including borrowing from foreign banks, issuance of equities and informal credit, are less effective in restructuring.

Restructuring occurred not only by firms but also by the government. In the beginning of the transition, many SOEs required an injection of capital in order to be able to survive, while some firms were not sustainable in the market environment. Hence, the government should distinguish firms with the potential to survive from firms that should be liquidated. Firm size was a different matter. Some firms were simply too big to be privatised, and thus needed to be de-bundled into smaller units. All of these problems would be better dealt with by the government in a coherent way. The prime example of this is the German unification, for which a specially designated institution, Truehandanstalt, was in charge of restructuring and privatising the national assets of East Germany, including large SOEs. SOEs that failed to be privatised and turned out to be unsustainable were allowed by the government to exit the market through liquidation. However, some countries preferred firm-led restructuring over the government-led, wholesale approach.

A recent evaluation of firm performance in Eastern Europe also suggests that *de novo* firms perform better than firms that have been privatised from SOEs (Havrylyshyn and McGettigan, 1999). This finding is consistent with the Chinese experience, where the performance of township enterprises based on non-state ownership is better than that of SOEs or privatised SOEs (Naughton, 2007). Sabirianova et al. (2012) maintain that new domestic firms are more efficient than existing domestic firms in the Czech Republic and Russia. This finding is line with a more recent study using a matched sample of Chinese and East European firms (Kim et al., 2014). They observe that new firms perform better than either SOEs or privatised firms in terms of productivity measures, and that such an ownership effect is particularly pronounced in China. In particular, small and medium-sized companies that were newly emerged during the transition played an important role in growth.

Newly created small and medium-sized companies, which require neither heavy investment nor well-developed institutions, can emerge overnight. Street vendors can become shopkeepers and a paid worker can become a self-employed employer. Yet the small private sector creates jobs, allocates resources efficiently and serves consumers' needs promptly. Hence, its development generates income and increases consumer welfare relatively rapidly. Among these people, entrepreneurs running large firms can emerge through learning and doing. Furthermore, the expansion of the private sector, where small and medium-sized companies dominate, can be a platform to push market reforms further. McMillan and Woodruff (2002) emphasise that one of the key determinants in the performance differential between Russia and Poland is the development of small and medium-sized companies. New enterprises in transition countries play a key role in creating jobs. Using data from Romania, Bulgaria and Hungary, Bilsen and Konings (1998) found that *de novo* private firms outperform both state-owned firms and privatised firms in terms of job creation. For illustration, these authors report that more than 60 per cent of all jobs are created in *de novo* firms in Romania and Bulgaria, and 31 per cent in Hungary, although their share of employment is at most 7 per cent of total employment. This finding corroborates the earlier finding in Frydman et al. (1997) that

85 per cent of *de novo* firms in the Czech Republic, Poland and Hungary increased employment, while comparable figures in SOEs and privatised firms were only 9 and 43 per cent, respectively.

The above findings suggest that policy-makers should pay more attention to the creation of new firms. The early debate on transition policies had been dominated by privatisation of SOEs, while creation of new firms was not regarded as a policy priority. However, Kornai (1990) argued that the main driving force in establishing a market mechanism in transition economies is found in *de novo* firms. In a similar vein, McMillan and Woodruff (2002) contrasted the transition performance in Russia with that in China and Poland to highlight the importance of new entrepreneurs. More specifically, both China and Poland experienced more rapid entry of firms than Russia during transition, which accounted for better transition performance in the former than in the latter.

The experience of the Chinese transition reinforces the importance of creating new enterprises. The evidence from China suggests that, without privatisation, the generation of market environments for entry of new firms and facilitation of competition among firms yielded large benefits (McMillan and Naughton, 1992). Permitting non-state ownership allowed township village enterprises to enter and prosper, especially in the rural sector. Competition pressure from such non-state firms imposed hard budget constraints on SOEs, which were required to improve firm performance. This evolutionary approach led to rapid growth for an extended period beginning with the start of transition in the late 1970s. Of course, it is still debatable whether this approach was a sufficient condition for the success of the transition process in China and whether it is replicable in other countries whose initial conditions differ from those of China.

The entry of new firms depends on the presence of appropriate conditions. Various factors might affect the entry of new firms. The literature identifies three main groups of such factors: institutions, corruption and financial resources. Institutions which are related to the enforcement of contracts and the protection of property rights facilitate the growth of new firms. Starting a business is risky, so firms start up more easily in countries where institutions properly enforce commercial contracts and protect property rights than in those where they do not. A judiciary system is an important mechanism to ensure such enforcement and protection. Informal institutions such as social capital are also important insofar as they lower the risks associated with opening a business. Using a pseudo-panel data constructed from World Value Surveys, Kim and Kang (2014) found a positive correlation between social capital and the number of entrepreneurs. Corruption is likely to increase the cost of starting a new business and the uncertainty associated with it, although corruption can act as 'greasing the wheel' in places where bureaucracy chokes business activities. Entrepreneurs who are driven out of markets because of high corruption may be motivated to become government officials in order to take bribes (Shleifer and Vishny, 1998). Lastly, the lack of financial resources prohibits potential entrepreneurs from doing business. Transition countries often suffer from poorly functioning financial institutions that make it difficult for new firms to borrow or to raise capital from financial markets. Such financial constraints turn out to be an important bottleneck repressing entrepreneurship. Hence, policies should focus on the above factors to encourage the growth of new firms.

Sequencing

The classification schemas of big-bang vs. gradualism are useful in illustrating the advantages and the disadvantages associated with each strategy. However, in practice, not all transition policies can be implemented at the same time. There are differences in how long it would take to prepare and implement policies; stabilisation and liberalisation policies are relatively quick to implement compared to those related to privatisation. Furthermore, because of political constraints, policy-makers tend to pay attention to building up pro-reform constituencies in order to maintain momentum for further reforms. This suggests that feedback from electorates' economic experiences into the political arena should make policy-makers interested in sequencing.

If an optimal sequencing of transition policies exists, policy-makers should pay more attention to such sequencing rather than to making transition strategy 'trade-offs', such as between big-bang and gradualism. They are likely to implement popular transition policies, followed by other policies that exploit momentum for further reforms and to persuade the public using an argument based on the complementary nature of the reform policies. Hence, it is important to devise the optimal sequencing of implementation for reform policies.

Barlow and Radulescu (2005) examined whether particular types of reform increase the probability of implementing another type of reform. They find that small-scale privatisation is the most effective policy in that it advances large-scale privatisation, trade reform and banking reform. In addition, fiscal surplus and trade liberalisation tend to facilitate other reforms. These results are broadly in line with the findings of Kim and Pirtilla (2006), who looked at correlations among the different aspects of reform. Their main findings suggest that both price liberalisation and small-scale privatisation should take place at an early stage of a transition in order to create a momentum for further reform.

One problem in interpreting the above findings is the question of whether the sequencing that transition countries followed was, indeed, optimal. Was the sequencing the outcome of political considerations, and could it have sacrificed potential economic benefits? Alternatively, did it contribute both to overcoming political constraints and to increasing the welfare of the population? Staehr (2005) answered these questions to some extent by looking at the effects of different reform elements on growth. He found the following results: (1) broad-based reforms, including liberalisation, privatisation and structural measures, hurt the economy in the short term but are beneficial for growth from the second year onward; (2) early reform, which is correlated with price-liberalisation, small-scale privatisation and market-opening, has a negative effect on the economy in the short term but a positive effect from the second year onward; (3) large-scale privatisation affects the economy negatively not only in the short term but also in the period after one year; (4) early market opening is detrimental to growth; and (5) early bank-liberalisation has a negative effect on growth.

In sum, work on optimal sequencing suggests that small-scale privatisation can play an important role in transition; it increases output and mobilises support for further reforms. This corroborates the findings that entrepreneurship is a key determinant of economic growth in transition economies (McMillan and Woodruff, 2002; Berkowitz and Dejong, 2005). McMillan and Woodruff (2002) document that the development of entrepreneurship in China and Poland accounts for the robust growth in these countries, while the economic decline experienced by Russia in the early part of transition was caused by the slow development of entrepreneurial mechanisms. Berkowitz and Dejong (2005) present intra-national evidence for the relationship between entrepreneurship and growth. They use Russian regional data to estimate the effects of entrepreneurial development (measured by the regional registry of small, private enterprises per thousand inhabitants) on growth, and find that the two variables are positively associated.

Institutional Development

Before the transition experiences in Eastern Europe in the 1990s, one of the most neglected fields in economics was, perhaps, the role of institutions in economic development. Davis and North (1971) emphasised the importance of institutions in the 1970s, but institutional economics became 'mainstream economics' in the 1990s–2000s. Transition experiences contributed to the development of institutional economics. However, many issues regarding institutions remain unsettled. What institutions are critical for economic performance? Why was the experience of the East German transition so negative, in spite of the transplanting of nearly perfect West German institutions into East Germany? Why did China succeed in spite of the low quality of its institutions?

Some work has used institution-related variables as independent variables for a growth equation, and has shown the security of property rights, political stability, judiciary reliability and lack of corruption, all of which are perceived by respondents, to be significant in determining economic growth (Brunetti et al., 1997). These findings make sense. However, many institutions take time to improve and, thus, it is difficult to draw concrete policy implications from the results of these regressions. In particular, slow-moving institutions, such as culture, affect economic performance in the long run. Trust also influences the transition process and its outcomes. In this context, one can ask what policy-makers should do if institutions are not well developed.

Roland (2008) argued that a minimal set of institutions should be in operation if positive outcomes are to result from economic transition. He provided the following list of legal reforms: the introduction of the titling of property, easy entry for businesses, basic contract enforcement, law enforcement and judicial protection. Kim (2015) regards de-collectivisation and granting the freedom to exchange and to create companies as a minimal, basic set of transition policies needed for North Korea. Without these institutional arrangements, he argues, it would be difficult for any transition economy to experience sustainable growth.

Important consideration should be given to the question of what institutional incentives bring policy-makers' interests into alignment with economic growth. Roland (2008) suggested that Chinese policy-makers have had strong incentives in favour of economic growth because of fiscal decentralisation and yardstick competition. However, these institutions are not easily transposed to countries whose conditions are different from those of China. Appropriate incentive mechanisms should take country-specific conditions into account. One example from South Korea is the export promotion policy in the 1960s–1970s under President Park Chung-hee. The performance of bureaucrats as well as business owners was evaluated against their contribution to exports. Bureaucrats were promoted and business owners obtained some privileges, including soft loans from banks. President Park himself presided over the meetings around export promotion, which gave strong incentives for policy-makers.

3.1.b Chinese Transition: Experimentation and Dual-Track Approach

The Chinese story of transition is interesting and important, not only because it resulted in highly successful economic performance but also because it is in stark contrast to the big-bang approach adopted in many Eastern European transition countries. The Chinese experience of gradualism appears to support gradualism over big-bang. China's transition strategy includes experimentation and a dual-track approach. Given the fact that China was the first country to attempt a transition from socialism to a market economy, experimentation was necessary because of the high degree of uncertainty about the outcome of such a transition. In addition, the regional duplication of industrial structure, the so-called M-form of organisation (as opposed to the U-form), made experimentation feasible and useful (Qian et al., 2006). The initial introduction of the household responsibility system first in some regions and then spreading to other regions is an example of experimentation. The SEZs are another example: the government opened up Shenzhen, Zhuhai, Shantou and Xiamen cities as SEZs in 1980. A series of 'openings up' of cities or regions as SEZs took place afterwards, following the success of the initial SEZs. The dual-track approach was intended to satisfy political constraints as well as Pareto optimality (Lau et al., 2000).

There are heated debates as to whether Chinese gradualism was transposable to former CPEs in Eastern Europe. One group of economists believes that Chinese gradualism was a mere political compromise, not an economically optimal strategy, and was possible there because of a unique set of initial conditions (Woo, 1994; Sachs and Woo, 1994). The other group of economists argues that the experience of Chinese transition based on gradualism through experiments was a genuine invention applicable to other transition economies (Lau et al., 2000; Naughton, 1996; Lin et al., 2003). The successful Chinese transition was possible, perhaps, because of a special combination of initial conditions, strategies and policies. Chinese initial conditions were indeed unique: political centralisation, but regional decentralisation of the economy; a non-democratically elected government; an agriculture-based economy; high savings rates; the beginning of reforms under stable conditions, etc. All of this makes it difficult to transpose Chinese transition policies to other transition countries as a whole. However, there must be important lessons to be learned from the Chinese experience and applied to other countries, as we will discuss subsequently.

Aims of Reform and Initial Conditions

Deng Xiaoping took over control of the Communist Party in 1978. Deng, who had been a victim of the Cultural Revolution, believed that a strong ideological orientation would be an obstacle to China's development. Both a large number of the elites and the majority of the people suffered under the Cultural Revolution and, thus, supported reforms that aimed to improve economic conditions within the country. Citing a former Premier, Chow (2007) stated, 'The Cultural Revolution did great harm to China, but it freed us from certain ideological constraints (p. 47)'. At the same time, to strengthen his political hegemony, Deng Xiaoping needed policies to increase the income of the population. However, given high uncertainty about the outcomes of the reform, the Chinese leadership preferred gradualism through experiments (Crossing the River by Gripping the Stones) over an outright transition toward a market economy. Over time, accumulated reforms became a *de facto* transition toward a market economy.

Sachs and Woo (1994) argued that the differences in initial conditions and economic structures were so profound that it had been necessary for former Eastern European socialist countries to follow a fundamentally different type of reform than Chinese gradualism. For example, the large industrial sector in Eastern European socialist countries meant there was a need to lay off workers during transition, whereas the large agricultural sector in China provided the possibility for workers to move from agriculture to industry without massive layoffs. In addition, given the inefficiencies of a number of SOEs in the former Soviet countries, a financial collapse could be expected without rapid privatisation. In contrast, the SOE sector was relatively small in China, meaning the government could take a gradual approach to privatising it while retaining some control over the enterprises, such as the fulfilment of production quotas at plan prices. Hence, Sachs and Woo believed that the Chinese policies of gradual reform were not the first or best alternatives for economic transition, but rather a political compromise between the adherents of the old economy and the proponents of the new, market economy.

Furthermore, as documented by Qian and Xu (1993) and Qian et al. (2006), the organisational structure of the planning hierarchy differed substantially between the Soviet Union (and most Eastern European economies) and China. The former was a unitary form based on the functional or specialisation principle (the U-form economy), whereas the Chinese form is a regional form based on a territorial principle (the M-form economy). The M-form structure makes an experiment within a region possible, as the shock due to the experiment is contained within the region. If the experiment turns out to be successful, it can easily be implemented in other regions because of similarities in industrial structure across the regions. In contrast, such an experiment is difficult to apply in a U-form economy because the shock due to the experiment will affect other regions in a significant way.

Blanchard and Shleifer (2001) suggested that political centralisation, as in China, plays a positive role in the transition because the central government can reward or punish local administrators. This was a way to reduce local capture and competition for rents. In contrast, the democratisation process in Russia caused the central government to struggle for control of the distorted behaviour of local governments. Qian and Roland (1998) compared the Russian and Chinese experiences of transition in terms of fiscal competition. Fiscal decentralisation in China led to a hardening of SBC through the effects of competition. That is, in the presence of factor mobility and fiscal competition, regions competed with each other to create favourable conditions for capital and labour, which reduced the SBC. Additionally, the checks-and-balances effect works, which induces conflicts of interest when a local government takes advantage of the SBC. By contrast, Russia redistributed revenues from within regions widely across regions, which increased the SBC of local governments and enterprises.

Reform Strategies: Experimentation and Dual-Track Approach

The processes for various reforms in China displayed similar patterns: experimentation and the non-creation of losers. The former is understandable, as China was the first country to deviate from the principles of Marxism and to dismantle the structures of CPEs. The latter reflects the nature of the leadership: as a reformer who grasped power in a non-democratic way, Deng Xiaoping needed political support from the public. Hence, he was prepared to accept reforms as long as they would improve the welfare of the population. In addition, the strong possibility that Deng Xiaoping would remain in power over the long term induced incentives for gradualism and for not creating losers. Table 3.2 summarises the features of the Chinese transition, focusing on aims, initial conditions, strategies and policies, as compared with those in Eastern European economies.

China's economic reform started with rural agriculture in 1978. This reform was the result of initial experiments by a group of peasants in Anhui Province. They found a significant improvement in output when a piece of land was assigned to each farm household who had an obligation to deliver a certain quantity of agricultural output to meet the procurement requirement of the commune. At the same time, households were allowed to freely use the output remaining

Table 3.2 *The Features of Chinese Transition in Comparison with Eastern European Transition*

Features	Chinese transition	Eastern European transition
Aims	• Improvement in welfare of population (transition was *ex post* consequence, not the initial aim)	• Transition toward a market economy • Joining the EU, for most Eastern European countries
Initial conditions	• Agriculture-dominated industrial structure (approximately 70 per cent of workforce was employed in agriculture) • High savings rate – No need for foreign capital • Political changes before reform (Cultural Revolution, 1966–76, and change in leadership before reform) but in stable conditions • Prospects for long-term leadership • Low degree of economic centralisation (regional autonomy)	• Industry-based economy • Savings rates are lower than those in China • Transition after the collapse of the old regime • Democratisation accompanied with economic transition (keeping power over the long term is difficult) • Highly centralised economic structure
Strategies	• Experimentation, given high uncertainty about the outcome of reform and feasibility based on regional duplication • Dual-track approach aiming to satisfy political constraints	• Wholesale adoption of market economies (transition started because of the collapse of the old regime) • Relatively big-bang oriented (we know what we are doing and have initially high public support for transition)

Table 3.2 (cont.)

Features	Chinese transition	Eastern European transition
Policies	• Responsibility system – incentives • Market liberalisation – creation and expansion of markets • Special Economic Zones – experiments • Township village – competition, ownership change	• Stabilisation • Liberalisation – rapid price liberalisation and opening-up the whole economy to the world market • Privatisation – ownership change and restructuring

after fulfilling the quota according to their interests. When a remarkable increase in agricultural production was observed, the household responsibility system was accepted by the government, applied first to poorer agricultural regions, and then applied universally to all regions in China. By 1983, most collective farms had adopted the household responsibility system. Gradually the dual-track system was expanded to industry as well. As in the agricultural sector, firms were held responsible for supplying a fixed amount of production at pre-reform prices, but they were free to sell the remaining outputs at free-market prices.

Dual-track price liberalisation, which was first introduced in China in 1979, accompanied the household responsibility system. Before 1979, there was rationing of many essential consumer goods and services. As the dual-track approach was introduced, urban residents continued to be able to purchase these goods and services at pre-reform prices, up to the pre-reform, rationed quantities. Yet, consumers were allowed to purchase any quantity of any good on the free markets. Over time, rationing gradually reduced and planned prices converged to market prices. This dual-track approach achieves Pareto-efficiency while satisfying political constraints. In other words, the strategy minimises some costs of transition while allowing the fundamentally benevolent realloca-tion of resources.

According to Lau et al. (2000), the advantages of the dual-track approach are three-fold. First, the administration burden is reduced. It relies on pre-existing institutions, but their duties shift from making detailed plans and enforcing them to monitor-ing the delivery of pre-reform quantities at pre-reform prices. The latter duties can be regarded as being less challenging than the former duties in terms of information content and implemen-tation. In addition, it does not require the establishment of new institutions because pre-existing institutions take on the roles of monitoring and enforcement. Second, it satisfies political con-straints by making everyone better off than before. Potential losers in the reform are implicitly subsidised by this approach, which maintains the status quo for part of the economy, but makes potential winners strictly better off through liberalisation at the margin. Third, Pareto-efficiency is achieved, as in the big-bang approach. As transfers are made in lump sums, they are not distortionary. Hence, Lau et al. claim that the dual-track approach is an original and important method for both achieving economic efficiency and dealing with the political constraints of transition without necessitating explicit compensation schemes.

Reform Policies

In addition to the introduction of the household responsibility system, rural markets, which had been forbidden during the Cultural Revolution, began to reopen. Hence, farmers were able to sell their agricultural output in the market. The combination of incentives and marketisation brought about a significant increase in productivity. According to MacMillan et al. (1989), 78 per cent of the increase in the total factor productivity for Chinese agriculture during 1978–1984, which increased by 32 per cent from that in the pre-reform period, is due to such changes in incentive schemes. De

Brauw et al. (2004) estimated that the magnitude of efficiency gains from incentive schemes amounted to 7 per cent per annum.

Increases in the income of farmers attributable to the household responsibility system provided conditions for development of small, private businesses, notably in retailing, transportation and crafts, and for community-owned industrial enterprises (township and village enterprises – TVEs) in rural areas. Until the 1984 relaxation of private ownership, TVEs were community-owned and their operations were controlled by local governments. From 1984 onward, the forms of TVEs varied according to the regulations of the regions. TVEs became the most dynamic sector of China's economy. In 1980–1988, over 30 per cent of the output growth was due to rural TVEs.

Together with increased competition from imported goods, state-owned enterprises faced competition from non-state sectors especially in the sectors of distribution and consumer service. In addition, industries lost control of their monopoly position in regional markets and, as a result, they needed to compete with producers from other regions. All of these factors applied competitive pressure on SOEs.

The open-door policy included two components: the opening of foreign trade and foreign direct investment. As regards the latter, the government opened up Shenzhen, Zhuhai, Shantou and Xiamen as SEZs in 1980. This was regarded as a type of experiment because a series of cities or regions were opened up as SEZs following the success of the initial SEZs. Infrastructure was built and foreign investors were able to receive special tax breaks and enjoy inexpensive, skilled labour. As a result, foreign investments soared from an annual rate of less than US$1 billion in 1978 to nearly US$30 billion in 1998.

Partial Liberalisation and Co-ordination Failure
A key difference between Murphy et al. (1992) and Lau et al. (2000) is in whether the government can force input suppliers to meet planned obligations. If not, partial price liberalisation may lead to co-ordination failure, as argued by Murphy et al. (1992). A critical

question is whether the government has the credibility to enforce plan-mandated deliveries at plan prices.

Another important criticism of the dual-track system is that it increases corruption. The dual-track system may foster non-transparency and unfair rents for existing agents that already enjoy privileges. However, one can argue that the dual-track system is an interim process in the transition to complete liberalisation. Although it is possible for bureaucrats and enterprise managers to resist against the elimination of the dual-track system, the public, who benefit from economic growth, are likely to push for the completion of reforms.

The above discussion implies that a critically important element for adopting a dual-track approach is the quality of the government. If the government is credible, effective and relatively honest, a dual-track approach is optimal for starting and completing economic reforms. In contrast, if the government is of low quality, a dual-track approach may lead to evasion of supply obligations, substantial increases in corruption and a fostering of unfairness in the society.

Lessons from the Chinese Transition

The success of the Chinese transition was due to a combination of initial conditions, strategies and policies. Hence, it is difficult to transplant the Chinese way of transition to other transition countries as a whole. In particular, the experiments in China required a unique setting that other countries may lack. If the economy of a country is highly centralised with heavy governmental intervention, experiments might not be a good option. In addition, when China launched reforms, little was known about whether transition toward a market economy would bring about a positive outcome. Hence, experiments that would provide the option of less costly reversal aided in overcoming a bias toward the status quo. However, after observing the transition experience of European former CPEs, it is now accepted that a transition toward a market economy increases the welfare of the population in the long run. All of these conditions suggest a limited possibility that European former CPEs would benefit from experimentation. Nevertheless, it would not be appropriate to state that the Chinese experience was possible only because of its unique initial conditions. The following general lessons can be drawn from the Chinese experience for application to other transition countries.

First of all, the Chinese experience exemplified in dual-track price liberalisation satisfied political constraints while achieving Pareto-improvement. In addition, rural reform focusing on de-collectivisation worked as a sweet pill. Some economists argue that one of causes of instability during the early stages of Russia's transition was ignorance of political constraints.

Second, policy-makers should be aware that some important components of transition change only slowly. A socialist planning system can be dismantled overnight, but that does not necessarily mean that all economic agents will change their behaviour accordingly in a short time. In addition, a market economy requires market-supporting institutions, which take time to build. China used existing institutions as the basis of its reforms. Over time, old institutions were replaced with new ones. This approach appears to be effective in avoiding 'co-ordination failure'.

Third, China successfully exploited the complementarities of reform policies. A notable example is rural reform, in which the introduction of a household responsibility system was accompanied with the reintroduction of markets for agricultural output. This is in line with the basics of economics: the combination of incentives and markets. SOE reforms followed a similar approach: a responsibility system together with allowing markets for inputs and outputs.

Fourth, although China reformed its economy gradually, the reforms themselves were comprehensive from the beginning, ranging from liberalisation, the introduction of competition and non-state ownership and institution building. This suggests that what is most critical for transition may not be the speed of transition itself but its comprehensiveness and consistency.

Fifth, China implemented economic policies consistent with factor endowment. China has a rich but inexpensive labour force.

Reforms started with industries that use cheap and abundant labour. Foreign capital was attracted by this factor as well. This policy contrasts with that used for German unification, in which the minimum wage policy and conversion rate between the East German and West German marks prevented the leveraging of comparative advantages of East Germany.

3.2 MACROECONOMIC STABILISATION AND LIBERALISATION

3.2.a Price Liberalisation

Initial Conditions in North Korea

North Korea has been experiencing open inflation rather than hidden inflation since the 1990s. According to Table A.2.1, the average rate of annual inflation from 1997 to 2009 was 44.3 per cent. The following three reasons account for the presence of open inflation in North Korea. First, the public distribution system (PDS) that rationed food to the population nearly collapsed in the 1990s, so the majority of the population relied on markets to purchase consumer goods. Currently, more than 70 per cent of household monetary expenditures are spent in informal markets where prices are determined by supply and demand. Second, the partial opening of external trade allowed the import of consumer goods, mostly from China. Food provided by South Korea, international organisations and other countries increased the supply of food in North Korea as well. In particular, not only the North Korean authorities but also firms, institutions and private individuals were involved in importing or smuggling food from China. Hence, the response of supply in reaction to shortages of consumer goods was quicker and more flexible in North Korea than in other former socialist countries. Third, the North Korean authorities are known to have eliminated retail price subsidies in the July 1st Measures in 2002 to reduce state expenditures. [4] This policy implies an official recognition of the open nature of inflation.

The dominance of open inflation in North Korea suggests that the effect of full price liberalisation on inflation should be significantly smaller. Open inflation's continued existence for two decades implies that most of the monetary overhang in North Korea has disappeared. The elimination of retail price subsidies in 2002 contrasts with the cases of the Soviet Union and most of the Eastern European socialist countries, where retail price subsidies were abolished only when prices were liberalised. Hence, North Korea is unlikely to experience a substantial one-time price increase when prices are liberalised.

The channels of food supply are significantly diverse, with a dominant role played by markets. Food is supplied to the population from both the domestic and external sectors. The agricultural products of collective farms are procured by the government, which subsequently delivers them to government distribution centres for rationing. The government is also responsible for the rationing of food received from international organisations and from other countries in the form of foreign aid. Finally, various state institutions as well as individual firms import food, mainly from China. Individual institutions and firms must pay hard currency to purchase food abroad or make barter transactions, notably between natural resources and food. Hence, only those institutions and firms that have access to hard currency and exportable goods are able to import food. Food available at markets is sourced from private plots, smuggling and imports. Individuals visit China to purchase food for sale in North Korea at a profit. There are certain limits on the export of rice applied by the Chinese customs office, but by paying bribes North Koreans can carry more rice than the amount specified by the regulations. Food sold in markets is primarily supplied by individuals, but there are some reports that collective farms are able to make market sales of agricultural products that remain after government procurement. In addition, some rationed food is sold in markets. For example, some families who receive rationed rice sell it in markets and buy corn instead because the latter is cheaper but has a longer shelf life than rice.

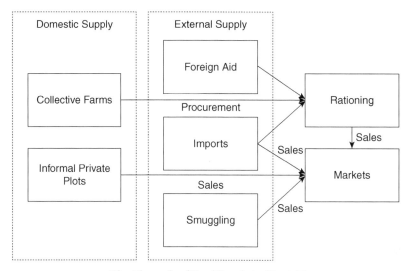

FIGURE 3.1 The Channels of Food Supply in North Korea

The share of the North Korean population regularly receiving rationed food is not exactly known. Government officials, the military and workers at core firms are known to receive food rationing regularly, although the amount of rationing may not be sufficient for sustenance of at least some part of the households belonging to this group. Interviews with North Korean refugees working in a special category of firms, such as Kimchaek Iron and Steel Company, suggest that there are different amounts of food rationing, depending on circumstances. According to reports from a refugee who escaped from North Korea in 2003, food was rationed irregularly, say, once every two or three months. In contrast, according to another refugee who left North Korea in 2010, food rationing was regular and increased to 15 kg per month in 2008 when Kim Jong-il visited Kimchaek Iron and Steel Company in a form of Spot Guidance.[5] A refugee who previously worked for a military unit reported that food rationing was regular until he left North Korea in 2010. In contrast, according to reports from a refugee who worked at an institution in charge of food rationing, food rationing from the government virtually stopped from 1996.

Instead, some companies and institutions that managed to import food in return for exports of natural resources and fish, etc., rationed such imported food to their workers. According to Table 2.18, only 24.4 and 13.0 per cent of food and consumer goods, respectively, are distributed by official channels such as rationing and the state retail network. These suggest a one-time increase in prices through the abolition of food rationing would not be substantial.

Applications to North Korea

It is likely that price liberalisation in North Korea will lead to a moderate, one-time increase in prices. However, it is possible that the political economic nature of such a policy would pose a significant threat to the sustainability of the transition process in North Korea. Unlike in most transition economies in Eastern Europe and the former Soviet republics, food rationing has traditionally been a more important mechanism of distributing food in North Korea than the purchase of food at state retail shops. The PDS of food broke down in the mid- and the late 1990s, but there are still those who rely on food rationing. Moreover, they are more likely to be government officials and workers in large, core companies. Although those who rely on food rationing are a minority of the total population, they might be able to effectively block the continuation of the transition process if they become worse off because of price liberalisation.

Gradual price liberalisation is likely to be preferred by the North Korean authorities when they decide to make the transition to a market economy. Food rationing is an effective control mechanism for the population. By attaching the access to food to their job and official residence, the North Korean authorities are able to monitor the work and life of the people. In addition, by targeting some part of the population, food rationing is less costly than retail price subsidies on food. Hence, the current political system will be damaged less if the authorities provide food to their key supporters at the same prices as before. Gradual price liberalisation is also attractive on economic grounds because, by allowing the reselling of food at markets, it improves the Pareto efficiency as much as full-price liberalisation would do (Lau et al., 2000).

Full price liberalisation would be a better policy option if the current North Korean regime were to collapse and the new authorities were to cooperate with or be represented by South Korea in implementing policies for transition to a market economy. This is because a need to take account of the political impacts of price liberalisation might diminish in the case, as above. The majority of the North Korean population is likely to support the elimination of the privilege enjoyed by government officials. In addition, financial resources provided by South Korea could be utilised to increase the salaries of those who previously relied on food rationing and to enable them to purchase food and consumer goods in markets. Additional benefits of full price liberalisation would include a reduction in costs involved in operating food rationing and the facilitation of institutional transparency.

3.2.b Trade Liberalisation

Initial Conditions in North Korea

The concerns of negative value-added and an increase in unemployment are less relevant to North Korea than to East European transition countries. The socialist economic system of North Korea has virtually collapsed. A large number of firms are unable to pay wages to their workers. Estimates suggest that the capacity utilisation rate of North Korean firms has been between 20 and 30 per cent in the 1990s and the 2000s (Daily NK, 2008).[6] Approximately 23 per cent of workers in a typical North Korean firm are involved in market activities instead of working in official workplaces (See Table 2.19). Although estimates of unemployment rates for North Korea are not available, one expects that they are substantially high. Interviews with North Korean refugees suggest that a number of men are at home because of the closure of firms but that their wives work in markets as informal traders. The dominance of female traders in the markets is influenced at least partially by heavier regulation on male involvement in informal

Table 3.3 *Comparison of Wages of North Korean Workers*

	Monthly wages (US$)	Ratio (KIC=1)
Kaesong Industrial Complex, North Korea	137.9	1
Chinese workers	400	2.9
Vietnam/Myanmar workers	238–285	1.7–2.1

Source: Kim and Jung (2015)
Notes: Wages of North Korean Workers in Dandong, China, include subsistence costs and administration costs such as visa processing fees. The original figures were in yuan, which were converted to US dollars using the exchange rate between US dollars and the Chinese yuan in June 2014. Wages other than for the KIC are for workers in the textile and clothes-making industry.

activities and by the traditional culture of despising trade conducted by men.[7]

North Korea's trade liberalisation should focus on increases in international competitiveness. Based on data from foreign trade, there are two main industries that could be internationally competitive. The extractive industry is the prime one in terms of potential for international competitiveness. It is known that North Korea possesses abundant natural resources, although no reliable statistics on the exact amount of reserves are available.[8] The textile and clothes-making industry is also believed to be competitive. The advantages of this industry are based on relatively low wages, given the skills of the workers. The clothes-making industry has been operating as an out-sourcing base for orders from South Korea, China and Europe.

Table 3.3 compares the wages of North Korean workers with those of Chinese, Vietnamese and Myanmar workers. The KIC was an industrial park inside North Korea in which South Korean firms hired North Korean workers in a city called Kaesong, located 60 km away from Seoul. The KIC was closed down in January 2016 by the decision of the South Korean government in reaction to North Korea's fourth nuclear test and long-range ballistic missile launch. Just before the closure of KIC, it housed 124 South Korean companies which employed over 54,000 North Korean workers. The monthly wage for workers in the KIC in 2013 was US$137.90. Chinese employees working in China receive, on average, US$400 per month, three times higher than the monthly salary of North Korean workers earned in the KIC. Monthly wages of workers in Vietnam and Myanmar are also higher than for North Korean workers by 42–52 per cent. Hence, the wages of North Korean workers can be regarded as being internationally competitive. On this basis, some labour-intensive industries can develop fast.

Trade liberalisation in North Korea should not undermine wage competitiveness. Rapid increases in wages would make it more difficult for the North Korean economy to catch up with other countries. During the catch-up period, the development of the North Korean economy should be based on price competitiveness supported by low wages. One condition for maintaining wage competitiveness is labour market flexibility. In other words, labour markets should allow wages to be determined by supply and demand. Minimum wage laws that stipulate wages to be paid above the equilibrium level undermines wage competitiveness. Another condition involves adopting exchange rates that are compatible with price competitiveness. That is, if North Korea adopts a fixed exchange rate regime, it should maintain a significantly undervalued currency for a sustained period in order to encourage exports based on price competitiveness.

Applications to North Korea

Trade liberalisation would be supported by the majority of the North Korean population because it would decrease the price of food and consumer goods. Currently, the bulk of food and consumer goods are imported from China. Both government institutions and firms are involved in importing food. Shuttle traders are also active in trading food and consumer goods not only for their own consumption but also for sale within North Korea. However, import prices for food and consumer goods are often higher than the sum of prices for the same commodities transacted in China and a normal margin for importers, partially because of the risks involved in doing business with North Korea and because of corruption in trade. According to surveys of Chinese companies trading with North Korean institutions and firms, 7 per cent of sales income is spent on average bribes and other related costs that are normally paid to North Korean brokers and individuals who have the authority to decide on trade matters (Kim and Jung, 2015). Trade liberalisation can decrease such costs by facilitating competition and by eliminating the risks attached to doing business with North Korea. It would also help to reduce corruption by making institutions behave in a more transparent way.

Trade liberalisation should start with abolishing the waku system. That is, any registered companies should be allowed to export and import commodities. In addition, non-tariff measures should be reduced. However, certain restrictions on trade can be applied to exports of certain commodities, such as natural resources. Otherwise, there is a risk that these natural minerals will be extracted too rapidly and sold at too low a price during the initial period of transition. Another policy on trade liberalisation is to abolish restrictions on specific countries as trading partners. Currently, South Korean products cannot be imported into North Korea. The abolishment of such restrictions should be mutually agreed upon and executed by both trading partners. Tariffs on imported goods should not be too excessive, and should be determined with consideration for various factors such as effect on inflation, revenue and domestic industry. In general, though, tariffs should not be employed against the promotion of openness of the economy. Lastly, the North Korean currency, the won, should be made convertible, and a proper exchange rate system should be established.

Like price liberalisation, the speed of trade liberalisation will be affected by which of the two Koreas will implement it. If the North Korean authorities decide to liberalise trade, they are likely to prefer a gradualist approach with some government control on trade, which would reduce over a relatively long time span. In contrast, full trade liberalisation would be preferred if the South Korean authorities were to exert influence on such a policy change. In such a case, South Korean trade policy would be used as a benchmark for North Korea's trade liberalisation.

With regard to the speed of trade liberalisation, it must be implemented in a way that will not undermine the price competitiveness of North Korean exports. The lack of domestically produced food and basic consumer goods implies that rapid trade liberalisation is likely to increase the cost of living for North Koreans. North Koreans would have to purchase food and other goods imported from foreign countries whose prices would likely be higher than those for domestically produced food and goods. As a consequence, there will be pressure to increase wages. There are two possible ways to prevent wages from increasing rapidly in response to higher prices for imported food and consumer goods.

First, tariffs imposed on imported food and basic consumer goods, particularly from China, should be sufficiently low. Prices for food and goods imported from China must be lower than those for food and goods imported from South Korea and Japan. As a result, the pressure to increase wages would be lower if food and other goods were imported from China rather than from South Korea or Japan. Of course, lower tariffs on imported food and goods would mean less protection for North Korean agriculture and consumer goods industries. However, the large difference in per capita income between China and North Korea would provide ample opportunities for North Korean industries to grow on the basis of price competitiveness and to enable them to compete with Chinese firms.

Second, wage subsidies could be utilised for financial support of households without undermining the price competitiveness of North Korean goods. By receiving such subsidies, North Korean firms would be able to produce goods at lower cost. If the two Koreas cooperate, South Korea could consider providing financial resources for such wage subsidies. Alternatively, subsidies could be given for necessary consumer goods, including food. Such in-kind subsidies would be preferable to monetary subsidies in terms of disinflation because in-kind subsidies would increase supply or reduce demand, whereas monetary subsidies would increase demand in the markets.

3.2.c   Exchange Rate Regime

Initial Conditions in North Korea

North Korea traditionally employs three exchange rates: basic exchange rates, exchange rates for trade and exchange rates for tourism. Basic exchange rates apply to the conversion of North Korean economic statistics in North Korean currency to those in international currency, and differ from the rates used for trade and for tourism. It is said that the most important exchange rate is that used for trade, which is regarded as the official rate.

However, exchange rates at informal markets became more important for everyday transactions than official ones (Lee et al., 2012). Informal currency markets are prevalent in North Korea, where the North Korean won is traded for US dollars and Chinese yuan. These markets began to emerge in the 1990s when the economy experienced a severe crisis. In 1992, US$1 was equivalent to 80 to 100 North Korean won. Reflecting higher inflation in North Korea than in the Unites States, the won began to lose value over time. In 2003, it climbed to 1,000 won per US$1, and reached 3,500 to 3,900 before the currency reform at the end of 2009. In November 2009, North Korea implemented a currency reform in which the old and new currencies were transacted at 100:1. A plunge in the exchange rate during 2010 reflected the effect of that policy. However, exchange rates rapidly began to climb. During 2014–2015, the ratio of the exchange rate at the informal currency markets to the official exchange rate was around 1:8,000. As of this writing, it stands at US$1 to 8,100 to 8,300 won (Daily NK, 12 Feb 2016). In contrast to informal exchange rates, the official exchange rate showed little variation from 1996 to 2002: US$1 was worth 2.1 to 2.3 won. After 1 July 2002, the official exchange rate was adjusted to reflect inflation, and US$1 was

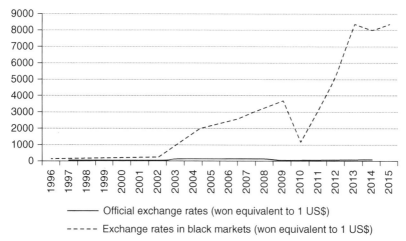

Official exchange rates (won equivalent to 1 US$)

----- Exchange rates in black markets (won equivalent to 1 US$)

FIGURE 3.2 Official and Informal Market Exchange Rates in North Korea, 1996–2015
Sources: Daily NK; Korean Statistical Information Service

exchanged for 90 to 150 North Korean won. Figure 3.2 displays the trend of the official and informal market exchange rates from 1996 to 2015.

Some argue that the dollarisation or yuanisation of the North Korean economy is already underway (Lee et al., 2012). That is, economic agents utilise hard currency instead of the North Korean won for transactions, especially for those involving large amounts of money. For example, households who want to buy an apartment in Pyongyang are requested to pay the price in US dollars rather than North Korean won. It is natural that the economy, which lacks production capacity and experiences high inflation but is open to external trade, finds it safer to employ international currency rather than the domestic currency for economic transactions. In particular, the currency reform in 2009 imparted an important lesson to economic agents: maintaining savings in North Korean currency is quite dangerous because the authorities forcibly take savings in won by refusing to allow the old money to be converted into new money, beyond a certain amount. This experience appears to have accelerated the process of dollarisation or yuanisation of the economy.

| | EURO | ERM II | Fixed exchange rate | | Managed floating | | Flexible floating | |
			Currency board	Traditional pegged one	Limited band	Managed floating	Broad band	Free floating
Czech Rep.					▒▒▒ →(May 1997)			
Estonia	◄ (Jan. 2011)	(June 2004)						
Hungary				▒▒▒ →(Feb. 2008)				
Lithuania	◄ (Jan. 2015)	(June 2004)						
Poland				▒▒▒ →(April 2000)				
Slovenia	◄ (Jan. 2007)	(June 2004)						

FIGURE 3.3 The Patterns of Exchange Rate Regime Movements of Some Selected Transition Countries
Sources: European Central Bank (http://www.ecb.europa.eu/euro/changeover/html/index.en.html); IMF (2014).
Notes: (1) The month and the year in parentheses refer to when the change in the exchange rate regime occurred. (2) The currency of the Czech Republic floated freely during the early 2010s but its exchange rate regime reversed to the managed floating one from Nov. 2013 according to IMF (2014).

Applications to North Korea

The first step in reform regarding exchange rates is to abolish the official exchange rate set by the authorities and let it be determined primarily by the markets. At the same time, an appropriate exchange rate regime should be introduced. The literature on the performance of transition countries suggests that countries adopting a fixed exchange rate regime experienced faster growth than those that introduced a floating exchange rate (Fischer et al., 1996; Kim and Pirtilla, 2006). One possible reason is that the fixed exchange rate regime facilitated economic stabilisation and thus promoted productive economic activities.

Figure 3.3 presents patterns of the movements of the exchange regimes in some advanced-transition economies. Among six countries, five started their transition with a fixed exchange rate regime. The only exception is Slovenia. Over time, most of these countries followed two distinct patterns: the first one was to adopt a more flexible exchange rate regime by moving to the flexible floating exchange regime; the second was to move toward a less-flexible exchange regime, namely adopting the Euro (Estonia, Slovenia, and Lithuania) following the membership of the

European Exchange Mechanism II (ERM II). These patterns can be explained in terms of the economies' plans to adopt the euro. The flexible exchange rate regime is a sound policy because it allows a country to find a sustainable equilibrium exchange rate on which the euro could be introduced. An alternative is to test the stability of an exchange rate at a certain level by adopting the fixed exchange rate regime for an extended period. If it is successful, the exchange rate is regarded as being a defendable, and perhaps sustainable, rate. Hence, the currency can be permanently pegged to the euro at such a rate.

The above patterns shed important light for possible currency conversion between South Korea and North Korea. Finding the exchange rate of the North Korean won would be a task similar to that of the East European transition economies if North Korea were to seek monetary integration with South Korea. The common characteristic of the East European economies is that they sought a pegged rate through a market mechanism for an extended period, regardless of the type of the exchange rate regime. This is distinctively different from the currency conversion method used between the West German mark and East German mark. The conversion rate in Germany was decided without a period during which market exchange rates could be established. There are numerous criticisms of the conversion rate between West German mark and East German mark having been established at 1:1, for flow variables such as income and pension (Neumann, 1992; Sell, 1995; Lange and Pugh, 1998). That decision was made on political rather than economic grounds. The West German authorities were afraid of the possibility of mass migration from East Germany to West Germany if they did not grant substantial favour to the East German mark against the West German mark. However, other types of subsidies (e.g. wage subsidies) could be provided if the purpose of the subsidies were to prevent mass migration (Akerlof et al., 1991). As a result of substantial increases in wages in excess of the productivity of East German workers, a number of East German firms went bankrupt, even some months after reunification (Roland, 2000).

If North Korea makes a transition without taking account of imminent integration with South Korea, North Korea is advised to adopt a fixed exchange rate regime for an initial period of transition, for the following reasons. First, a fixed exchange rate is effective at reducing expected inflation. North Korea has been experiencing relatively high open inflation for more than a decade. Hence, economic stabilisation could be facilitated by adoption of a fixed regime. Second, a fixed exchange rate could serve as a nominal anchor for stabilisation policies. During the initial period of transition, North Korea would likely suffer from the underdevelopment of money markets and associated institutions that are required for the conduct of sound monetary policy. A nominal anchor based on a fixed exchange rate would increase economic activities by enhancing certainty in economic environments. Following this period, North Korea would need to move toward a floating rate. Otherwise, any real appreciation of the North Korean currency would undermine the competitiveness of North Korean industries. If an equilibrium exchange rate is more or less established, a permanent peg to South Korean won could be introduced. However, if necessary, a system similar to ERM II could be tried before any decision is made on a permanent currency conversion rate between the two Koreas.

Pegging of the North Korean won to a hard currency during the initial period of transition would require a substantial devaluation of the North Korean currency. This would make the exchange rate more defendable, and economic growth based on exports would be promoted. However, the lack of hard currency in North Korea indicates that pegging would not be durable, and the currency may be exposed to speculation. Hence, international help would be necessary to maintain the fixed exchange rate regime. The creation of a currency stabilisation fund or swap arrangements with other governments might be considered for such a purpose.

Pegging immediately after abolition of the socialist system of exchange rates would require an understanding of a sustainable exchange rate. Although informal market exchange rates in North

Korea could give some guidance, these are usually overshot. One rule of thumb is to employ the exchange rate that equals the estimate of North Korea's GDP per capita in North Korean won to that in US dollars. The Bank of Korea estimates North Korean GDP per capita only in South Korean won. Although the United Nations reports North Korea's GNI both in North Korean currency and US dollars, the reliability of the former data is not high. For example, the United Nations reports the GNI per capita of North Korea in 2013 as 66,907 North Korean won,[9] but we understand this figure to be lower than the monthly expenditure of a member of a typical North Korean household. From the surveys of North Korean refugees, typical North Korean households of four members spent about 300,000 North Korean won per month in the same year. This translates into 900,000 North Korean won per person per annum. Assuming that the share of consumption in North Korea's GNI is 70 per cent, the GNI per capita of North Korea is estimated to be 1,285,714 North Korean won. We estimated North Korean GDP per capita in 2013 to be US$749 (Table 2.6). Hence, an exchange rate that takes into account the value of the North Korean won per US$1 is 1,716. This is much higher than the official exchange rate for 2013, but substantially lower than is reflected in informal market rates.

3.2.d Establishment of Monetary and Fiscal Policy

Initial Conditions in North Korea

The North Korean financial system follows the principle of the mono-bank system adopted in other socialist countries. Unlike the two-tier banking system in a market economy, where the central bank and commercial banks are separated, the monobank system combines the roles of the central bank and commercial bank into one. North Korea's central bank, Chosun Joongang Eunhaeng, is based on the socialist banking system.

There were recent attempts to adopt the two-tier banking system in North Korea. For instance, it first revised the Central Bank Act in September 2004 and adopted the Commercial Banks Act in January 2006. These two acts laid the legal foundation for transforming the financial system from a monobank to a two-tier banking system. However, there is little evidence that commercial banks currently operate in North Korea. One of the reasons appears to be the lack of lending resources. The low level of trust in the banking system in North Korea encourages economic agents to keep saving in cash, but not in the bank.

The underdevelopment of the banking system for households can be observed in data from the surveys of North Korean refugees. According to Table 3.4, only 4.9 per cent of North Koreans had any experience with utilising banks at least once in their life. In contrast, the share of households that borrowed money from informal creditors amounted to 11.1 per cent in the period from 1996 to 2008, and this share tended to increase over time.

A number of other types of banks exist in North Korea. Chosun Trade Bank (Chosun Mooyeok Eunhaeng) is a bank that addresses foreign trade. This type of specialised bank has existed in other socialist countries. However, unlike many former socialist economies, North Korea has small, specialised banks either for international finance or for equity joint financial institutions. North Korea began establishing specialised banks in the late 1970s. This was related to the hard currency crisis, which led to its default on its foreign debt. Hence, the authorities decentralised foreign trade to allow various state institutions to conduct foreign trade on their own. State institutions such as the Workers' Party, the army and the cabinet established their own banks to address the demands of their external businesses. This led to the establishment of some small banks specialising in settlements involving foreign trade. North Korean authorities also encouraged foreign investment, especially from ethnic Koreans living in Japan who supported North Korea over South Korea. Some specialised banks were established to address the demand for currency conversion for this foreign investment.[10] In addition, equity joint financial institutions were established, reflecting efforts by North Korean authorities to attract hard currency.

Table 3.4 *The Experiences of Utilising Banks and Informal Credit of North Korean Refugees*

		Total respondents (%)	Refugees who left before 2000 (%)	Refugees who left in 2000–2006 (%)	Refugees who left in 2007 (%)	Refugees who left in 2008 (%)
Experience with utilising bank	Yes	4.9	2.4	10.8	8.3	3.3
	No	95.1	97.6	89.2	91.7	96.7
Experience with utilising informal credits	Yes	11.1	0.0	5.4	25.0	19.2
	No	88.9	100.0	94.6	75.0	80.8

Source: The surveys of North Korean refugees conducted in 2007 and 2009 (refer to Section 2.3 for details of these surveys)

The traditional North Korean fiscal system follows the Soviet-style model in which the state budget allocates financial resources between industries. However, there are some qualitative differences between the Soviet fiscal system and the traditional North Korean system. First, the share of fiscal revenue in GDP was higher in North Korea than in the Soviet Union: the average of annual share of fiscal revenue in GDP from 1970 to 1987 was approximately 70 per cent in North Korea, while that in the Soviet Union in 1980 was 65 per cent (Kim, 2009a). Second, the share of expenditures on financing the national economy, including capital investment in the economy, was also higher in North Korean than in the Soviet Union. For example, the share of total budget expenditures allocated to financing the national economy was 60.5 per cent in North Korea in 1980, but the share in the Soviet Union from 1965 to 1980 ranged from 40 to 55 per cent. These differences suggest that the traditional North Korean economy was more centralised than that in the Soviet Union.

The North Korean fiscal system began to collapse in the 1990s, affected by the economic crisis in the same period. Both the share of fiscal revenue in GDP and the share of expenditures on the national economy declined in this period (Kim, 2009a).[11] For instance, the share of expenditures on financing the national economy of North Korea decreased from 60.5 per cent of total expenditures in 1980 to 20 to 40 per cent in the period starting with the 1990s. The share of fiscal revenue dropped to 13 to 24 per cent of GDP starting in 2003, although the reasons for such a large decrease are not clearly understood (Kim, 2009a). One suggested reason was that the North Korean economy fragmented into different institutions (the Workers' Party, the army, the cabinet and regional governments) and the state budget began to reflect only the sector managed by the cabinet. This indicates that fiscal policy in North Korea fails to play the role of resource allocation amid severe economic crisis and disintegration of the economic system.

Applications to North Korea

The transition of the banking system in North Korea should start with the introduction of a two-tier banking system. That is, the current central bank of North Korea should be split into two parts: one being the central bank, which is responsible for monetary policy and for overseeing banking, and the other being commercial banks, which lend money to firms and households and receive their deposits. The household savings bank (Jeogeumso), which obtains savings from households under the central bank, should also be separated from the central bank and made into a commercial bank.

The next step in the transformation of the banking system should be to restructure the commercial banking system. The commercial banks should include the household savings bank, a foreign trade bank and specialised banks dealing primarily with international finance and investment. Initially, these banks would be state-owned, but they should subsequently be privatised. However, given the small size of the many banks – especially the specialised banks – some banks should be merged into larger banks. Recapitalisation, restructuring and privatisation of these banks would occur eventually, although it would take some time to complete the process of establishing private commercial banks. During this process, some banks would likely be sold to outsiders, including South Koreans and foreigners, although this issue may cause a heated debate in North Korea, depending on the specific circumstances of North Korea's transition. At the same time, bank licensing should be given to newly entering banks to encourage competition among banks.

Creation of money markets and securities markets is also necessary. The interest rates should be determined in money markets, which is the central bank's basis for conducting monetary policy. The development of stock markets would be heavily affected by privatisation of state-owned enterprises. The convertibility of North Korean currency and the adoption of an appropriate exchange rate regime in accordance with the market economy system would be the precondition to the development of money markets and securities markets, especially for foreign investors.

The transformation of the fiscal system would require changes in the tax system and government expenditures. These changes would be more or less routine, following the examples of previous transition economies. The most difficult part would be reduction of the budget deficit. The amount of the budget deficit in North Korea is unknown, but high inflation during the 1990s and the 2000s implies that the fiscal deficit was substantial and was financed by printing more money. However, fiscal stability would require not only administrative changes but also the recovery of the economy. Furthermore, the informal economy, which tended to increase rapidly during the transition period in Eastern Europe and the former Soviet republics, prevented tax revenues from increasing. Hence, certain measures should be put in place to ensure the formalisation of currently informal economic activities. These measures could include application of low or no taxes on small businesses, one-stop procedures for business registration and the provision of subsidies for the creation of small businesses, with the condition that they utilise bank services for business transactions.

3.3   PRIVATISATION AND NEW ENTRY OF FIRMS

3.3.a   Privatisation

Initial Conditions in North Korea

Three main differences exist between North Korea and other former socialist economies. These differences are related to the structure of firms and the industry. First, the agricultural sector in North Korea is larger than those in Eastern Europe were in the 1980s, but smaller than that in China before the country started reforms in 1978. The contribution of agriculture to GDP is 23 to 30 per cent of the total GDP of North Korea from 1991 to 2013 (Table 2.5; Bank of Korea 2014). The proportion of the population working on farms in 2008 was 36.8 per cent of the total population (Bank of Korea, 2014).

By contrast, 71 and 13 per cent of the population in China in 1978 and in Russia in 1990, respectively, were employed in agriculture. This fact implies that the transition strategy for North Korea should be different from that for China and Eastern Europe. North Korea should find an optimal combination of the Chinese transition strategy, based on agricultural reform, and the Eastern European transition strategy, based on privatisation and restructuring of SOEs.

Second, the crisis in North Korean industry is more severe than conditions in Eastern Europe and China before their transitions to market economies. Long-term stagnation from the 1950s to the 1980s and the serious North Korean economic crisis in the 1990s resulted in a virtual standstill for a number of firms. The current capacity utilisation rate of North Korean industries is estimated at 20 to 30 per cent, and much capital equipment is old and obsolete.[12] Some refugees complained that the machines used in Kimchaek Iron and Steel Company, one of the most important firms in North Korea, were almost scrap metal. A former worker in a North Korean construction firm said that because of an insufficient number of shovels, many workers used their bare hands in digging soil. Eastern European countries did not experience such serious crises before their collapse. China's transition did not occur in a period of economic crisis but in normal economic conditions, despite the country's low productivity.

Third, North Korean households rely more on the informal economy than on the official economy for their income. An informal economy existed in Eastern Europe and China, but North Korea's is considerably larger. As discussed in Chapter 2, the share of informal income in total household income in North Korea is 58 to 74 per cent, compared with 16 per cent of the income of Soviet households from 1969 to 1990 (Kim, 2003). Thus, Eastern European countries could undergo transition from the official, but inefficient, SOEs to the official and efficient private industry. The growth of the Chinese economy is based on a shift of the industrial structure from agriculture to manufacturing. North Korea's transition should include changes from the informal private economy to the formal private economy, as well as changes from inefficient SOEs to efficient private firms.

North Korea has not provided a list of its firms since the 1990s, so researchers have employed alternative sources, such as information on firms as revealed through North Korean mass media. Lee and Lee (2014) compiled a list of North Korean firms based on two North Korean newspapers from 2000 to 2013, and found a total of 2,891 firms in North Korea. Out of these firms, 2,258 are manufacturing firms, 261 are power plants and 360 firms are mining firms. The study shows that 55 and 45 per cent of the manufacturing firms belong to light and heavy industries, respectively. In terms of the number of firms, those that manufacture food, beverages and tobacco are the largest, followed by textile and clothing firms. Only 215 firms were established or constructed between 2000 and 2013.[13] Only 40 and 60 per cent of the 2,891 firms engaged in investment and production activities, respectively. These findings reveal severe difficulties in the North Korean industrial sector.

The most recent data reported by a North Korean official source indicate that the total number of manufacturing firms was 5,489 in 1987 (Kim et al., 1987).[14] The discrepancies between 5,489 firms in 1987 and 2,258 firms in the 2000s do not necessarily mean that the number of firms decreased during this period. A likely explanation is that Lee and Lee (2014) underestimated the number of firms because it counted only firms that appeared in North Korean newspapers.

The majority of North Korean manufacturing firms appear to be small. Another North Korean official source reveals the distribution of North Korean firms located in Pyongyang in 1986 in terms of the number of workers. This finding shows that 32.1 per cent of the firms employ fewer than 100 workers, whereas the share of manufacturing firms that employ more than 500 workers is 17.6 per cent. The weighted average of the number of workers in such firms is 426.[15]

We can compare the aforementioned figures with the estimated number of workers based on the number of manufacturing firms and the number of people working in the manufacturing sector. According to the North Korean population survey of 2008, the number of people who work in the manufacturing sector was 2.89 million. By dividing this figure by the number of manufacturing firms, we can obtain an average number of workers per firm, which is 525. This is higher than the estimated number of workers per firm in Pyongyang, but the discrepancies are small. On this basis we can conclude that the average number of workers in manufacturing firms is approximately 400 or 500.

Applications to North Korea

The privatisation method will differ depending on the scenario of transition to a market economy. If North Korean authorities initiate such transition by themselves, they are unlikely to implement rapid and wholesale privatisation that involves large-scale enterprises. The speed of privatisation of such enterprises will be gradual, as shown by the experience of China. Furthermore, insufficient financial resources will increase the difficulty of restructuring. Given these problems, North Korea should consider focusing on the privatisation of small firms and liberalising the creation of new private firms, and should put aside the problem of large-scale privatisation for a later time.

The privatisation of SOEs following the unification of the two Koreas will be speedier than if it is implemented by the current North Korean authorities. Moreover, improvement in firm efficiency due to privatisation will be high because an ideal privatisation method can be selected under such a scenario. Speed, efficiency and fairness should be considered when selecting the appropriate privatisation methods, but emphasis on each of the three can differ. For example, speed is more important than efficiency in privatising small and medium companies. A speedy privatisation can provide opportunities for employment and contribute to social and economic stabilisation. By contrast, efficiency improvements should be a top priority in the privatisation of large firms. A hasty privatisation may fail and lead to a plunge in North Korea's industrial output because many of these large firms would not be viable without substantial investment and restructuring. Fairness should always be considered: privatisation should be viewed as fair by North Koreans insofar as it provides additional benefits to North Koreans vis-à-vis South Koreans.

Small firms that employ fewer than 100 workers can be privatised quickly by auction, recognition of *de facto* ownership and insider privatisation. The objects of small-scale privatisation will include cafeterias, kiosks, small shops and small manufacturing firms. Privatisation of medium-sized enterprises that employ more than 100 workers but fewer than, say, 250 or 500 workers may take longer, given the complexities associated with the transition. Privatisation by managers and employees who understand the characteristics of the firms and their environments is preferable because it can be implemented in a speedy manner. Following insider privatisation, auction to outsiders restricted to North Koreans can be considered as a subsequent measure of privatisation. The ownership of small and medium companies as a result of privatisation should be acquired by North Koreans rather than by South Koreans. Auctions restricted to North Koreans should be implemented for this purpose. If the transfer of ownership fails at the stage of such a restricted auction, South Koreans should be permitted to participate in subsequent auctions. If no bidders emerge, such firms should be closed down.

As regards large enterprises, a privatisation method to improve firm performance should be considered the default option. This approach indicates that core outsider ownership, including sale to outsiders, particularly to South Koreans and foreigners, is the best option. However, this method of privatisation may be perceived by North Koreans as unfair. One possible option is to combine sales to outsiders as a main privatisation method, with voucher privatisation as a secondary method. The proportion of shares obtained through vouchers in total shares could be allowed up to 49 per cent, and more than 50 per cent of the total shares could be sold to core outsiders. The case of Polish voucher privatisation should be considered in order to ensure that vouchers are exchanged only with shares of privatisation funds. This approach is expected to increase concentration of ownership.

Large-scale privatisation will be less important in North Korea than in most Eastern European countries and former Soviet republics because of the low proportion of North Korean firms that will be viable and transferable to private owners. The viability of these firms should be evaluated at the initial stage and classified into the following categories: (1) firms privatised within one or two years; (2) firms privatised within three or more years; and (3) firms that need to be closed down immediately. Labour-intensive firms that produce final goods, particularly firms that export goods abroad, are likely to belong to the first category. For example, firms that manufacture clothing are known to be competitive in the world market and can be viable in market environments. Most of the firms that are related to the extraction of mineral resources may be classified in the second category. Some firms in the military sector and heavy industries may also be included in this category. However, given the long-term stagnation of the economy, a larger proportion of North Korean enterprises will belong to the third category than was true of Eastern European countries and former Soviet republics.

3.3.b   Creation of New Enterprises

Initial Conditions in North Korea

The industrial sector in North Korea has virtually collapsed, except for some heavy, defence and garment industries. Many firms are still at a standstill because of a lack of inputs and financial resources. The lack of investment for an extended period indicates that a large number of firms suffer from obsolete equipment (Lee and Lee, 2014). Given this finding, one can argue that the majority of firms should be allowed to go bankrupt because the creation of new firms is more important than the privatisation of SOEs.

Despite the maintenance of state ownership of productive assets, small-scale informal privatisation continues to take place, particularly in the service sector. For example, an SOE enters into an informal contract with individuals who pay the firm for the use of its properties, such as trucks and buses. These individuals start a transport business and pay part of their profits to the firm. This contract appears to place the individuals in a position somewhere between an owner and an employed manager. From the legal point of view, the assets belong to the state property and thus should not be sold off. However, the individuals are likely to regard such properties as their own because they tend to pay to the firms a substantial amount of money for their use for business. In a similar manner, some cafeterias, kiosks and public baths that were previously owned and operated by SOEs are informally contracted out to individuals who possess or mobilise sufficient financial resources to run them.

The large informal economy of North Korea provides various opportunities for making money. Producing and supplying goods and services outside the planned sector is one of these opportunities. The majority of activities in the informal economy involve trading rather than manufacturing goods, mainly because of the high risk of investment in the manufacturing industry. Most of the goods supplied to the informal economy are basic ones, such as food, drinks and clothing. Some reports indicated that the division of labour in the informal economy facilitates increases in productivity, which may have been affected by Kim Jong-un's lenient approach toward the informal economy, as compared with that practised during his father's era (Chang et al., 2014). These informal economic activities may develop into self-employed and entrepreneurial businesses when the transition to a market economy begins and private ownership is introduced.

Applications to North Korea

The development of the North Korean economy depends on the emergence and sustained growth of new firms because the effect of privatisation on economic growth is likely to be small in North Korea. A jump-start is required to encourage the establishment of new firms. Small firms can emerge and grow quickly when property rights are introduced and borrowing constraints are relaxed. The following policies are necessary for this purpose.

First, property rights should be given to private owners on the condition that they have a contract with a firm to use its asset or facility. Contracts and practices are of various types. One classification is close to informal ownership, whereas another resembles a lease. Policy-makers should act quickly and should not devote much time to deciding on ownership. Rather, ownership should be granted on the basis of simple and clear rules, such as the existence of written contract and the amount one paid to use the asset or facility of the firm. If the amount is less than the evaluated worth of the asset or facility, the person can be asked to pay an additional amount to claim its full ownership. Second, unless the transfer of ownership involves a large sum of assets, the courts do not need to get involved. The East German case shows that too much time was devoted to decisions over the ownership of assets through the court system. Unclear property rights undermined the development of firms. Third, the government should provide subsidies or loans to potential self-employed and entrepreneurial businesses to help them overcome borrowing constraints. In addition, they should be allowed to borrow using collaterals, such as privatised houses.

An informal economy should be formalised as soon as possible. For this purpose, the government should streamline the process of registering properties. For example, filing for a simple registration document without the payment of fees should be considered for someone who wishes to open a small firm. One could also propose registration by mail or registration by visiting a residence or nearby place (e.g. a post office). An incentive can be introduced for formal registration and operation of a business. Such incentives may include a lump-sum subsidy paid through the banking institution on the condition that the firm be registered. Additional loans or discounts on interest rates could be tied to use of transaction records in a bank.

A positive growth at the early stage of transition is important. Such growth facilitates productive economic activities and the cooperation of economic agents from a long-term perspective. Conversely, economic crisis and a highly uncertain economy increase the rent-seeking motives of economic agents based on short-sighted views. Comprehensive measures to encourage business activities, particularly the establishment of new businesses, should be introduced immediately when transition begins in North Korea.

3.4   ECONOMIC INTEGRATION WITH SOUTH KOREA

3.4.a   Experiences of Integration and Unification

Several economic integrations occurred in the previous and current centuries. The four prominent cases are provided in Table 3.5. One case refers to a rapid economic integration with political unification. The other three cases, which are yet to reach political unification, achieved a certain degree of economic integration. The German case is an example of rapid economic integration, which took place as a result of the German unification in 1990. The cases of the European Union (EU), the China–Taiwan integration and the China–Hong Kong integration reveal the experiences of gradual integration.

The major driving force of economic integration was the recovery of the historical status of one country. The German case and the two China-related cases belong to this category. The EU is the only example of integration that was pursued without the historical status of having been one country. Nevertheless, the extent of integration is more advanced in the EU than in the two China-related cases. The reasons include the tragic memories of the World Wars, which were strong enough to form an international community beyond national boundaries. Homogeneity in the political and economic systems also contributed to progress in such integration. By contrast, the China–Hong Kong and China–Taiwan relations are complicated, partly because of different political systems and the lack of consensus on the aim of integration. The relationships between China and Taiwan are volatile, possibly because of the experience of the civil war between the communists, led by Mao Zedong, and nationalists,

Table 3.5 *Cases of Unification and Integration*

	West–East Germany	EU	China–Taiwan	China–Hong Kong
Background	Historically one country	Avoiding wars	Historically one country	Historically one country
Political and economic systems at the start of integration	Different political and economic systems	Homogeneous political and economic systems	Different political systems	Different political systems
Market integration (coverage and extent)	Comprehensive and complete integration	Deep and comprehensive (commodities, capital and labour, but some countries apply restrictions on labour movements)	Deep but not comprehensive (free movement of commodities, restricted capital movements but no labour mobility)	Deep and comprehensive, with restrictions (free movement of commodities and capital but restricted labour mobility)
Process of integration	Radical and formal integration	Gradual, following formal stages	Gradual, from informal to formal developments	Gradual, with formal stages
Driving force	Political and economic	Political and economic	Mainly economic, with some political purpose from the Chinese side	Mainly economic, but with political purpose of unification mainly from the Chinese side

Table 3.5 (cont.)

	West–East Germany	EU	China–Taiwan	China–Hong Kong
Stage of integration	Unification	Economic and monetary union	Stage toward FTA and service agreements (finance and labour)	Stage toward FTA and service integration (finance and labour)
Differences in objectives of integration	No difference (unification)	Few differences on economic areas, but differences on the future stage of integration	Difference (unification vs. economic benefits without political integration)	Difference (unification vs. economic benefits with political autonomy)
Main treaties/ MOU	GEMSU	Maastricht Treaty	ECFA	CEPA

led by Chiang Kai-shek. Despite the economic opportunities offered by the Chinese reform in 1979, the Taiwanese government forbade any trade and investment involving mainland China before 2001. Trade and investment were conducted informally between the two, via Hong Kong and the United States.

German unification was completed within a year or so. The five East German states joined the Federal Republic of Germany in 1990 following elections, but the actual process was an absorption of the East by the West. The German Economic, Monetary and Social Union (GEMSU) adopted in May 1990 laid the most important foundation for integration and unification. The EU achieved advanced integration, an economic union where factors of production including capital and labour are free to move and a monetary union in which the common euro currency is used in euro-zone countries. The Maastricht Treaty signed in 1992 played a key role in creating the economic and monetary union. The Economic Cooperation Framework Agreement (ECFA) and the Closer Economic Partnership Arrangement (CEPA) between China and Taiwan and between China and Hong Kong, respectively, stand for limited economic integration. Such a level of integration is far behind that achieved by the EU. The two cases of Chinese integration with Taiwan or Hong Kong are close to the Free Trade Agreement (FTA), with some degree of integration in the service and financial sectors. Table 3.5 summarises the main features of these four cases of unification and integration.

The relationships between South Korea and North Korea are more similar to those between China and Taiwan in terms of political and military tension than to those reflected in the other three cases of integration. Political and economic systems in North Korea are in stark contrast to those in South Korea. Political peculiarities of North Korea and military tension between South Korea and North Korea are not comparable with those in any country that has experienced integration. These circumstances imply that any form of integration between the two Koreas will be either radical, as displayed in Germany, or very slow, as exemplified in China–Taiwan integration.

Several attempts have been made at economic cooperation between South and North Korea. The Sunshine Policy announced by Kim Dae-jung encouraged economic aid and businesses with North Koreans. As a result of this policy, tours to the Kumgang Mountain started in 1998 and the KIC began to operate in 2005. However, the tours to the Kumgang Mountain stopped because a South Korean tourist was shot dead by a North Korean soldier in 2008. The KIC was also closed as a sanction against North Korea in response to its fourth nuclear weapon test and the launch of a long-range ballistic missile in early 2016. These events resulted in the lack of any official economic relationships, including trade between the two Koreas, as of March 2016. This result indicates that progress in economic integration was reversed from 2008 to 2016, and the stage of inter-Korean integration is lower than in the two Chinese-related integrations.

3.4.b   Integration Scenario

The various scenarios of unification of the two Koreas were proposed by scholars and South Korean research institutes (Ahn and Mun, 2007; Choi, 2011; Mun and Yoo, 2012; Lee, ed., 2012; Kim, 2014b). The main factors that determine the type of scenarios are the speed of unification (rapid vs. gradual) and the entity that has the initiative that leads to unification (absorption by South Korea vs. mutual consent of South Korea and North Korea). The four scenarios become possible when these factors are combined. However, the scenario of rapid unification led by North Korea is not realistic at all, leaving three feasible unification scenarios. The first scenario, which is rapid unification in the form of absorption of the North by the South, is similar to the German unification. The second scenario, which is the gradual unification in the form of absorption by the South, is based on temporary political separation between the two Koreas prior to unification (Ahn and Mun, 2007). This unification scenario assumes that the transition of North Korea toward a market economy and its economic integration with South Korea takes places prior to political unification. This   scenario   is   also   called   'one   with   special administration region' or 'two regions with one economic system' (Ahn and Mun, 2007; Lee, ed., 2012; Kim, 2014b).

The third scenario, which is adhered to by the South Korean official unification policy, is based on a gradual and consensual mode of unification. South Korea's official policy for unification, which was initially announced in 1989 and revised in 1994, states that unification should take place step-by-step and should be agreed upon peacefully by both Koreas. The first stage refers to reconciliation and cooperation. The Korean commonwealth, which acknowledges different systems under each of the two governments, is established at the second stage. Complete unification is achieved on the basis of the results of democratic election. North Korean official policy for unification is based on the confederation of the two Koreas. South and North Korea will be transformed into a confederate state, wherein political, diplomatic and military powers are held by each government. The June 15 South–North Joint Declaration, which was announced in 2000, was a result of the first summit between South Korean President Kim Dae-jung and North Korean leader Kim Jong-il. This declaration finds a common element in the unification policies of South and North Korea and states that South and North Korea should recognise the commonality between South Korea's proposal for a complete unification and the North's proposal for a low-level federation.

Under the current political system of North Korea, gradual unification on the basis of mutual consent is theoretically conceivable but practically impossible. The fundamental institutions in South Korea are different from those of North Korea. South Koreans will give up neither democracy nor a market economy to be united with North Korea. Thus, unification actually means the transformation of North Korea's political and economic systems into South Korea's regardless of the speed of transformation. Although the majority of North Koreans may prefer political and economic freedom over dictatorship and socialism, the North Korean leader and the elites are likely to oppose such a transformation. Given the atrocities imposed on

North Koreans, he is likely to lose power and face criminal charges for human rights violations when unification occurs. Furthermore, South Korea's economic capacities far exceed those of North Korea. Given its advantage, South Korea wants to exercise leadership and initiative in the unification process of the two Koreas. The federation of the two Koreas to preserve its own economic system implies the continuous flow of large subsidies from the South to the North because the possibility of economic growth is limited as long as North Korea maintains a socialist economic system. This model of unification is not likely to be accepted by the South Korean electorate.

The above discussion indicates that a gradual and consensual mode of unification is possible only if North Korea adopts a market economy and follows a path toward democratisation. Although the probability of these changes does not appear to be high, they could occur when the current North Korean leader embraces the Chinese style of transition, either voluntarily or as a result of being forced to do so. Alternatively, it is possible that the next leader after the current one may make a decision toward a market economy. Political changes may take place over time through the impacts of market forces on the political regime.

In sum, there are two feasible scenarios for unification, broadly defined. One scenario is radical unification, wherein democracy and market economy are established simultaneously. In this case, South Korean institutions will likely be transplanted into North Korea in a relatively short time. The other scenario is gradual unification on the basis of sequencing; that is, economic transition and integration followed by political unification.[16] Two main sub-scenarios can be proposed under this gradual unification. A North Korean leader may launch a Chinese-style reform prior to political unification (Chinese-style scenario). Alternatively, the current North Korean regime could collapse, which will lead to absorption by South Korea. Yet, this scenario temporarily separates the North from the South and implements policies for transition and integration before eventual unification (Temporary separation scenario). These sub-scenarios are common in that economic transformation occurs with North Korea separated from South Korea for the time being. Thus, we focus on economic policies for integration of the two Koreas in accordance with the two unification scenarios.

3.4.c   Economic Policies for Radical Unification

'Radical unification' refers to the absorption of North Korea by South Korea through the implanting of institutions and mechanisms from South Korea into North Korea in all spheres, including the economy. During this process, most of the economic institutions in North Korea will be transformed and integrated with those in South Korea. Radical unification also means that economic integration and transition take place simultaneously in North Korea in a short-time span. It has also an important political implication: North Koreans become citizens of the unified Korea with full rights to vote.

Kim and Roland (2012) propose various policy measures under the radical unification scenario, followed by the regime collapse in which a power vacuum paralyses the North Korean government. One critical issue that determines policy measures under this scenario is the possibility of a massive inflow of North Korean refugees into South Korea. They argue that closure of the border between the two Koreas violates the constitution of South Korea and fails to respect the human right to settle down and move freely with their fortunate kin to the South. Instead, they propose policies to persuade North Koreans to stay in the North voluntarily, even under this scenario. The most important policy is the provision of incentives and social safety nets on the condition that North Koreans continue to live in North Korea without migrating to South Korea. However, North Koreans should be required to give up such incentives and welfare provisions when they settle in South Korea.

Their proposed economic policies include the distribution of land to all inhabitants of North Korea. Such lands can be used for renting purposes but cannot be sold before a certain minimum period has passed. They also propose the provision of government-guaranteed entrepreneurship loans and a favourable tax system to encourage entrepreneurial activities. North Koreans will be required to use banks in order to obtain such loans. This approach will contribute to the shifting of the domain of economic activities from the informal sector to the formal sector. They also emphasise the importance of facilitating entry into market activity, which should be supported by simple procedures for opening a business and the protection of property rights.

As regards currency conversion, they propose adopting a conversion rate that is determined by market forces. The South Korean won is used in parallel with the North Korean won to facilitate free trade, leading to the establishment of the market exchange rates between the two currencies.[17] The stable exchange rates for a certain period imply that the North Korean won is ready to be converted into South Korean won. This conversion is based on market forces as a way to prevent the negative effects of a currency conversion based on arbitrary decisions.

Kim and Roland (2012) explore the German unification, and they believe that keeping unprofitable firms in operation with government subsidies is less costly than providing a social safety net for the unemployed. Thus, they propose a sequential approach for privatisation and enterprise restructuring. Rapid privatisation is necessary for small shops, restaurants and small enterprises, whereas the majority of manufacturing firms are privatised gradually. As long as these firms produce goods that are sold in the domestic market, they are allowed to operate. After a certain length of time, firms are privatised and sold, mainly to outsiders, when the firms that have the capacity to survive have become obvious. Restructuring also takes place gradually. Large Yeonhap Giupso disintegrate into small firms and units, but large firms that cannot be disintegrated further are allowed to operate for some time under existing conditions. These firms will then be required to choose between privatisation and complete closure.

3.4.d Economic Policies for Gradual Unification

A Chinese-Style Scenario

This scenario, which assumes that a North Korean leader decides to transition toward a market economy, is similar to the Chinese reform launched in the late 1970s by Deng Xiaoping. This form of transition in North Korea does not necessarily lead to political unification with South Korea. However, economic integration with South Korea will be more likely because it economically benefits both the North and the South.

North Korea's transition can start with policies that have been proven effective in the Chinese reform process. These policies include (1) de-collectivisation of collective farms; (2) provision of private ownership with freedom to start businesses; (3) freedom to engage in market transactions; and (4) establishment of SEZs. Kim (2015) calls the first three policies the minimum requirements for transition toward a market economy. The fourth element, which was introduced in four regions in China at the initial stage of its reform, aims to exploit advantages from geographical proximity to neighbouring South Korea, China and Russia.

Policies for liberalisation of prices and foreign trade were discussed in Section 3.2. Such policies are easy to implement because prices and foreign trade are already liberalised in North Korea to a substantial extent. The privatisation of large enterprises is more complicated because the supreme leader and the Workers' Party might be concerned about the effect such privatisation would have on their control over the society and the economy. One option is to follow the approach adopted by Chinese authorities, wherein they encouraged the entry of private firms and competition with the existing SOEs, whereas privatisation of SOEs was delayed.

Kim and Roland (2012) discuss the process of winning political support for transition among bureaucrats; they propose that bureaucrats are allowed to engage part-time in private businesses. Through this approach, the government can save the cost of paying a full salary to the bureaucrats. Furthermore, bureaucrats are incentivised not to block a reform but to support it. They would want to use their power to repress competition at a later stage, but this matter should be resolved at a higher level.

Integration with South Korea will benefit the economic performance of North Korea during the transition period in the following ways. First, investment from South Korea will significantly contribute to the North Korean economy. One of the most binding constraints in North Korea at the early stage of development will be its insufficient rate of domestic savings and the difficulty it has in borrowing from international capital markets. South Korean investment will fill this gap. Second, North Korean goods, which might be competitive mainly on the basis of low price, can be exported to South Korean markets. Third, knowledge spillover from the South to the North can be expected, particularly given the homogeneity in culture and language between the two Koreas. Fourth, institutions that support the market economy, such as the two-tier banking system and capital markets, can be designed based on is what is learned from South Korea. These systems can even be integrated with those of North Korea, if necessary.

The question of how to sequence policies for transition and integration with South Korea needs to be explored. The optimal speed of integration in tandem with transition in North Korea can be adopted. Otherwise, economic costs of integration will increase fast. For example, North Korea will experience a rapid increase in wages and lose international competitiveness if South Korean investment into North Korea is large, given the stage of its economic development. Complementarities between South and North Korea will quickly disappear if the integration of the two Koreas occurs too rapidly.

According to Kim (2015) and Park et al. (2010), transition and integration policies should be sequenced. Kim (2015) presents the stage of transition that should be matched with the relevant stage of integration with the South. The following graph shows the matched

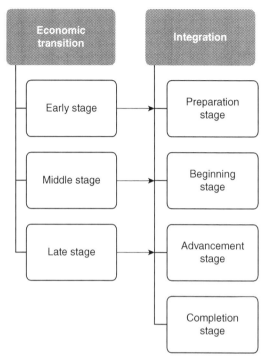

FIGURE 3.4 Stages of Economic Transition and Integration
Source: Kim (2015)

stage of North Korean transition and the integration with South Korea. Figure 3.4 indicates that the early stage of transition should be accompanied with the preparation stage of integration. The middle and late stages of transition should be matched with the beginning and advancement of integration, respectively. Completion of integration should take place after the stage of integration.

Table 3.6 provides the detailed policies for each stage of transition and integration. Policies that need to be implemented at the early stage of transition are equivalent to those categorised as the minimum requirements for transition toward a market economy. Policies for the preparation stage of integration include economic aid from the international community to North Korea. These policies pursue a backward or forward linkage with an existing industrial complex

Table 3.6 *Proposed Policies at Each Stage of Transition and Integration*

Transition Stage	Policies	Integration Stage	Policies
Early	De-collectivisation Liberalisation of market activities Liberalisation of starting businesses	Preparation	Economic aid Linkage of an existing industrial complex with the economy Technical assistance Human capital development
Middle	Small-scale privatisation Introduction of competition Liberalisation of prices and foreign trade Two-tier banking system	Beginning	Development of new industrial complexes Commodity market integration Joint development of infrastructure Joint development of natural resources
Late	Large-scale privatisation Development of capital markets Capital market liberalisation	Advancement and completion	Participation in large-scale privatisation Free mobility of capital Free mobility of labour Institutional integration

Source: Modified from Kim (2015)

in the North Korean economy and the provision of technical assistance and programmes for human capital development in North Korea. Policy-makers are advised to implement the following: small-scale privatisation, competition policy, liberalisation of prices and foreign trade, and a two-tier banking system. At the beginning stage of integration, which is matched with the middle stage of transition, free mobility is allowed for commodities and limited mobility for capital, such as South Korean investments in North Korean infrastructure and the development of natural resources. The late stage of transition completes the transformation of the economic system to a market economy by implementing complicated policies that remain to be done after the middle stage. These policies include large-scale privatisation, development of a capital market and capital market liberalisation. North Korean authorities should abolish the socialist economic system based on state ownership and central planning. As regards the advancement stage of integration, free capital and labour movement between the two Koreas should be guaranteed. South Koreans are allowed to participate in large-scale privatisation. Most of the institutional integration takes place at the completion stage of integration.

Temporary Separation Scenario

This scenario assumes that, following the collapse of the North Korean regime, South Korea and North Korea are temporarily separated with a view to accomplishing unification at a later stage. One case would have South Korea governing North Korea as a special administrative region, but postponing political integration. The duration for implementation of policies before unification might be shorter under the temporary separation scenario than that under the Chinese-style scenario, but longer than that under the radical unification scenario.

The most important difference between the radical unification scenario and the temporary separation scenario, from the policy-making perspective, is whether or not policy-makers need to consider the possibility of mass migration from the North to the South. Unlike the radical unification scenario, the temporary separation scenario is supposed to prohibit migration from the North to the South, at least at the early stage of unification. As a result, expenditure on social safety nets will be lower in this scenario than that in radical unification. During the period of separation, transition policies will be introduced in the North with the aim of aligning the economic system to that of South Korea. Given that per capita income is lower in the North than in the South, the North Korean economy will be expected to catch up with the economy of South Korea. In this way the economic shock to South Korea will be lower later on, when unification takes place.

Policies for a temporary separation scenario can be modified from those for both radical unification and the Chinese-style scenario. If the duration of this temporary separation were sufficiently long, policy-makers would be able to adopt an evolutionary approach for the development of the North Korean economy. For example, export-led growth based on low wages could be pursued. In addition, policies up to the beginning and middle stages for transition and integration presented by Table 3.6, respectively, could be implemented at the same time in the early stages of this scenario. Large-scale privatisation and institutional integration would be carried out slowly. By contrast, if the temporary separation were not to last long, policies for radical unification would be more relevant. In either scenario, free mobility of labour will be one of the last policies to be implemented.

3.4.e Unification Costs and Benefits

From the viewpoint of South Korea, unification brings costs and benefits. The amount of cost depends heavily on how unification unfolds. South Korea will spend less under the scenario of gradual unification than under the scenario of radical unification. The main reason is that a large amount of spending is required to provide social safety nets for

North Koreans if unification takes place according to the radical scenario, but such expenditures will decrease if the unification process is gradual.

Table 3.7 presents the recent estimates of unification costs. Such costs are computed by utilising one of the following methods. In the first method, the costs incurred for each item are summed up to give an aggregate cost for unification. The main cost items include emergency relief, construction of infrastructure, provision of education and health care, and integration of institutions. The second method uses a model to compute the cost of unification. A target income per capita for North Koreans or a ratio of North Korean to South Korean income per capita is selected first. This model will then compute the amount of money needed to achieve such a target. The models used in estimations of Korean unification costs include a computable general equilibrium (CGE) model, a model based on incremental capital output ratio (ICOR) and a macroeconomic model.

Three of the estimates in Table 3.7 use a model-based approach, while the remaining two are based on the aggregated cost of each item that was expensed on unification. Estimated unification costs range from US$50 to US$3,947 billion and from 3.8 to 12.0 per cent of annual South Korean GDP. Such estimates cannot be compared on the same grounds because the methodology and assumptions used in estimating the costs differ significantly. For example, Wolf and Akramov (2005) define unification costs as the costs required to increase North Korean income per capita by 100 per cent. Lee (2003) assumes that North Korean income per capita in the year of unification is 20 per cent that of South Korea, but our estimate indicates that it is less than 3 per cent that of South Korea. Recent estimates that used a model-based approach, such as those by Choi (2008), two Korean public research institutes (Korea Institute for International Economic Policy and Korea Institute for Industrial Economics and Trade (KIEP and KIET, 2012)) and the National Assembly Budget Office (2014), estimated high unification costs. Under the radical unification scenario, the share of

Table 3.7 *Various Estimates of Unification Costs of the Two Koreas*

Studies	Unification scenario	Unification costs	Methodology	Assumptions
Lee (2003)	Radical	US$182.7 to US$561.4 bn	CGE model	In the base year, income per capita of North Korea is 20 per cent of that of South Korea
Wolf and Akramov (2005)	N.A.	US$50 to US$670 bn	ICOR	Achieving a doubling of North Korea's per capita GDP in four to five years
Choi (2008)	Radical	7 to 12 per cent of annual South Korea's GDP	Macro model	North Korea's productivity becomes 80 to 90 per cent of that of South Korea within 50 to 60 years.
KIEP and KIET (2011)	Radical	US$954 bn for 20 years	Aggregation of expenses	Based on German unification cost
	Radical, medium and gradual	3.8 to 9.5 per cent of annual South Korea's GDP	CGE model	Radical, medium and gradual unification are assumed to start in 2020, 2030 and 2040, respectively.
National Assembly Budget Office (2014)	Radical	US$3,947 bn (in 2005 price) for 45 years	Aggregation of expenses	Costs from 2016 to 2060, assuming that unification occurs in 2016

Sources: Lee (2003); Wolf and Akramov (2005); Choi (2008); KIEP and KIET (2011); National Assembly Budget Office (2014)

Table 3.8 *Various Estimates of Benefits of Unification of the Two Koreas*

Study	Unification scenario	Unification benefits	Methodology
Choi (2008)	Radical	North Korea's annual growth rates: 5 to 18 per cent for 30 years South Korea's annual growth rates: increase by 0.1 per cent point	Macro model
KIEP and KIET (2011)	Gradual	North Korea's annual growth rates: 8.5 to 14.5 per cent for 40 years South Korea's annual growth rates: 2.1 to 7.3 per cent for 40 years	DSGE model
Kang et al. (2014)	Gradual	North Korea's annual growth rates: 6.19 per cent or lower for 35 years South Korea's annual growth rates: increase by 0.32 per cent point or lower for 35 years	Growth accounting based on Cobb–Douglas function
National Assembly Budget Office (2014)	Radical	North Korea's annual growth rates: 4.8 to 13.9 per cent for 45 years South Korea's value-added: increase by 1.0 per cent point for 45 years	Growth accounting/ Inter-industry analysis
Sung (2014)	Gradual	North Korea's GDP: increase by 656 per cent at maximum for 35 years South Korea's GDP: decrease by at least 2.03 per cent for 35 years	CGE model

Table 3.8 (*cont.*)

Study	Unification scenario	Unification benefits	Methodology
Kim (2014b)	Gradual	North Korea's annual growth rates: 13.1 per cent for 35 years South Korea's annual growth rates: increase by 0.7 to 0.8 per cent point for 35 years	Empirics of economic growth

Sources: Choi (2008); KIEP and KIET (2011): Kang et al. (2014): National Assembly Budget Office (2014): Sung (2014); Kim (2014b).

unification costs in annual GDP is estimated up to 9.5 to 12 per cent. This estimation translates into US$130 to US$170 billion in 2015 when South Korea's GDP in 2015 was approximately US$1.4 trillion. Estimates that use aggregated costs indicate that the costs incurred through radical unification will be US$954 billion for 20 years, or US$3,947 billion for 45 years.

Two estimation methods can be utilised to determine the benefits of unification. First, a model-based approach is used (Choi, 2008; KIEP and KIET, 2011; Kang et al., 2014). This method initially sets up a model of unification, wherein parameters are specified. A simulation is then conducted to estimate the effect of unification on growth. Several models, including the dynamic stochastic general equilibrium (DSGE) model and the Cobb–Douglas function, are employed. Second, an empirics-based approach is used (Kim, 2014b). Based on the existing literature on the empirical studies of growth, this approach first identifies changes in the variables that affect growth because of unification. The effects are then aggregated to estimate the total effect of unification on growth in the South and the North.

Similarly to estimates on the costs of unification, estimates of its benefits vary substantially. According to these estimates, the North Korean economy is estimated to grow at 6 to 18 per cent per annum for an extended period as a result of integration or unification with South Korea. By contrast, the estimated benefits accrued to South Korea from the integration or unification with North Korea are relatively modest. Most estimates indicate that the increase to South Korea's growth rate will be less than 1 per cent per annum.

The aforementioned studies suggest that capital accumulation is a major growth engine for North Korea. For example, the National Assembly Budget Office (2014) estimates that a South Korean investment into North Korea of 1 per cent of South Korea's GDP will increase North Korea's GDP by approximately 40 times over a period of 55 years. Without such investment, North Korea's GDP will increase only tenfold. This finding is consistent with that of KIEP and KIET (2011), which assume that South Korea will spend 2 to 5 per cent of its annual GDP on North Korea and subsequently estimates that North Korea's GDP will increase by 8.5 to 14.5 per cent for 40 years.

Kang et al. (2014) and Kim (2014b) provide a detailed discussion of the growth-enhancing effect of different channels. Kang et al. (2014) specify the following channels through which unification benefits are brought about: reduction in personnel and expenditures for national defence; inter-Korean economic cooperation; and inter-Korean trade. If North Korea transitions to a market economy and implements the aforementioned three policies, the country will achieve 6.19 per cent growth per annum from 2015 to 2050. Kim (2014b) considers other channels of growth such as improvements in labour force and human capital, economic stabilisation and institutional reforms. Assuming that most of the variables that affect North Korea's GDP will converge to South Korea's level within 35 years, he estimates that North Korea's growth rate will be 13.1 per cent on average from 2015 to 2050. South Korea will benefit from the unification through the reduction of personnel in the defence sector, increased economic integration and improved efficiency from the use of resources for productive activities. He estimates that the aggregated effect on growth will increase South Korea's GDP by 0.7 to 0.8 per cent point per annum.

A strong consensus exists among researchers and policy-makers in South Korea. They agree that the economic benefits accrued from the unification will be larger than the costs associated with it mainly because the benefits will last far longer than the costs will. However, the sharing of costs across generations is not easy to resolve. Taxpayers who will bear the burden of unification will prefer debt-financing, whereas the younger generations will prefer tax-financing.

NOTES

1. We use 'Eastern Europe' in a broad sense, to include the former Soviet republics.
2. For example, vouchers in Russia were transferrable to other persons, while those in the Czech Republic were not transferrable. Hence, citizens in the Czech Republic were able to use vouchers for exchange with shares of firms to be privatised or those of the IPFs. The voucher privatisation in Poland was different from that of Russia or the Czech Republic in that vouchers in Poland could only be exchanged for shares of the IPFs.
3. The following reasons were suggested for the passive role of the IPFs. First, there was a legal requirement that a single fund and funds founded by the same investment company could hold up to 20 per cent and up to 40 per cent of a firm's equity, respectively. This limited the motivation for people to be actively involved in the running of firms. Second, funds lacked the technical and managerial know-how needed for management of a firm (Kenway and Chlumsky, 1997).
4. The price of food rationed by the PDS is very low, and even negligible in comparison with actual market prices. This suggests that retail price subsidies are implicitly given for this rationed food.
5. In the case that a worker at Kimchaek Iron and Steel Company has a meal in a company cafeteria, the worker's food ration is reduced by 14 kg per month. Hence, he or she tends to have lunch at home, although it takes some time to get home.
6. A South Korean analyst at a research institute of the Korean intelligence service claims that the capacity utilisation rate of North Korean firms ranges between 20 and 30 per cent on average (www.dailynk.com/korean/read.php?cataId=nk00400&num=55275 as of June 2016).

7. The Chosun Dynasty, which was the last kingdom in the Korean peninsula, was based on Confucian culture. According to this culture, there are four different occupational groups in terms of respect. The highest respect is given to scholars, followed by farmers and then manufacturers. The group of traders is least respected. In addition, gender discrimination against women is another factor in the more active participation of women in informal trading in markets.

8. Some estimates suggest that it is approximately US$5.7 trillion (North Korean Resources Institute, 2013). However, there is some criticism that some of the natural resources are not valuable in the world market and large costs will be incurred to extract them (Lee, ed., 2013).

9. This figure is derived by dividing GNI in 2013 by the number of the population in the same year.

10. For more detailed discussion, refer to Kim (2009a).

11. These are based on the official figure of fiscal revenue reported by North Korea and the estimates of North Korea's GDP.

12. www.dailynk.com/korean/read.php?catId=nk00400&num=55275 as of June 2016.

13. The majority of these 197 newly established firms are small-scale power plants (107 firms), followed by food processing firms (100 firms), which reflects the emphasis of the North Korean authorities on overcoming shortages of energy and food.

14. This is derived from the figure for the number of manufacturing firms located in Hamkyungnamdo, which is 763, and is 13.9 per cent of total manufacturing firms in North Korea. However, this figure may not include the total number of firms in that region because only the numbers of firms belonging to the first, second, third and fourth categories are reported.

15. The middle number of the workers in each category is multiplied by the share of the number of the firms in that category, except for the category of the firms that employ more than 3,000, for which we use the number 3,000.

16. Some scholars may argue that integration rather than unification should be the goal of South Korean policies toward North Korea (Park et al., 2010). This scenario can be regarded as the gradual transformation of North Korea and its integration with South Korea, but without pursuing political unification. The EU-type of integration is similar to this scenario.

17. Kim (2012) discusses various methods for identifying the equilibrium conversion rate between the South Korean won and the North Korean won, and proposes a method that equalises the North Korean won figure for North Korean income per capita to that in US dollars. Income of North Koreans in won can be surveyed, whereas that in the US dollars can be estimated using a similar method that we discussed in Chapter 2.

Conclusion

This book can be seen as proceeding in chronological order. We began with a discussion of the socialist economy. Given the experiences of the Soviet economy, we argued that the socialist economic system achieved neither efficiency nor a balance between aggregate supply and demand. Furthermore, the system proved to be unsustainable, which led to its collapse. Using the framework established during our discussion of the Soviet economy, we then investigated North Korea's economic system, performance, the activities of households and firms, and the stability of the North Korean regime. Lastly, the experiences of transitions in Eastern Europe and China were summarised and we identified lessons which could be applied to the future of the North Korean economy.

The events and circumstances under which North Korea's present-day economy will undergo transition in the future are uncertain. In other words, how can North Korea begin the transition process? Where is North Korea heading? The most important factor determining North Korea's future is perhaps Kim Jong-un. A decline of support for the regime or changes in his health could trigger a power struggle inside North Korea. Two possible outcomes include the explosion of the regime and a normal power transfer to an individual or group of individuals. If the regime explodes, violence and military conflicts could erupt. External forces such as that of South Korea may have to enter North Korea in order to maintain order. After an interim period and once the situation has stabilised, a decision can be made to determine the future of the country, with the reunification of the two Koreas being a likely outcome. Alternatively, a subset of the North Korean elites could be placed in power. Given the 'fear politics' currently used by Kim Jong-un, it is unlikely that his child or sister,

Kim Yeo-jong, will succeed him. If the newly established leader is relatively free from extreme ideological orientations, he or she may prioritise economic development.

The best outcome would be for Kim Jong-un himself to transform the economy of North Korea into a market economy and agree to de-nuclearisation. While this outcome is fairly unlikely, given that he appears to believe that his power would be substantially undermined by adoption of a market economy and the giving up of nuclear weapons, one cannot rule out a scenario in which he is unwillingly forced to do so. Markets will transform the structure of the economy and the mind-sets of people. Relationships among people, firms and institutions will change in accordance with the advancement of markets. At a certain point, the demand from the beneficiaries of market activities for reform of the economy may become extremely hard for Kim Jong-un to resist.

He will consequently have two ultimate choices. He may try to repress such demand, even using military force as Stalin did when he collectivised farms. However, this option is risky for him because he may lose his power in the process of repression. Another option involves a compromise. Kim Jong-un loosens his tight hold on power and grants autonomy to the economy. This circumstance can be viewed as the beginning of the Chinese style of transition. For the time being, Kim Jong-un may attempt to keep his absolute power using indoctrination of the Juche ideology and various surveillance mechanisms. At the same time, he wants to exploit gains from marketisation for his own benefit while controlling market activities so as not to threaten the stability of the regime. However, our analysis predicts that this subtle balance between the power of markets and that of the state cannot sustain long term, and economic considerations will ultimately prevail among North Koreans. Kim Jong-un will have to face difficult choices.

The second determinant of North Korea's destiny is the North Koreans, including the elites and the public. Jeong et al. (2015) show interesting results in this regard from the surveys of North Korean refugees who recently arrived in South Korea. According to this work, a majority of North Koreans still support Kim Jong-un and the Juche ideology. However, those who support individualism over collectivism have been increasing over time, and more than 80 per cent of the refugees reply that the former is more important than the latter in present-day North Korea. In addition, 47 per cent of these refugees answered that the most important reasons for economic stagnation are the North Korean leader and the lack of reform and opening-up. These findings imply that North Koreans are becoming increasingly critical of the existing system. The elites also experience the power of money when they take bribes and engage directly or indirectly in lucrative businesses, including external trade and market activities. Some elites and private financiers called donju are believed to have accumulated a substantial amount of money (Yang, 2010b). These people may be tempted to protect their money and power using their financial resources against possible punishments from Kim Jong-un.

The third factor is external. Normal relations between South Korea or China and North Korea may facilitate the marketisation of the North Korean economy, resulting in important changes to the regime. By contrast, North Korea's development of nuclear weapons and intercontinental ballistic and submarine-launched ballistic missiles will lead to coordinated reactions from relevant countries against such provocations. An example is the imposition of economic sanctions in 2016 by the United Nations Security Council. Further testing of nuclear weapons is likely to invoke stronger sanctions. The United States may attempt to find other solutions including diplomacy and direct coercive means if it judges that its mainland can be threatened by North Korea in the future. The consequences there are uncertain. What is certain, however, is that the status quo cannot be maintained in the long term, as long as North Korea keeps developing nuclear weapons.

South Korea's attempt for unification faces tough challenges. The desired unification should be a peaceful one accompanied by economic integration between South and North as well as North

Korea's economic transition and advancing growth. Solving these three economic tasks will be difficult. Each requires considerable resources and effort. In most Eastern European countries, only economic transition was required. Germany needed to solve two tasks – that is, transition and integration. The German case, which involves closing the income gap between West and East, appears easier than the Korean one, where the gap in income per capita between South Korea and North Korea is immense.

The good news is that Koreans can learn from the transition experiences of Europe and China as well as the German unification. These countries had to start their transition and unification without a blueprint or a roadmap. Policies were often improvised and thus incoherent and ineffective. Now, such valuable experiences can provide important lessons for North Korea's transition toward a market economy and can assist in drawing up appropriate strategies and policies. It is highly likely that crucial events will unfold in the Korean peninsula within the next ten years. All kinds of scenarios are possible. Although we are not able to predict which one will occur, we can prepare with plans drawn from an accurate understanding of the North Korean economy and experiences from countries that have undergone similar transitions. Policies that South Korea and the outside world apply to North Korea should be based not on wishes or naïve belief, but on scientific knowledge of North Korea. This book is intended to contribute to such preparations for the future of North Korea, the Korean peninsula and the world beyond.

References

Academy of Social Sciences (1970), *Dictionary on the Economy 1* (경제사전 1), Pyongyang: Press of Social Sciences.

Academy of Social Sciences (1985), *Dictionary on the Economy 2* (경제사전 2), Pyongyang: Press of Social Sciences.

Acemoglu, Daron, Johnson, S., and Robinson, J. A. (2001), The Colonial Origins of Comparative Development: An Empirical Investigation. *American Economic Review* 91(5): 1369–1401.

Acemoglu, Daron, Johnson, S., and Robinson, J. A. (2002), Reversal of Fortune: Geography and Institutions in the Making of the Modern World Income Distribution. *Quarterly Journal of Economics* 117: 1231–1294.

Acemoglu, Daron, and Robinson, James (2012), *Why Nations Fail*, New York: Crown Publishing Group.

Adam, J. (1989), *Economic Reforms in the Soviet Union and Eastern Europe since the 1960s*, London: MacMillan Press.

Aghion, P., and Blanchard, O. (1994), On the Speed of Transition in Central Europe. *National Bureau for Economic Research Macroeconomics Annual* 9: 283–320.

Ahn, Ye-Hong, and Mun, Sung Min (2007), A Study on Methods of Economic Integration after Unification (통일 이후 남북한 경제통합 방식에 대한 연구), Research on Finance and Economics. Bank of Korea, Research Paper No. 291.

Akerlof, George, Rose, Andrew, Yellen, Janet, and Hessenius, Helga, (1991), East Germany in from the Cold: The Economic Aftermath of Currency Union. *Brookings Papers on Economic Activity* 1991(1): 1–105.

Alexeev, M. (1988), Are Soviet Consumers Forced to Save? *Comparative Economic Studies* 30(4): 17–23.

Andvig, J. C., and Fjeldstad, O. H. Amundsen, I., Sissener, T., and Søreide, T. (2000), Research on Corruption: A Policy Oriented Survey. Chr. Michelsen Institute and Norwegian Institute of International Affairs.

Bank of Korea (2002), Meaning of Recent Economic Measures of North Korea and Prospects (최근 북한 경제조치의 의미와 향후 전망). Material for public report.

Bank of Korea (various years), *Gross Domestic Product Estimates for North Korea*, Seoul: Bank of Korea.

Bardhan, P. (1997), Corruption and Development: A Review of Issues. *Journal of Economic Literature* 35(3): 1320–1346.

Barlow, David, and Radulescu, Roxana (2005), The Sequencing of Reform in Transition Economies. *Journal of Comparative Economics* 33(4): 835–850.

Barro, R., and Grossman, H. (1971), A General Disequilibrium Model of Income and Employment. *American Economic Review* 61(1): 82–93.

Barro, R., and Grossman, H. (1974), Suppressed Inflation and the Supply Multiplier. *Review of Economic Studies* 41(1): 87–104.

Bennett, John, Estrin, Saul, and Urga, Giovanni (2007), Methods of Privatisation and Economic Growth in Transition Economies. *Economics of Transition* 15(4): 661–683.

Bergson, Abram (1961), *The Real National Income of Soviet Russia Since 1928*, Boston: Harvard University Press.

Bergson, Abram (1987), Comparative Productivity: The USSR, Eastern Europe and the West. *American Economic Review* 77(3): June, 342–357.

Bergson, Abram (1992), Communist Economic Efficiency Revisited. *American Economic Review Papers and Proceedings* 82(2): May, 27–30.

Berkowitz, D., and Dejong, D. N. (2005), Entrepreneurship and Post-Socialist Growth. *Oxford Bulletin of Economics and Statistics* 67(1): 25–46.

Bilsen, Valentijn, and Konings, Jozef (1998), Job Creation, Job Destruction and Growth of Newly Established, Privatized and State-Owned Enterprises in Transition Economies: Survey Evidence from Bulgaria, Hungary and Romania. *Journal of Comparative Economics* 26(3): 429–445.

Blanchard, Oliver, and Shleifer, Andrei (2001), Federalism with and without Political Centralisation: China versus Russia. IMF Staff Papers, Vol. 48, Special Issue, 171–179.

Boretsky, M. (1987), The Tenability of the CIA Estimates of Soviet Economic Growth. *Journal of Comparative Economics* 11(4): 1987, 517–542.

Boycko, Maxim, Shleifer, Andrei, and Vishny, Robert W. (1994), Voucher Privatization. *Journal of Financial Economics* 35(2): 249–266.

Boycko, Maxim, Shleifer, Andrei, and Vishny, Robert (1996), A Theory of Privatisation. *Economic Journal* 106(March): 309–319.

Brunetti, Aymo, Kisunko, Gregory, and Weder, Beatrice (1997), Institutions in Transition: Reliability of Rules and Economic Performance in Former Socialist Countries. World Bank Policy Research Working Paper No. 1809.

Brus, W., and Laski, K. (1989), *From Marx to the Market: Socialism in Search of an Economic System*, Oxford: Oxford University Press.

Carlin, Wendy, Fries, Steven, Schaffer, Mark, and Seabright, Paul (2001), Competition and Enterprise Performance in Transition Economies: Evidence from a Cross-Country Survey. *CEPR Discussion Paper* No. 2840.

Central Intelligence Agency (CIA) (1991), Sector of Origin and End Use GNP for the Soviet Union 1950–90. Update of JEC estimates in 1982 rubles, processed, 29 March 1991.

Central News Agency of Democratic People's Republic of Korea (various years), *Chosun Joongang Yeongam* (Yearbook of Democratic People's Republic of Korea: CJY), Pyongyang: Central News Agency of Democratic People's Republic of Korea.

Chai, Won-Ho, Son, Ho-Jung, and Kim, Ok-Il (2006), The Bureaucratic Corruption and Its Causes in North Korea: A Survey of Perception of North Korean Refugees (북한 관료부패의 실태와 원인에 관한 연구). *Journal of the Korean Association for Governance* 13(1): 297–321.

Chang, Yong Seok, Eun-mee, Jeong, and Park, Myoung-Kyu (2014), *Social Changes in North Korea, 2014: Marketisation, Inequality and Economic Reforms* (북한 사회변동 2014: 시장화, 불평등, 경제개혁), Seoul: Seoul National University Institute for Peace and Unification Studies.

Charemza, W. (1989), Disequilibrium Modelling of Consumption in the Centrally Planned Economy. In *Models of Disequilibrium and Shortages in Centrally Planned Economies*, Davis, C., and Charemza, W., eds. London: Chapman and Hall.

Charemza, W. (1990), Parallel Markets, Excess Demand and Virtual Prices: An Empirical Approach. *European Economic Review* 34(2–3): 331–339.

Chawluk, A., and Cross, R. (1994), The Real Balance Effects of Price Liberalization in Poland. *Economics of Transition* 2(4): 487–499.

Chawluk, A., and Cross, R. (1997), Measures of Shortage and Monetary Overhang in the Polish Economy. *Review of Economics and Statistics* 79(1): 105–115.

Choi, Jin Wook (2011), Unification Scenario and Preparation (통일 시나리오와 통일준비). In *Tasks and Strategies for Unification Diplomacy* (통일 외교 과제 와 전략), Choi et al., eds. Seoul: Korea Institute for National Unification.

Choi, Joonook (2008), *Fiscal Impact of Economic Integration of Two Koreas* (남북경 제통합과 재성성책), Seoul: Korea Institute of Public Finance.

Choi, Soo-young (1991), Foreign Trade of North Korea, 1946–1988: Structure and Performance, Unpublished Doctoral Dissertation, Northeastern University.

Chow, Gregory (2007), *China's Economic Transformation*, 2nd edn. Oxford: Blackwell Publishing.

Chung, Chung-Gil, and Jeon, Chang-Gon (2000), The Analysis of the State of Farmer's Markets in North Korea (북한 농민시장의 실태 분석). *Agricultural Economy* 23(2): 103–120.

Chung, Young-chul (2007), The Suryong System as the Institution of Collectivist Development. *Journal of Korean Studies* Vol. 12, Fall: 43–74.

Claessens, Stijn, and Peters, Kyle (1997), State Enterprise Performance and Soft Budget Constraints: The Case of Bulgaria. *Economics of Transition* 5(2): 305–322.

Crafts, N., and Toniolo, G. (1996), Postwar Growth: An Overview. In *Economic Growth in Europe Since 1945*, Crafts, N. and Toniolo, G, eds. Cambridge: Cambridge University Press.

Cumings, Bruce (1997), *Korea's Place in the Sun: A Modern History*, New York: W.W. Norton & Company.

Davis, Christopher (1988), The Second Economy in Disequilibrium and Shortage Models of Centrally Planned Economies, Berkeley–Duke Occasional Papers on the Second Economy in the USSR, No. 12. Duke University, Durham, NC.

Davis, Lance, and North, Douglass (1971), *Institutional Change and American Economic Growth*, New York: Cambridge University Press.

De Brauw, Alan, Huang, Jikun, and Rozelle, Scott (2004), The Sequencing of Reform Policies in China's Agricultural Transition. *Economics of Transition* 12(3): 427–465.

Dewatripont, M., and Maskin, E. (1995), Credit and Efficiency in Centralized and Decentralized Economies. *Review of Economic Studies* 62(4): 541–555.

Dewatripont, M., and Roland, G. (1992), The Virtues of Gradualism and Legitimacy in the Transition to a Market Economy. *Economic Journal* 102(March): 291–300.

Dewatripont, M., and Roland, G. (1995), The Design of Reform Packages under Uncertainty. *American Economic Review* 85(5): 1207–1223.

Djankov, Simeon (1999), The Restructuring of Insider-Dominated Firms: A Comparative Analysis. *Economics of Transition* 7(2): 467–79.

Djankov, Simeon, and Murrell, Peter (2002), Enterprise Restructuring in Transition: A Quantitative Survey. *Journal of Economic Literature* 40(3): 739–792.

Dong, Yong-Seung (2010), The Conditions and Prospects of the North Korean Iron and Steel Industry (북한 철강산업의 현황 및 전망). *EXIM North Korea Economic Review* 7(3): 59–74.

Eberstadt, Nicholas (2009), *The North Korean Economy: Between Crisis and Catastrophe*, New Brunswick: Transaction.

Ericson, R. (1990), The Soviet Statistical Debate: Khanin vs. TsSU. In *The Impoverished Superpower: Perestroika and the Soviet Military Burden*, Rowen, H., and Wolf, C., eds. Oakland: Institute for Contemporary Studies Press.

Estrin, Saul and Stone, Robert, (1997), A Taxonomy of Mass Privatisation. In *Between State and Market: Mass Privatization in Transition Economies*, Lieberman, I. W., Nestor, S. S and Desai, R. M., eds. Washington DC: World Bank.

Estrin, Saul, Hanousek, Jan, Kocenda, Evzen, and Svejnar, Jan (2009), The Effects of Privatization and Ownership in Transition Economies, *Journal of Economic Literature* 47(3): 699–728.

Falcetti, Elisabetta, Lysenko, Tatiana, and Sanfey, Peter (2006), Reform and Growth in Transition: Re-examining the Evidence. *Journal of Comparative Economics* 34(3): 421–445.

Fernandez, R., and Rodrik, D. (1991), Resistance to Reform: Status-Quo Bias in the Presence of Individual-Specific Uncertainty. *American Economic Review* 81(5): 1146–1155.

Fischer, Stanley, Sahay, Ratna, and Vegh, Carlos A. (1996), Stabilization and Growth in Transition Economies: The Early Experience. *Journal of Economic Perspectives* 10(2): 45–66.

Food and Agriculture Organization of the United Nations (FAO) and World Food Programme (WFP) (2012, 2013), FAO/WFP Crop and Food Security Assessment Mission to the Democratic People's Republic of Korea, Special Report.

Frank, Ruediger (2005), Economic Reforms in North Korea (1998–2004): Systemic Restrictions, Quantitative Analysis, Ideological Background. *Journal of the Asia Pacific Economy* 10(3): 278–311.

Free North Korea Radio (2008), Lectures by Hwang Jang-yop on Juche Ideology and Sooroung Dictatorship (황장엽 강좌: 주체사상과 수령독재사상에 대하여) (www.fnkradio.com/).

Fyrdman, Roman, Gray, Cheryl, Hessel, Marek, and Rapaczynski, Andrzej (1999), When Does Privatization Work: The Impact of Private Ownership on Corporate Performance in the Transition Economies. *Quarterly Journal of Economics* 114(4): 1153–1191.

Frydman, Roman, Gray, Cheryl, and Rapaczynski, Andrej (1997), Private Ownership and Corporate Performance: Some Lessons from Transition Economies, New York University Working Paper 9827, New York.

Funke, Norbert (1993), Timing and Sequencing of Reforms: Competing Views and the Role of Credibility. *Kyklos* 46(3): 337–362.

Gaddy, Clifford. (1991), The Labour Market and the Second Economy in the Soviet Union, Berkeley-Duke Occasional Papers on the Second Economy in the USSR, 24.

General Accounting Office (GAO) (1991), Soviet Economy: Assessment of How Well CIA Has Estimated the Size of the Economy, Report to the Honorable

Daniel Patrick Moynihan, United States General Accounting Office. GAO/NSIAD91:274.

Goodkind, Daniel, and West, Loraine (2001), The North Korean Famine and Its Demographic Impact. *Population and Development Review* 27(2): 219–238.

Graham, Edward M. (2007), How North Korea Finances Its International Trade Deficit: An Educated Guess, *Korea's Economy* 23: 74–82 (http://keia.org/sites/default/files/publications/17.Graham.pdf).

Gregory, Paul (2004), *The Political Economy of Stalinism*, Cambridge: Cambridge University Press.

Gregory, Paul, and Stuart, Robert (2004), *Comparing Economic Systems in the Twenty-First Century*, 7th edn. Boston: Houghton Mifflin Company.

Greif, Avner (2006), *Institutions and the Path to the Modern Economy: Lessons from Medieval Trade*, Cambridge: Cambridge University Press.

Grossman, Gregory (1977), The 'Second Economy' of the USSR. *Problems of Communism* 26(5, September-October): 25–40.

Grossman, Gregory (1987), Roots of Gorbachev's Problems: Private Income and Outlay in the Late 1970s. In *Gorbachev's Economic Plans*, Vol. 1. Joint Economic Committee, US Congress, Washington, DC: US Government Printing Office, pp. 213–229.

Grossman, Gregory (1998), Subverted Sovereignty: Historic Role of the Soviet Underground. In *The Tunnel at the End of the Light: Privatization, Business Networks and Economic Transformation in Russia*, Cohen, Stephen S., Schwartz, Andrew, and Zysman, John, eds. Berkeley: University of California Press, pp. 24–50.

Haggard, Stephan, Euijin, Jung, and Melton, Alex (2013), Is China Subsidizing the DPRK? Part One: Food (https://piie.com/blogs/north-korea-witness-transformation/china-subsidizing-dprk-part-one-food) as of June 2016.

Haggard, Stephan, and Noland, Marcus (2007), *Famine in North Korea: Markets, Aid and Reform*, New York: Columbia University Press.

Haggard, Stephan, and Noland, Marcus (2009), Repression and Punishment in North Korea: Survey Evidence of Prison Camp Experiences. MPRA Chapter no. 17705.

Haggard, Stephan, and Noland, Marcus (2010), Reform from Below: Behavioral and Institutional Change in North Korea. *Journal of Economic Behavior and Organization* 73(2): 133–152.

Han, In Sup (2006), The 2004 Revision of Criminal Law in North Korea: A Take-Off? *Santa Clara Journal of International Law* 5(1): 122–133.

Harrison, Mark (1993), Soviet Economic Growth since 1928: The Alternative Statistics of G. I. Khanin, *Europe-Asia Studies* 45(1): 141–167.

Harrison, Mark (2002), Coercion, Compliance and the Collapse of the Soviet Command Economy. *Economic History Review* 55(3): 397–433.

Harrison, Mark, and Kim, Byung-Yeon (2006), Plans, Prices and Corruption: The Soviet Firm under Partial Centralization, 1930 to 1990. *Journal of Economic History* 66(1): 1–41.

Havrylyshyn, Oleh, and McGettigan, Donal (1999), Privatization in Transition Countries: A Sampling of the Literature, Working Paper 99/6, International Monetary Fund.

Hayek, F. A. (1944), *The Road to Serfdom*, Chicago: University of Chicago Press.

Hayek, F. A. (1948), *Individualism and Economic Order*, Chicago: University of Chicago Press.

Heal, G. (1969), Planning without Prices. *Review of Economics Studies* 36(3): 347–362.

Heinzen, James (2007), The Art of the Bribe: Corruption, Law and Everyday Practice in the Late Stalinist USSR. *Slavic Review* 66(3): 389–412.

Howard, D. (1976), The Disequilibrium Model in a Controlled Economy: An Empirical Test of the Barro–Grossman Model. *American Economic Review* 66(5): 871–879.

Huntington, S. P. (1968), *Political Order in Changing Societies*, New Haven: Yale University Press.

Hwang, Eui-Gak (1993), *The Korean Economies: A Comparison of North and South*, Oxford: Clarendon Press.

International Monetary Fund (2014), *Annual Report on Exchange Arrangements and Exchange Restrictions*, Washington: IMF Publications Services.

International Monetary Fund, The World Bank, Organisation for Economic Co-operation and Development, and European Bank for Reconstruction and Development (1991), *A Study of the Soviet Economy*, Vol.1. Paris: Organisation for Economic Co-operation and Development.

Jeong, Eun-mee, Kim, Philo, Park, Myoung-Kyu, and Song, Young-Hoon (2015), *Perceptions on Unification of North Koreans* (북한 주민 통일의식), Seoul: Seoul National University Institute for Peace and Unification Studies.

Jeong, Hyung-Gon, Kim, Byung-Yeon, and Lee, Suk (2012), Current Marketization of North Korea and Prospects on Changes in Its Economic System (북한의 시장화 현황과 경제체제의 변화 전망). Korea Institute for International Economic Policy.

Jo, Dongho (1993), Labour Productivity and Optimal Wage in North Korea: A Study on the Quality of North Korean Labour (북한의 노동생산성과 적정임금: 북한 노동력의 질에 관한 고찰). *KDI Journal of Economic Policy* 15(4): Winter, 37–68.

Jung, Eun-Lee (2009), A Study on the Organic Developmental Process of Markets in North Korea: Focusing on the March of Hardship in 1990s (북한의 자생적 시장발

전 연구: 1990 년대 고난의 행군 이후를 중심으로). *North Korean Issues* 52: 157–199.

Jung, Seung-Ho (2014), North Korea's Trade with China: Aggregate and Firm-Level Analysis, Unpublished Doctoral Dissertation, Seoul National University.

Jung, Seung-Ho (2016), Effects of Sanctions on North Korea-China Trade: A Dynamic Panel Analysis, *Seoul Journal of Economics* 66(3): 481–503.

Kang, Moonsung, Lee, Jong-Hwa, and Pyun, Ju Hyun (2014), *Benefits of Korean Unification and the Roles of the Unified Korea* (남북한 경제통합의 혜택과 한반도 통일국가의 역할), Seoul: Asiatic Research Institute Korea University.

Kenway, Peter, and Chlumsky, Jiri (1997), The Influence of Owners on Voucher Privatised Firms in the Czech Republic. *Economics of Transition* 5(1): 185–193.

Khanin, Grigorii (1991), *Dinamika ekonomicheskogo razvitiia SSSR* (The Dynamics of Economic Development of the USSR), Novosibirsk: Nauka.

Khanin, Grigorii, and Selyunin, V. (1987), Lukavaya Tsifra, Novyi Mir, 63(2): 181–202.

Kim, Byung-Yeon (1997a), Soviet Household Saving Function. *Economics of Planning* 30(2): 181–203.

Kim, Byung-Yeon (1999), The Income, Savings and Monetary Overhang of Soviet Households. *Journal of Comparative Economics* 27(4, December): 644–668.

Kim, Byung-Yeon (2002), Causes of Repressed Inflation in the Soviet Consumer Market, 1965–1989: Retail Price Subsidies, the Siphoning Effect and the Budget Deficit. *Economic History Review* 55(1): 105–127.

Kim, Byung-Yeon (2003), Informal Economy Activities of Soviet Households: Size and Dynamics. *Journal of Comparative Economics* 31(3, September): 532–551.

Kim, Byung-Yeon (2005a), Poverty and Informal Economy Participation: Evidence from Romania. *Economics of Transition* 13(1): 163–185.

Kim, Byung-Yeon (2005b), The Political Constraints of Economic Reforms and Transition: The Implications of Experiences of Former Soviet Union, Eastern Europe and China for North Korea (사회주의 경제개혁과 체제이행의 정치적 조건). *Comparative Economic Studies* 12(2): 215–251.

Kim, Byung-Yeon (2008), North Korean GDP: Estimates and Evaluation (북한의 국민소득: 추정치와 평가), *EXIM North Korea Economic Review* (Autumn).

Kim, Byung-Yeon (2009a), The Financial System of North Korea: A Comparative Perspective. In *Financial Sector Reform in Transition Economies: Implications for North Korea*, Kim, Byung-Yeon, and Lim, Cheng-Hoon, eds. Seoul: Seoul National University Press and International Monetary Fund.

Kim, Byung-Yeon (2009b), The Marketization of the North Korean Economy: Evaluation of the Informalization Hypothesis (북한경제의 시장화: 비공식화 가설을 중심으로). In *North Korean Economy and Society after the July 1st*

Economic Management Improvement Measures (7·1 경제관리개선조치 이후 북한 경제와 사회), Young-kwan Yoon and Un-Chul Yang, eds. Korea Peace Institute Series 2, Seoul: Hanul.

Kim, Byung-Yeon (2010a), Markets, Bribery and Regime Stability in North Korea, EAI (East Asia Institute) Asia Security Initiative Working Paper, No. 4.

Kim, Byung-Yeon (2010b), *Economic Evaluation of North Korean Currency Reform* (북한 화폐교환의 경제학적 평가), Korea Peace Institute.

Kim, Byung-Yeon (2011), The Determinants of North Korean Economic Growth (북한 경제성장의 결정 요인). *POSRI Management and Economic Research* 11(1): 63–81.

Kim, Byung-Yeon (2012), Monetary Integration of the Two Koreas (남북한 화폐통합). In *The Government of the Unified Korea*, Kim, Byong Seob and Im, Tobin, eds. Seoul: Nanam.

Kim, Byung-Yeon (2014a), North Korea's Economy in the Era of Kim Jong-un (김정은 시대 북한의 경제). In *Today's North Korea*, Yoon, Young-kwan ed. Seoul: Neulpoom.

Kim, Byung-Yeon (2014b), Economic Vision of the Unified Korea (통일 한국의 경제 비전). In *National Image of the Unified Korea and Cooperation between Korea and China*, Bae, Jung Ho, et al., Seoul: Korea Institute for National Unification.

Kim, Byung-Yeon (2015), Transition and Integration: Scenarios, Strategies and Policies (체제전환과 경제통합: 시나리오, 전략 및 정책) in *Economic Integration of the Two Koreas: Strategies and Policies*, Lee, Jangro, Kim, Byung-Yeon and Yang, Un-Chul, eds. Seoul: Hanul.

Kim, Byung-Yeon, and Jung, Seung-Ho (2015), *China's Trade and Investment with North Korea: Firm Surveys in Dandong*, (중국의 대북무역과 투자: 단둥시 현지기업 조사), Seoul: Institute for Peace and Unification studies, Seoul National University.

Kim, Byung-Yeon, and Kang, Youngho (2014), Social Capital and Entrepreneurial Activity: A Pseudo-Panel Approach. *Journal of Economic Behavior and Organisation* 97(Jan.): 47–60.

Kim, Byung-Yeon, Kim, Suk-Jin, and Lee, Keun (2007), Assessing the Economic Performance of North Korea, 1954–1989: Estimates and Growth Accounting Analysis. *Journal of Comparative Economics* 35(3): 564–582.

Kim, Byung-Yeon, and Koh, Yu Mi (2011), The Informal Economy and Bribery in North Korea. *Asian Economic Papers* 10(3): 104–117.

Kim, Byung-Yeon, and Park, Jieun (2016), Financial Systems and Enterprise Restructuring in Eastern Europe, *Eastern European Economics* 54(6): 503–520.

Kim, Byung-Yeon, and Pirtilla, Jukka (2006), Political Constraints and Economic Reform: Empirical Evidence from Post-Communist Transition in the 1990s. *Journal of Comparative Economics* 34(3): 446–466.

Kim, Byung-Yeon, and Roland, Gerard (2012), Scenarios for a Transition to a Prosperous Market Economy in North Korea. *International Economic Journal* 26(3): 511–539.

Kim, Byung-Yeon, and Song, Dongho (2008), The Participation of North Korean Households in the Informal Economy: Size, Determinants and Effect. *Seoul Journal of Economics* 21(2): 361–385.

Kim, Byung-Yeon, Wang, Jin, and Xu, Chenggang (2014), Understanding Firms in Transition Economies: China and Central-Eastern Europe Compared, Paper presented at the Pacific Rim Economics Conference, Hawaii.

Kim, Byung-Yeon, and Yang, Moon Soo (2012), *Markets and the State in the North Korean Economy* (북한 경제에서의 시장과 정부), Seoul: Seoul National University Press.

Kim, Il-sung (1982, 1983, 1985), *Collected Works of Kim Il-sung* (김일성 저작집), Pyongyang: Korea Workers' Party Press.

Kim, Jong-Wook (2006), A Study on the Transformation of the Bureaucracy and Ruling Structure in North Korea (북한의 관료체제와 지배구조의 변동에 관한 연구), PhD Dissertation submitted to Dongguk University, South Korea.

Kim, Keun-Sik, and Lee, Mu-Cheol (2007), Military-First Politics and Building a Strong and Prosperous Country of North Korea, (북한의 선군 정치와 강성대국론). *Research on Unification Issues* 48(2): 69–94.

Kim, Suk-Jin (2007), The Reconstruction of North Korean Industries Using Trade Data (무역통계로 본 북한의 산업재건 실태), KIET Issue Paper Series 2007–223.

Kim, Suk-Jin (2013), Factors of Increases in Economic Co-operations between North Korea and China and their Effects on the North Korean Economy (북중 경협 확대 요인과 북한경제에 대한 영향). *KDI North Korean Economic Review* January 2013.

Kim, Suk-Jin (2014c), North Korean Trade Statistics: Analysis and Evaluation (북한 무역통계: 해설과 평가) in *Understanding the North Korean Economy through Statistics* (통계를 이용한 북한 경제 이해), Seoul: Bank of Korea.

Kim, Yeon-chul (1997b), *Crisis in North Korea's Rationing System and Prospects on Market Reform* (북한 배급제의 위기와 시장개혁 전망), Seoul: Samsung Economic Research Institute.

Kim, Yeonho (2014d), Use of Mobile Phones in North Korea, US-Korea Institute at SAIS (http://uskoreainstitute.org/wp-content/uploads/2014/08/Kim-Yonho-Cell-Phones-in-North-Korea-Korean.pdf) (as of June 2016).

Kimura, Mitsuhiko (2001), *North Korean Economy from Emergence to Collapse* (북한의 경제: 기원·형성·붕괴), translated by Kim, H., Seoul: Hyean.

Korea Development Institute (KDI) (2009), Main Contents of the North Korean Currency Reform in 2009 and its Effects (2009년 북한 화폐개혁의 주요 내용 및 영향). *KDI Review of the North Korean Economy* December: 29–37.

Korea Institute for International Economic Policy (KIEP) and Korea Institute for Industrial Economics and Trade (KIET), (2011), *Plan for Pursuing Economic Community of the Two Koreas* (남북경제공동체 추진 구상), Seoul: Research Report Submitted to Ministry of Unification.

Korea Institute for National Unification (2011), *Trends of Kim Jong-il's Spot Guidance, 1994–2011* (김정일의 현지지도 동향, *1994–2011)*, Research Report, Seoul: Korea Institute for National Unification.

Korea National Statistical Office (2012, 2013), *Economic Statistics of North Korea* (북한의 주요통계 지표), Seoul: Korea National Statistical Office.

Kornai, J. (1971), *Anti-Equilibrium*, Amsterdam: North Holland.

Kornai, J. (1986a), *Economics of Shortage*, Amsterdam: North Holland.

Kornai, J. (1986b), The Soft Budget Constraint. *Kyklos* 39(1): 3–30.

Kornai, J. (1990), *The Road to a Free Economy: Shifting from a Socialist System; The Example of Hungary*, Norton: New York.

Kornai, J. (1992), *The Socialist System: The Political Economy of Communism*, Oxford: Oxford University Press.

Kornai, J., Maskin, E., and Roland, G. (2003), Understanding the Soft Budget Constraint. *Journal of Economic Literature* 41(4): 1095–1136.

Lange, Thomas, and Pugh, Geoffrey (1998), *The Economics of German Unification*, Cheltenham: Edward Elgar.

Lau, L., Qian, Y., and Roland, G. (2000), Reform without Losers: An Interpretation of China's Dual-Track Approach to Reforms. *Journal of Political Economy* 108(1): 120–143.

Lee, Jong-Kyu (2015), What Determines the DPRK's Anthracite Exports to China?: Implications for the DPRK's Economy (북한의 대중 무연탄 수출 감소: 원인과 의미), *KDI Journal of Economic Policy* 37(2): 40–63.

Lee, Ki-baik (1984), *A New History of Korea*, Cambridge, MA: Harvard University Press.

Lee, Seog Ki, Kim, Suk-Jin, and Yang, Moon Soo (2012), Dollarization in North Korea (북한의 외화통용 실태 분석), *KIET Research Report 2012-656*.

Lee, Seog Ki, and Lee, Seung-Yup (2014), *The Situations of North Korean Firms in the 2000s* (2000 년대 북한기업 현황), Seoul: Korea Institute for Industrial Economics and Trade Press, 2014–13.

Lee, Shinhyo (1992), The Characteristics and Superiority of the New System of Foreign Trade (새로운 무역체계의 본질적 특성과 우월성). *Economic Studies* 4(2).

Lee, Suk (2004), North Korean Famine: Occurrence, Impacts and Characteristics (1994–2000 년 북한기근: 발생, 충격 그리고 특징). Working Paper 04–20, Korea Institute for National Unification.

Lee, Suk (2007a), North Korean Statistics: Availability and Reliability (북한의 통계: 가용성과 신뢰성). Korean Institute for National Unification Research Paper 07–17.

Lee, Suk (2009), North Korea Markets: Estimate of Size and Analysis of their Structure (북한의 시장: 규모 추정과 구조분석). KDI Policy Research Report, 2009–12.

Lee, Suk, ed. (2012), *A Study of Inter-Korean Economic Integration: Strategies and Policy Issues for Economic Reform and Transition in North Korea* (남북한 경제 통합 연구: 북한 경제의 개혁 및 이행 전략), *KDI Research Report*, Seoul: Korea Development Institute.

Lee, Suk, ed. (2013), Economic Foundation of North-South Korean Integration (남북 통합의 경제적 기초: 이론, 이슈, 정책), KDI Policy Research Series, 2013–04.

Lee, Suk, et al. (2013), Determinants of Trade between North Korea and China: Analysis of Trade and Survey Data (북중무역의 결정요인: 무역통계와 서베이 데이터의 분석), KDI Research Report, 2013–05.

Lee, Suk, and Lee, Jae-Ho (2012), Trade between South Korea and North Korea and Changes in Trade between North Korea and China after the 5.24 Sanction: Data and Implications (5.24 조치 이후 남북 교역과 북중무역의 변화: 데이터와 시사점), *KDI North Korean Economic Review* May 2012.

Lee, Suk, Lee, Jae-Ho, Kim, Suk-Jin, and Choi, Soo-Young (2010), The Analysis and Reconstruction of North Korean Trade Data 1990–2008 (1990–2008 년 북한무역 통계의 분석과 재구성), KDI Research Report, 2010–07.

Lee, Yong-Hwa (2013), Evaluation of the Period Three Years after the North Korean Currency Reform (북한 2009년 화폐개혁 3년 평가), Unification Economy, 2013, No. 1, Hyundai Research Institute, pp. 75–86.

Lee, Young-Hoon (2000), A Study on Economic Growth and Accumulation Mechanism in North Korea, 1956–64: An Analysis of Kaleckian CGE Model (북한의 경제성장 및 축적체제에 관한 연구, (1954–1964년) Kaleckian CGE 모델 분석). PhD Thesis submitted to Korea University, Seoul.

Lee, Young-Hoon (2005), The Spontaneous Marketization and Development of North Korean Economic Reform (북한의 자생적 시장화와 경제개혁의 전개). *Research on Unification Issues* 44: 25–54.

Lee, Young-Hoon (2006), The Status of North Korea-China Trade and its Impact on North Korean Economy (북중무역의 현황과 북한경제에 미치는 영향). Finance and Economic Studies, Bank of Korea Issue 246.

Lee, Young-Hoon (2007b). A Survey of North Korean Economic Conditions Using Data from Refugees' Survey (탈북자를 통한 북한경제 변화 상황 조사), Bank of Korea.

Lee, Young-Sun (2003), Unification Costs of the Korean Peninsula and Its Financing Methods (한반도의 통일비용과 그 조달 방법). in *Handbook of Korea Unification IV* Sung-hee, Jwa, Chung-In, Moon, and Roh, Jeong-Ho, eds. Seoul: Korea Economic Research Institute.

Leff, N. H. (1964), Economic Development through Bureaucratic Corruption. *American Behavioral Scientist* 8(3): 8–14.

Lim, Kang-Taeg (2009), A Study on the Marketization of the North Korean Economy, Korea Institute for National Unification (북한 경제의 시장화 실태에 관한 연구), Research Paper Series 09–04.

Lim, Kang-Taeg, Yang, Moon Soo, and Lee, Seog Ki (2011), A Study on North Korea's Official Economy for Understanding the Costs and the Benefits of Unification (통일비용 편익 추계를 위한 북한공식경제부문의 실태 연구), Korea Institute for National Unification Working Paper 2011–03.

Lin, Justin, Cai, Fang, and Li, Zhou (2003), *The China Miracle: Development Strategy and Economic Reform*, revised ed. Hong Kong: The Chinese University Press.

Little, Ian, Scitovsky, Tibor, and Scott, Maurice (1970), *Industry and Trade in Some Developing Countries: A Comparative Study*, London: Oxford University Press.

Maddison, Angus (1995), *Monitoring the World Economy, 1820–1992*, Paris: Organisation for Economic Co-operation and Development.

Maddison, Angus (1998), *Chinese Economic Performance in the Long Run*, Paris: Organisation for Economic Co-operation and Development.

Martinelli, Cesar, and Tommasi, Mariano (1997), Sequencing of Economic Reforms in the Presence of Political Constraints. *Economics and Politics* 9(2): 115–131.

Mauro, P. (1995), Corruption and Growth. *Quarterly Journal of Economics* 110(3): 681–712.

McKinnon, Ronald (1991), *The Order of Economic Liberalization*, Baltimore: Johns Hopkins Press.

McMillan, John, and Naughton, Barry (1992), How to Reform a Planned Economy: Lessons from China. *Oxford Review of Economic Policy* 8(1): 130–143.

McMillan, John, Whalley, John, and Zhu, Lijing (1989), The Impact of China's Economic Reforms on Agricultural Productivity Growth, *Journal of Political Economy* 97(4): 781–807.

McMillan, John, and Woodruff, Christopher (2002), The Central Role of Entrepreneurs in Transition Economies. *Journal of Economic Perspectives* 16 (3): 153–170.

Megginson, William, and Netter, Jeffry (2001), From State to Market: A Survey of Empirical Studies on Privatization. *Journal of Economic Literature* 39(2): 321–389.

Ministry of Unification, Republic of Korea (1990), *Comparative Studies on South and North Korean Economy for Forty-Five Years since Division* (분단 45년 남북한경제의 종합적 비교연구), Seoul: Ministry of Unification.

Mun, Sung Min (2008), An Empirical Analysis on North Korean Prices and Exchange Rates: Employing the Purchasing Power Parity Theory (구매력평가 이론에 근거한 북한 가격 및 환율 분석), *Research on Unification Policy* 17(2): 83–115.

Mun, Sung Min, and Yoo, Byoung Hark (2012), The Effects of Inter-Korean Integration Type on Economic Performance: The Role of Wage Policy. *International Economic Journal* 26(3): 447–470.

Murphy, K., Shleifer, A., and Vishny, R. (1991), The Allocation of Talent: Implications for Growth. *Quarterly Journal of Economics* 106(2): 503–530.

Murphy, K., Shleifer, A., and Vishny, R. (1992), The Transition to a Market Economy: Pitfalls of Partial Reform. *Quarterly Journal of Economics* 107(3): 889–906.

Murrell, Peter (1995), The Transition According to Cambridge, Mass. *Journal of Economic Literature* 33(1)(March): 164–78.

Mussa, Michael L. (1984), The Adjustment Process and the Timing of Trade Liberalization, NBER working paper, No. 1458.

Nakagawa, Masahiko (2003), The Formation of North Korean Yeonhap Giupso (북한 연합기업소의 형성). *KDI North Korean Review*, 2003–3, pp. 48–75.

Nanto, D., and Chanlett-Avery, E. (2008), The North Korean Economy: Leverage and Policy Analysis, CRS Report for Congress, Congressional Research Service.

National Assembly Budget Office (2014), *Economic Effects of the Unification of the Korean Peninsula* (한반도 통일의 경제적 효과), Seoul: National Assembly Budget Office.

Naughton, Barry (1996), *Growing Out of the Plan: Chinese Economic Reform, 1978–1993*, Cambridge: Cambridge University Press.

Naughton, Barry (2007), *The Chinese Economy: Transition and Growth*, Cambridge, MA: MIT Press.

Nellis, John (2002), *The World Bank, Privatization and Enterprise Reform in Transition Economies: A Retrospective Analysis*, Washington DC: World Bank.

Neumann, Manfred (1992), German Unification: Economic Problems and Consequences. *Carnegie-Rochester Conference Series on Public Policy* 36: 163–210.

Niwa, Haruki, and Goto, Fujio (1989), Estimates of the North Korean Gross Domestic Product Account 1956–1959. *Asian Economic Journal* 3(1, March): 133–169.

Noland, Marcus, Robinson, Sherman, and Wang, Tao (2001), Famine in North Korea: Causes and Cures. *Economic Development and Cultural Change* 49(4): 741–767.

North, Douglass (1990), *Institutions, Institutional Change and Economic Performance*, Cambridge: Cambridge University Press.

North, Douglass (2005), *Understanding the Process of Institutional Change*, Princeton, NJ: Princeton University Press.

North Korean Resources Institute (2013), Reserves of North Korea's Natural Resources (<통계자료> 북한 지하자원 매장량), mimeo.

Ofer, G., and Vinokur, A. (1992), *The Soviet Household under the Old Regime*, Cambridge: Cambridge University Press.

Park, Hyeong-Jung (2002), *System of North Korean Economic Management* (북한의 경제관리체계), Seoul: Hainaim.

Park, Keong-Suk (2012), The Economic Hardship and Famine Since the 1990s in North Korea and Its Impact on the Population Dynamics (북한의 식량난 및 기근과 인구변동). *Study on Unification Policy* 21(1): 127–156.

Park, Myoung-Kyu et al. (2010), *Flexible and Complex Unification* (연성복합통일론), Seoul: Seoul National University Institute for Peace and Unification Studies.

Portes, R. (1981), Macroeconomic Equilibrium and Disequilibrium in Centrally Planned Economies. *Economic Inquiry* XIX: 559–578.

Portes, R., Quandt, R. E., Winter, D., and Yeo, S. (1987), Macroeconomic Planning and Disequilibrium: Estimates for Poland, 1955–80. *Econometrica* 55(1): 19–41.

Portes, R., Quandt, R. E., Winter, D., and Yeo, S. (1988), Tests of the Chronic Shortage Hypothesis: The Case of Poland. *Review of Economics and Statistics* 70(2): 288–295.

Qian, Yingyi, and Roland, Gerard (1998), Federalism and the Soft Budget Constraint. *American Economic Review* 88(5): 1143–1162.

Qian, Yingyi, Roland, Gerard, and Xu, Chenggang (2006), Coordination and Experimentation in M-Form and U-Form Organisations. *Journal of Political Economy* 114(2): 366–402.

Qian, Yingyi, and Xu, Chenggang (1993), Why China's Economic Reforms Differ: The M-Form Hierarchy and Entry/Expansion of the Non-State Sector. *Economics of Transition* 1(2): 135–170.

Rhee, Yeongseop (2009), Currency Conversion during the Period of Transition: The Case of North Korea. In *Financial Sector Reform in Transition*

Economies: Implications for North Korea, Kim, Byung-Yeon and Lim, Cheng-Hoon, eds. Seoul: Seoul National University Press and IMF.

Roberts, Andrew and Kim, Byung-Yeon (2011), Policy Responsiveness in Post-Communist Europe: Public Preferences and Economic Reforms. *British Journal of Political Science* 41(4): 819–839.

Robinson, W., Courtland, Myung, Lee, Ken, Hill, Kenneth, and Burnham, Gilbert (1999), Mortality in North Korean Migrant Households: A Retrospective Study. *Lancet* 354(July–December): 291–295.

Rock, M., and Bonnett, H. (2004), The Comparative Politics of Corruption: Accounting for the East Asian Paradox in Empirical Studies of Corruption Growth and Investment. *World Development* 32(6): 999–1017.

Rodrik, Dani (1989), Credibility of Trade Reform: A Policy Maker's Guide. *The World Economy* 12(1): 1–16.

Roland, G. (2000), *Transition and Economics: Politics, Markets and Firms*, Cambridge, MA: MIT Press.

Roland, G. (2008), Transposable and Non-Transposable Lessons from the Transition Experience. *Seoul Journal of Economics* 21(2): 265–283.

Rose-Ackerman, S. (1978), *Corruption: A Study in Political Economy*, New York: Academic Press.

Sabirianova, Klara Peter, Svejnar, Jan, and Terrell, Katherine (2012), Foreign Investment, Corporate Ownership, and Development: Are Firms in Emerging Markets Catching Up to the World Standard? *The Review of Economics and Statistics* 94(4): 981–999.

Sachs, Jeffrey, and Woo, Wing Thye (1994), Structural Factors in the Economic Reforms of China, Eastern Europe, and the Former Soviet Union. *Economic Policy* 9(April): 101–145.

Sah, R. (1987), Queues, Rations and Market: Comparisons of Outcomes for the Poor and the Rich. *American Economic Review* 77: 69–77.

Schroeder, G. (1997), The Soviet Economy and the Fate of the USSR, mimeo, June 1997.

Sell, Friedrich (1995), The Currency Conversion Controversy. *MOCT-MOST* 5: 27–53.

Shleifer, A., and Vishny, R. (1993), Corruption. *Quarterly Journal of Economics* 108 (3): 599–617.

Shleifer, A., and Vishny, R. (1998), *The Grabbing Hand: Government Pathologies and Their Cures*, Cambridge, MA: Harvard University Press.

Smith, Adam (1976), *An Inquiry into the Nature and Causes of the Wealth of Nations*, Campbell, R. H., Skinner, A. S., and Todd, W. B., eds. Oxford: Clarendon Press.

Staehr, Karsten (2005), Reforms and Economic Growth in Transition Economies: Complementarity, Sequencing and Speed. *European Journal of Comparative Economics* 2: 177–202.

Sung, Hankyoung (2014), *The Effects of Economic Integration between South and North Korea* (남북한 경제통합의 효과), Seoul: Korea Institute for International Economic Policy.

Treml, Vladimir G., and Alexeev, Michael (1994), The Growth of the Second Economy in the Soviet Union and Its Impact on the System. In *The Postcommunist Economic Transformation*, Campbell, Robert W., ed., Boulder, CO: Westview Press, 221–247.

United Nations DevelopmentProgramme (UNDP) (1998), Thematic Roundtable Meeting on Agricultural Recovery and Environmental Protection in the Democratic People's Republic of Korea.

Van Wijnbergen, Sweder (1992), Intertemporal Speculation, Shortage and the Political Economy of the Price Reform. *Economic Journal* 102(November): 1395–1406.

Weitzman, M. (1980), The 'Ratchet Principle' and Performance Incentives. *Bell Journal of Economics* 1980: 302–308.

Wellisz, S., and Findlay, R. (1986), Central Planning and the 'Second Economy' in Soviet-type Systems. *Economic Journal* 96: 646–658.

Wolf, Charles Jr., and Akramov, Kamil, (2005), *North Korean Paradoxes: Circumstances, Costs and Consequences of Korean Unification*, Santa Monica: RAND Institute.

Woo, Wing Thye (1994), The Art of Reforming Centrally Planned Economies: Comparing China, Poland and Russia. *Journal of Comparative Economics* 18 (3): 276–308.

Xu, Chenggang (2011), The Fundamental Institutions of China's Reforms and Development. *Journal of Economic Literature* 49:(4): 1076–1151.

Yang, Moon Soo (2001), *The Structure of the North Korean Economy: Mechanism for Economic Development and Decline* (북한경제의 구조: 경제개발과 침체의 메커니즘), Seoul: Seoul National University Press.

Yang, Moon Soo (2008), Institutions and Practice of North Korean Trade (북한 무역의 제도와 실태), KDI Research Report.

Yang, Moon Soo (2010a), North Korea's Marketization during the Repression Period, 2007–2009: Facts and Implications (시장억제기 북한의 시장화: 실태와 함의 2007–2009). Symposium Chapter presented at Institute for Peace and Unification Studies, Seoul National University.

Yang, Moon Soo (2010b), *The Marketization in North Korean Economy* (북한경제의 시장화), Seoul: Hanul.

Yoon, Suk-Bum (1986), Macroeconometric Analysis of North Korea's Economy (북한 경제의 거시계량적 분석), mimeo, Ministry of Unification.

Yoon, Young-kwan and Yang, Un-chul, eds. (2009), *Economic and Social Change in North Korea after the July 1ˢᵗ Economic Measures: From Plan to Market!* (7.1. 경제관리 개선 조치 이후 북한 경제와 사회: 계획에서 시장으로), Seoul: Hanul.

Yu, Shi-Eun, Kim, Byung-Yeon, Jeon, Woo-Taek, and Jung Seung-Ho (2012), Determinants of Labour Market Participation and Wages of North Korean Female Refugees in South Korea. *Asian Economic Policy Review* 7(1): 113–129.

Zang, Hyoung Soo (2009), Balance of Foreign Exchanges of North Korea from 2000 to 2008 (북한의 2000년대 외화수급 추정). *Comparative Economic Studies* 16 (2): 1–48.

Zang, Hyoung Soo (2013), Estimation and Analysis on the Balance of Foreign Exchanges of North Korea for 1991–2012 (북한의 외화수급 추정과 분석: 1991–2012년). *Studies on Unification Policies* 22(2): 165–190.

Index

Adam Smith, 7, 8, 10
Alexeev, M., 19, 33, 175
asymmetric information, 25

Barlow, D., 238
Barro, R., 23
Bennett, J., 232
Bergson, A., 12, 13, 14, 15, 71, 87
Berkowitz, D., 239
big-bang, 4, 217, 218–221, 225,
    237–238, 247
Bilsen, V., 235
Blanchard, O., 243
bribery, 174, *See also* corruption
    informal markets, 181
    market-related, 180
    redistribution, 181
    regime stability, 176
Brus, W., 29
Bulgaria, 235
businessmen in Dandong, 133
    advantages, 153
    Chinese (Hanjok), 133, 145
    Chinese-North Koreans (Chosun
        Hwagyo), 133, 145, 149
    constraints, 153
    Korean-Chinese (Chosunjok), 133, 145
    South Korean group, 133

Carlin, W., 234
Central Intelligence Agency (CIA), 12, 13, 14,
    71, 88, 89
central planning, 3, 10
centrally planned economies (CPEs), 2,
    17, 19
Charemza, W., 17
Chawluk, A., 18
Chiang Kai-shek, 281
China
    Cultural Revolution, 58, 67, 242, 247
    Dandong, 132
    decollectivisation, 250
    Great Leap Forward, 44, 48, 58, 67

household responsibility system, 246,
    247, 248
initial conditions, 242
open-door policy, 248
Special Economic Zones (SEZs),
    241, 248
township and village enterprises, 248
Chinese investment
    equipment investment, 135, 136, 168
    hiring workers, 135
    ioint investment, 135
    joint management, 135
Chinese trade
    export, 134
    import, 135
    outsourcing, 135
    wholesale/retail trade, 135
Choi, Joonook, 293
Chow, G., 242
Cobb–Douglas function, 15, 296
collapse, 34, 38
    coordination failure, 31
    corruption, 31, 35
    forced surrender, 31
    informalisation, 31, 33, 39
    North Korea, 3, 284
    radical unification, 285
    socialist economies, 4, 16, 187
    Soviet economy, 31, 32
computable general equilibrium (CGE)
    model, 293
coordination mechanism, 28, 32, 33
    capitalist system, 8, 10
    economic performance, 6
    failure, 31
    socialism, 3, 9
corruption, 4, 173, *See also* bribery
    'bad', 181, 187
    'good', 181
    defined, 34
    effect on production, 181
    market activities, 180
    quality, 36

Printed in the United States
By Bookmasters